WITH THE SPIRIT'S SWORD

6-3-71

BASEL STUDIES OF THEOLOGY
edited by the Faculty of Theology, Basel
No. 3

WITH THE SPIRIT'S SWORD

The Drama of Spiritual Warfare in the Theology of John Calvin

by

CHARLES A. M. HALL

JOHN KNOX PRESS · RICHMOND, VIRGINIA

6-3-71

Library of Congress Catalog Card Number: 68—13 492
Joint publication by
EVZ-Verlag, Zürich, and John Knox Press, Richmond, Virginia
© EVZ-Verlag, Zürich, 1968

Printed by P. G. Keller — 8053 Zürich
Printed in Germany

To the women and children who by their action and suffering immeasurably deepened and sharpened Calvin's perception — and mine — of the Good Fight to be waged With the Spirit's Sword.

Finally, be strong in the Lord and in the strength of his might. Put on the whole armor of God, that you may be able to stand against the wiles of the devil. For we are not contending against flesh and blood, but against the principalities, against the powers, against the world rulers of this present darkness, against the spiritual hosts of wickedness in the heavenly places. Therefore take the whole armor of God, that you may be able to withstand in the evil day, and having done all, to stand . . . And take the helmet of salvation, *and the sword of the Spirit,* which is the word of God.

Ephesians 6:10—13, 17.

PREFACE

The completion of this book gives me a very special pleasure and sense of accomplishment, because it represents the culmination of a long-term labor of love. Almost fifteen years ago in theological seminary I became convinced that what Gustav Aulen called the classic view of the atonement, a combination of the Christus Victor motif with the conception of God's reconciliation, had profound theological significance. I had already become a follower of John Calvin by accident of denominational affiliation, and as my convictions deepened I discovered that I was also one by inclination. I considered myself fortunate, then, to be able to combine two great interests in my doctoral dissertation, for it dealt with Calvin's conception of the Christian's participation in the warfare of the Victor.

The intensive work of research and formulation uncovered the limits of my Calvinism. I became aware that Calvin's own discoveries, in his existential investigation of the problem of evil and its overcoming, would have to be reshaped to be effective weapons in the warfare against evil today. At the same time, my respect for Calvin as the man he intransigently was could only be strengthened the deeper I probed. It is for this reason that this book must remain about him, his thought, his life in his time, while the usefulness of his discoveries in dealing with the problem of evil in the twentieth century must await another occasion which shall give the twentieth century its full due. In the almost ten intervening years my work has not involved solely theology's interior dialogue — that of Calvin with Calvin and his peers — about the Word of God and *spiritual* warfare. It has also been a wrestling with many kinds of words of man about man and his world and works. It has been that engagement with philosophy and literature, with sciences and arts, which I call *The Common Quest*. The common quest for the relevance of Truth and Humanity to the life of man today has led my theology beyond theologians to sociologists, economists, musicologists, and historians of art, of literature, and of culture. This quest has introduced me to many a great thinker and writer, but when I return to concentrate on the mind of John Calvin its impact is, if anything, more forceful than ever. I have listened sympathetically to unsympathetic words about Calvin in the secular Academy, and even to statements from scholars of religion who read the manuscript of my dissertation and said, in substance: The author tickles up a bit of interest in tired old Calvin through a showy metaphor, "but this on the tail of the dog is not going to make the dog bark loud enough" to arouse interest. Then I have reread Calvin and discovered that the editors of the Great Books, in according him unique status among Protestant theologians, are right and the uncritically hasty critics are wrong. There is much to criticize in Calvin and we today possess perhaps a better perspective than any preceding generation from which to do it. But beside the featherweight words we bandy, his still weigh a pound apiece.

I have already implied that this book has profited from the expert critical readings associated with rejections by numerous publishers. As a result of them the manuscript has received needed chastening and astringent baptisms of discipline in certain specific areas, though the substance remains unchanged. Most clearly, however, the comments of other scholars have led to increasing confidence in the integrity of the initial conception, but also to awareness that it will be useful to clarify the approach employed. I seek here to allow Calvin to speak, "as the man he intransigently was"; but what Calvin is that? One of those giants who condemn subsequent generations to the task of explaining him, Calvin has been considered as a leading Church Father of Protestantism, as a great thinker — orderly, comprehensive, profound, as a brilliant exegete of Scripture, as a superb scholar versed in vast expanses of the intellectual history of his past, as the teacher of a whole culture, as the architect of the Puritan ethic, as a religious leader — preacher, organizer, shepherd of souls. His detractors have deemed him legalist (or Jew), Biblicist, economic opportunist, political tyrant, inhumane theologian, brutal policeman, psychopath (schizoid), or simply sick. Scholars have thought of him in some of these terms, but also as sixteenth century Frenchman, as child of the northern Renaissance, that is — with paradoxically real point — as humanist. It is my task and privilege, however, to portray Calvin as a consistent and conscious "spiritual warrior" and as such a theologian. I believe that this is an essential Calvin — though not the only or the whole Calvin — the man he deliberately and intransigently was. This is not to suggest that we are presenting a biography of Calvin — except insofar as he lived his theology and the story of his theology is the story of his life. For this is a book by a theologian about a theologian, originally conceived and formulated under the direction of a theologian. We discover in Calvin as theologian one of humanity's truly great systematic thinkers, a man who loved to see and expound truth in its wholeness and scope, one who could follow a conception wherever it might lead and still find its connection with the total fabric of experience and of revealed reality. Of revealed reality above all, because the richness and power of Calvin's thought was borrowed: he was always and everywhere dependent upon the Spirit and upon the fifteen centuries of Hebraic diversity and intensity which are the Christian Bible. The Calvin who speaks to us, however, is also a theological artist; for, in spite of all partial understandings which speak of his rigidity and pedestrian plainness, this was a man who knew what symbols — the stuff of art — are about [1]. This was a man who took *seriously* the Biblical *metaphor* of spiritual warfare, who developed a whole theology based on this metaphor, who became consciously a spiritual warrior, and who as

---

1) The aesthetic dimensions of Calvin's work have received considerable attention: Leon Wencelius, *L'Esthétique de Calvin;* F. Blume, *Die Evangelische Kirchenmusik;* A. M. Hunter, "Calvin's Attitude to Art, Music, Science", Ch. XV in *The Teaching of Calvin, a Modern Interpretation;* etc. Two aspects have been stressed, his literary style and his role in the creation of the Reformed (including Presbyterian) tradition of psalmody. B. B. Warfield saw in Calvin fundamentally "the man of letters as saint" *(Calvin and Calvinism),* while Doumergue called him *"l'homme de la parole",* the man of the word: the Word of God and the word of man. Quirinus Breen, "John Calvin and the Rhetorical Tradition", *Church History* XXVI (1957), pp. 3—21, claims that Calvin wrote rhetorically (i. e. in the conventions of rhetoric) not syllogistically (i. e. in the conventions of logic). On the other hand, Calvin is known to have composed a poem to the victorious Christ during his stay at Worms in 1541, while the Genevan liturgy of 1542 has, according to H. D. Foster, "Calvin's Programme for a Puritan State in Geneva, 1536—41", *Harvard Theological Review,* Vol. I, No. 4, October 1908, "a swinging militant lilt that runs through psalm and prayer", and Doumergue called the psalm of battle "the Protestant Marseillaise of the victorious Huguenots". What I am referring to here, however, is *the artistry of Calvin's theology itself,* taken as a whole synthesis of form and content, conception and execution. A fuller discussion of such artistry is given in "Theology as an Art", Chapter V of *The Common Quest,* Philadelphia, Westminster Press, 1965 by the present author.

artist — a creator at one with his art — lived his metaphor of thought.

Upon the validity of the John Calvin who steps forth from these pages armed *with the Spirit's sword,* depends the success, the justification, of the approach essayed in this study. For we are proceeding here by the risky, but perhaps fruitful, method of following one consistently used metaphor throughout Calvin's entire literary oeuvre. It is important to understand from the beginning that we have chosen to do this, and that in so doing we have willingly given up several proven scholarly approaches to Calvin and to the history of Christian thought. Above all, our choice has deprived us of the excitement of historical discovery, or rediscovery with Calvin, of ideas, of triumphant experiments or bitter mistakes, of the excitement of reliving Calvin's reactions to the ever-changing landscape of human history. In place of the adventure of traversing ever higher mountain ranges as Calvin reformulates his thought, our method of study takes us into the vast interior expanses of his mind. It leads us through room after inter-connecting room arranged and fitted with consumate skill, especially in the superb architectonic of the *Institutes* of 1559. As we enter upon our exploration we are reminded of Kierkegaard's disparaging claims that intellectual giants such as Hegel built mansions of thought — and lived in hovels next door. We will find Calvin's castle neither evanescent nor un-inhabited. Since Calvin lived his theology we shall find it furnished plainly, even severely, but with every piece of equipment needed for living — or, as we shall contend, for waging war. In addition to eschewing the historical-biographical approach, we have chosen not to consider Calvin's work as one organic unit participating in the historical development of Western intellectual history. Finally we have not chosen to represent a single *transverse* slice through Calvin's theology, to study his treatment of one doctrine, or one article or subarticle of the creed: for example, Calvin's doctrine of God, or of man, of atonement, or eschatology. Instead, although we have made use of many studies made from these approaches, we have tried to listen to Calvin as systematic *theologian,* as a theological artist developing one consistent metaphor — spiritual warfare as the necessary response to the problem of evil — throughout the whole range of Christian doctrines. Thus we have taken, so to speak, a *longitudinal* slice through Calvin's work, following an historical development — though not that of his personal biography or of the stream of culture which flowed around and through his life. Our history is, rather, *Heilsgeschichte,* the history of God's mighty acts for men in time. This is our history because we believe it was Calvin's history, not as though he were a member of that later school of *Heilsgeschichte* theologians but because the outline of his theology, like those of all theologies based on the Apostles Creed [2], is structured by the *Heilsgeschichte.* What we mean by *Heilsgeschichte* here is what Calvin meant when he said in defending the authority of the Apostle's Creed: "We consider to be beyond controversy the only point that ought to concern us: *that the whole* history of our faith *is summed up in it succinctly and in definite order,* and that it contains nothing that is not vouched for by genuine testimonies of Scripture" [3].

A further word ought to be said about our relentless emphasis on Calvin's militant career "with the Spirit's sword". Comments of limited enthusiasm for our treatment have ranged from, "There is nothing new in laying stress on Calvin's fighting qualities and on the conflicts that marked his career", to, "Almost anything the Reformer did or said *can* be represented as a 'battle area'". In response to the former comment my grateful acknowledgement extends to such brief but important writings as those of Karlfried Fröhlich (especially, *Gottesreich, Welt und Kirche bei Calvin*), E. Mülhaupt, "Die Predigt Calvins ...," Albert De Quervain, *Calvin, Sein Lehren und Kämpfen,* and important sections of such works as Wm. Niesel, "The Church Militant", (*The Theology of Calvin*), and Wm. Kolfhaus, "Das christliche Leben nur möglich in stetem Kampf", (*Vom christlichen Leben nach Johannes Calvin*). None of these illuminating vignettes, however, has represented more than 10 % of the iceberg, more than a fraction of the range of Calvin's conscious struggle with the reality of evil. Only a study from such a perspective as that of the present one could reveal the tenacity

---

2) I make this assertion in spite of the valuable suggestion by T. H. L. Parker (*The Doctrine of the Knowledge of God,* p. 42) that the 1559 *Institutes* are structured by the *duplex cognitio* (twofold knowledge, of God and of ourselves, I, i, l) rather than by the Apostles' Creed, so that Book I is set apart from II—IV. In any case, the events through which God uniquely reveals himself and knowledge of ourselves make up the *Heilsgeschichte.*

3) II, xvi, 18. The use of *Heilsgeschichte* to describe a central organizing principle of Calvin's theology is confirmed by Berger's result: "Calvin's concept of history is founded on the facts *(Tatsachen)* of the *Heilsgeschichte*". (*Calvins Geschichtsauffassung,* p. 109).

with which Calvin conceived of his role in the *militia Christi.* I have added nothing. All of the more than one thousand citations [4] which stand behind Chapter IV, for example, were written by Calvin. It is not that I *could* represent almost anything Calvin did or said as a "battle area"; the entire striking point is that *he did.* In selecting and synthesizing — in just such a way as he might himself have done — his words about wielding the Spirit's sword, we have unavoidably relegated all the other well-known aspects of his thought to a subsidiary role. It may be that the resulting hyperbole does not go very far toward the interpretation of Calvin; but continuing to delve into the literature about Calvin brings awareness that something essential is consistently underestimated there [5]. I am convinced that there is a real place for a study which portrays the spiritual warrior in internal and external combat. This portrait of a man who lived by the Spirit's sword thrusts us into the turmoil of the life of the sixteenth century — a time so like our own — and perhaps even into the very presence of him whose theology and

---

4) I have drawn principally from the *Institutes* and *Commentaries,* the formal writings of Calvin published during his lifetime, because it was for these that he intended and expected to be held responsible. This approach obviates the frequent criticism that Luther's Satan prances principally across the pages of his polemic writings and informal utterances and is, therefore, merely theological tabletalk. Thus we are deliberately reversing the methodology of H. Obendiek, whose studies of Luther are definitive in this area, for he excluded from his brief work on Calvin's Satan the systematic works (suspect of yielding a theological *Fündlein,* a consideration handled out of theoretical necessity and "enclosed in the prison of a theological seminary") and turned to the correspondence for more "original, living and pictorial" material (*Der alt boese Feind,* 1930, p. 67).

5) There are, of course, a few striking exceptions to this such as those listed above. Still more significant, however, is a remark such as that of Walter E. Stuermann. Concerning other works on the same topic he says they ". . . overlook the whole matter of . . . the tensions faith introduces into human life, and the significance of the urgent heroic warfare with sin, Satan and death which is initiated in faith" (*Calvin's Concept of Faith,* p. 380). Most striking of all is the extent to which Heinrich Berger finds spiritual warfare, the *militia christiana,* penetrating Calvin's conception of history. It was perhaps inevitable that his study should have discovered spiritual warfare as the content of Calvin's *Heilsgeschichte,* while the present investigation of that warfare with the Spirit's sword had to be organized according to the *Heilsgeschichte* which is *Heilsdrama,* the Redemptive History which is Redemptive Drama. It can be no accident that both works were first formulated in the atmosphere of a "theological existence" shaped by the living memory of the *Kirchenkampf,* the 1933—45 Church Struggle against Hitler.

concrete ethical decisions forged the strategy which guided Protestantism in the battles of succeeding centuries.

My debt to investigators of things Calvinic — among the countless army of scholarly weavers who have contributed warp and woof to the fabric of human knowledge — has been formally acknowledged in the Bibliography. But certain specific debts are too great to be left unappreciated. Particular recognition, therefore, must be given to John T. McNeill, whose edition of the 1559 *Institutes* in the Westminster Library of Christian Classics provides material for an entire theological education within itself;

to Leonard J. Trinterud, who introduced me to the scope, the extensive dimension, of Calvin's thought;

to Joseph Haroutunian, who introduced me to the depth, the intensive dimension, of Calvin's thought;

to Karl Barth, who set me free from Calvin — for Calvin;

and, finally, to him whose spiritual energy, theological artistry, clarity of style, subtle sardonic wit, and intellectual relentlessness, have put the whole of Western civilization in his debt: the soldier of Christ, Jean Cauvin.

TABLE OF CONTENTS

ACT I: THE LION ON A LEASH

Satan and Man: Rebellion and Servitude . . . . .

An Historical-Theological Background of Demonology . . .
> The sixteenth century was the devil's golden age 55 — the place of Satan in Anselm's theology 55 — in the system of St. Thomas Aquinas 57 — the Lutheran devils 59 — the background of the *Teufelliteratur* 60 — Calvin rejected the devils of popular superstition 64 — Pelagian view of evil (man as its sole creator) is unbiblical and unrealistic 65.

The Creation of Satan and His Fall . . . .
> Satan was created good (Manichean view rejected) 65 — his fall was voluntary but irrevocable 66 — his plan is to overthrow God and enslave man 66 — attacks man's worship of God 66 — attacks God's truth 67.

The Fall of Man . . . .
> Man's fall as an act of rebellion 68 — results of the fall 69 — man enslaved by Satan 71 — by sin 71 — by death 72 — by the flesh 73 — fallen man makes himself God's enemy 73 — allies himself with Satan and becomes his slave 75 — Satan's dominion over man threatens Calvin's distinction between elect and *reprobi* 76.

The Kingdom of Satan . . . .
> Calvin elevates Satan to magisterial role over other powers of evil 77 — the New Testament view 77 — a modern view 78.

God is the Lord . . . .
> Satan's power is minute compared to God's 79 — Satan is a dragon on a chain 79 — Luther's Manichean tendency 80 — the goodness of Calvin's God endangered 80 — Satan as the instrument of God's justice 81 — God's election is man's only hope 82.

ACT II: THE DIVINE INVADER

Christus: Invader, Victor and Restorer . . . . . .

Jesus Christ: The Divine Invader . . . .
> appeared to destroy the work of the devil 84 — as Mediator between God and fallen man 85 — strong doctrine of the two natures of Christ 86 — Calvin's tendency to separate the two natures 87.

ACT III: THE GOOD FIGHT

ACT IV: TOWARD COSMIC VICTORY

INTRODUCTION: JOHN CALVIN, SOLDIER OF CHRIST

John Calvin was a battler. He would gladly have accepted this appellation, if it clearly connoted that he was a warrior of God, a good soldier of Jesus Christ. He would have rejected the term on any other basis, for he never stopped thinking of himself as the poor, timid student who sought refuge and anonymity for the sake of his studies and writing. It was thus that he presented himself to William Farel when the latter accosted him at the inn where Calvin was making an overnight stop in Geneva on the road to Strasbourg in 1536. It was thus that he still presented himself in 1552 when writing Dryander not to think that a lust for power led him to seek out enemies and battles, but to consider that he much preferred quiet scientific work[1]. However, in Farel's importunate demands that he remain in Geneva as a practical help to God's Church, Calvin heard the Spirit's battle trumpet, and he never heard it sound "retreat". Calvin believed he had not chosen the warfare into which he whole-heartedly entered, but that it was thrust upon him as a Christian: "If I would live to Christ . . . the present life is appointed as the field of conflict"[2]. Furthermore, this spiritual warfare was no war game, no set of perfunctory maneuvers, for Calvin, but a *dura militia,* a hard campaign[3].

Justifying such a hard struggle requires clear and worthy goals. One of Calvin's most poignant statements of them was addressed to the five French students of the Lausanne academy imprisoned (and eventually executed) at Lyon for their faith. They (and he) were said to be fighting for the glorification of God, the truth of his Gospel, and the praise of Christ's kingdom[4]. (Elsewhere, he

---

1) CR XLII, 434.
2) CE I, 187.
3) CR XLIII, 18.
4) CG II, 256.

often said that this warfare defines our present status as Christians and leads to our future blessing.) Calvin was convinced that he kept these goals before him at every step of his own march, but his career demonstrates to us in disinterested retrospect how inevitably the smoke of battle dims the soldier's vision. The necessity for using the proper weapons and equipment provided an important safeguard against this danger, for Calvin knew that the "spiritual" character of our warfare determines which arms are appropriate to it and how they are to be used [5]. For example, he writes to the Protector Somerset of England, in whose land the struggle was being carried out in quite literally military terms: "Let us not waste our energies upon men, but rather let us set ourselves against Satan to resist all his machinations against us" [6]. An even milder attitude, bordering on compassion, was evinced toward the opponents in Geneva — while Calvin was far from the battle line, in Strasbourg, it must be confessed — who were not to receive evil for evil but to be treated with a *zeal* for the service of God, *moderated* by his Spirit according to the rule of his Word, for "insofar as they are the adversaries of Jesus Christ, we do resist the wiles of our *spiritual* enemy" [7]. Yet in the heat of battle Calvin himself sometimes seems unable to renounce the destructive steel mace of bitter invective for the Spirit's sword, whose deepest thrusts bring health and life.

Calvin remained secure in the confidence that he fought only *the good fight* of faith. He believed that God had placed him at a series of military posts (Geneva being by far the most important of his assignments) [8] and that he must remain there to do battle in obedience to the Divine Commander. There could be no retirement from his service, no pensioned veterans in this life. Instead, Calvin considered the death of Christ's soldier to be the entrance into the promised rest and reward so longed for here. And over the whole reigned the complete assurance of victory: "We know for certain, that while we wage war under the banners of our Christ, and fight

---

5) II Cor. 10:4.

6) CE II, 244.

7) CE I, 60 f. e. a.

8) Calvin was by no means the only Reformer to use the metaphor of spiritual warfare. As Cecil Northcott points out, the Zürich pastors urging him to return to Geneva emphasized the strategic importance of Geneva, and all he might do there to "enlarge the ramparts of the kingdom of Christ" (*John Calvin,* p. 8).

with the weapons of his warfare, we shall be unconquerable" [9]. The victory of God *accomplished* in the life, death and resurrection of Christ and the *promised* final triumph stand as twin sentinels — past and future — guarding and assuring the success of God's warrior in the drama of redemptive history. This was Calvin's understanding of what is expected of the Christian soldier, and his own life and work was filled with conflicts, but also with plans and assurances of victory, recorded from his mention of Christ's victory in his greeting to Bucer in 1534 [10] until the end of his life. He regarded his flight from France in 1535 and his banishment from Geneva in 1538 as the enemies' successes over which Satan jubilantly rejoiced [11]. Although he shrank with inner timidity at the vigorous opposition, the "sorts of contests" he met in Geneva, that "place of torture" [12], he steeled himself for his return and considered that the arduous wrestlings in Strasbourg in the interim "only keep me in training" [13].

Therefore, from the time of his return to Geneva until his death, Calvin continued to be involved in struggle throughout every succeeding period and in every area of his life. He was in continual conflict with Roman Catholic theology and ecclesiastical practice; he had renewed disagreements with the Anabaptists, whose attempts to win for Christians freedom from the state seemed anarchistic to Calvin; he made himself the ally of evangelical Christians struggling to be free of the tyranny of the Church and of inimical states from Scotland to Italy, and from Poland to Spain; and, above all, he supported with every means at his disposal the cause of his Protestant fathers and brethren in his beloved France. His letter dedicating the 1536 *Institutes* to Francis I marked the beginning of a campaign extending through and beyond the Huguenot war of 1562—3 (the initiation of which he denounced, the successes of

---

9) CE I, 287.

10) This first letter to Bucer was formerly dated Sept. 4, 1532, but McNeill, among others, now places it with greater probability in 1534. Calvin's awareness of life as a battle certainly antedates this and, interestingly, roots in classic as well as Biblical soil. His first publication, the commentary on Seneca's *De Clementia* (1532), is said by Berger (*op. cit.,* p. 21) to be determined by the Stoic wisdom that to live is to be a warrior, *vivere militare est,* Seneca, ep. 96, 5.

11) CG I, 38.

12) CF VI, 228 and CF VII, 43.

13) CE I, 110.

which he cheered, the abandonment of which he deplored, and the projected resumption of which he opposed).

These spiritual contests did not, however, remain outside the camp of the Protestant Reformation. Calvin arrived on the scene when the disagreements between Luther and the followers of Zwingli were heated, and when the Genevan leader attempted to take up a middle ground and act as mediator he was shouted at, if not shot at, from both sides [14]. Calvin attempted to quiet all local disruptions in the ranks of the French-Swiss ministers marching under the banner of Christ [15], but also on the wider fronts he warned Bullinger that it is Satan who attempts to divide the Reformed [16], and even admonished Melanchthon that to further the kingdom of God and to defeat the plots of Satan he and the epigone of Luther must not interrupt their liaison, in spite of "widely different positions" [17]. As the situation degenerated into something of a running feud, however, Calvin emerged as the leader of the Reformed side and became the chief target of Lutherans. (Schwarz reports that in 1557—8 at Worms where Zwingli was declared a heretic, Calvin's name was linked with those of Andreas Osiander and Kaspar Schwenkfeld on the heretical list. Melanchthon was among the signers of the declaration.) Almost more painful than the necessity of defending *himself* against Evangelical brothers was the necessity of trying to ward off Lutheran attacks on French Reformed refugee congregations, particularly the one at Frankfort.

Yet more disturbing were the recurrent difficulties Calvin experienced in Geneva itself. He was called to the city because of the

---

14) Zwingli's successor in Zürich, Heinrich Bullinger, was one of Calvin's closest allies. But disagreement about the Eucharist remained, with Calvin's conception ultimately closer to the Lutheran than to that of Zürich (see Calvin's letters to Bullinger: Feb. 25, 1547 [CG I, 265] objecting to Bullinger's view; June 26, 1548 [CE II, 155], setting forth Calvin's own view at some length; CE I, 85 and also CE II, 318, which indicates that Calvin's respect for Zwingli does not approach his esteem for Luther). Although they supported him at certain decisive junctures, Calvin far more deeply mistrusted the Bernese whom he regarded as reinforcements stupidly taking pot shots at their own front line troops, i. e. himself (see Calvin's letter to the pastors of Bern, Sept. 1551, CG I, 421).

15) CE I, 387.

16) CE I, 89.

17) In this letter of Nov. 28, 1552, CE II, 362, Calvin was seeking agreement with the Lutherans on two exceedingly knotty problems: holy communion and divine election.

unrest and disorder there, and the struggle against the opposition he met was one of his longest and most strenuous. The people wished to be free from the tight rein of Roman Catholicism. Many of the aristocratic families of the older Geneva, however, after supporting the original call of Calvin to their city felt so restricted by the stringency with which he attempted to impose order that they secured his ouster. Eventually they were forced to admit their inability to control the forces of disorder in Geneva and to entreat the return of Calvin and his virtually martial severity. He wielded control primarily through the internal discipline of the Church, which he often referred to as the "sinews"[18] of the Body of Christ. He bridled social and moral excesses through the ministers' right to exclude Genevans from the communion table. Calvin's second line of action — and we must remember that it was an indirect one — was through the civil authorities, the town councils. The councils in turn, however, exerted a large measure of control over the ministers, and when the Libertine or "freedom" party of the older Genevans held the reins (as they did throughout much of Calvin's time in the city) the Reformer faced formidable opposition in his fight for the rights of the ministers to order the Church and the moral life of the people.

Morals and discipline did not account for all of the battlefronts in Geneva, however, for heresy charges frequently incited combat. The first of those accused of heresy during Calvin's Genevan period was Calvin himself. When Peter Caroli understood Calvin's refusal to accept the authority of the ancient Church symbols as a defection from the Trinitarian faith, he considered this sufficient grounds for linking Calvin in an alliance with Satan[19]. Calvin, on his side, believed that Caroli was an "apt tool" of Satan's attack on the sole authority of Scripture in the Church[20]. This skirmish set the pattern for Calvin's encounters with heterodoxy, which he viewed as frontal attacks of Satan and the forces of evil upon God's truthfulness, upon his Word, upon his revelation, the Christian's source of truth and assurance[21]. We must keep in mind that Calvin be-

---

18) E. g. IV, xii, 1. Schwarz translates the Latin word *nervi* into as *Muskulatur* (CG II, 385). Calvin similarly refers to *laws* as the sinews of the (political) commonwealth (IV, xx, 14).

19) CE I, 174.

20) CE I, 30.

21) CR XLII, 165.

lieved he was battling a hostile strategy more dangerous to the order of God than murder or political treason. For driven by this motivation, Calvin — although he denies that he possesses the resources to combat every insignificant heretic — sometimes seems to us not only too severe but also unduly hasty in donning the armor of polemics. Not only does Calvin resist the external Anabaptist and Roman Catholic allies of Satan's assault on the faith, he also seeks out destroyers of the truth in Geneva. They must be counter-attacked with *every* weapon, physical as well as spiritual. And so Calvin's list of Satan's miserable allies grows from Gruet to Bolsec to Servetus. Calvin's harsh abuse of the weapons of spiritual warfare in this area led Sebastian Castellio, the "father of tolerance" who almost alone opposed Servetus' execution, to say that Calvin's God is worse than the devil [22].

Calvin pressed the assault so hard because he believed that even indecision — anything short of the enemy's total defeat — was a victory for Satan. And he felt that responsibility for prosecuting the attack to the last bitter consequence fell upon him as the officer in charge of the spiritual forces of God in that particular theatre of operations. The course of his correspondence with and attitude toward Melanchthon centers in his conviction that the mild-spirited humanist chronically failed to stand fast in the face of the foe. Much is told by Calvin's scolding words: "And seeing that the Lord led us forth into the arena, it became us on that account to strive more manfully. Your position is different from that of many, as you yourself are aware. For the trepidation of a general or leader is more dishonorable than the flight of a whole herd of private soldiers [23]. Calvin was the commanding officer charged with the garrison at Geneva. This is the presupposition underlying his attitude toward its citizens. His Church discipline is military discipline. In this spirit De Quervain calls Calvin's *discipline ecclesiastique* an admonition not to desist from battle, and claims that Calvin considers the Church a corps of picked troops, every man reliable [24]. By this logic, the heretics are deserters, traitors, turncoats, the most dangerous foes of all. One imprisons captured enemies — one executes traitors.

---

22) See CG II, 126 and 266.
23) CE II, 259.
24) *Calvin, Sein Lehren und Kämpfen.*

Calvin was aware of the threat which a haughty, self-asserting and overly severe Christian commander posed to the cause of God — when the commander in question was one of the *other* Protestant Reformers. His comments in a letter to Bullinger concerning Luther are most instructive: "Consider how eminent a man Luther is, and the excellent endowments wherewith he is gifted, with what strength of mind and resolute constancy, with how great skill, with what efficiency and power of doctrinal statement, he has hitherto devoted his whole energy to overthrow the reign of Antichrist, and at the same time to diffuse far and near the doctrine of salvation ... But while he is endued with rare and excellent virtues, he labours at the same time under serious faults. Would that he studied to curb this restless, uneasy temperament which is so apt to boil over in every direction. I wish, moreover, that he had always bestowed the fruits of that vehemence of natural temperament upon the enemies of truth, and that he had not flashed his lightning sometimes also upon the servants of the Lord. Would that he had been more observant and careful in the acknowledgement of his own vices ... It is our part, however, so to reprove whatsoever evil qualities may beset him as that we make some allowance for him at the same time on the score of these remarkable endowments with which he has been gifted" [25].

No heir of Calvin, bearing the glory and the burden of his legacy, could write a more accurate accolade for Calvin himself, and the subsequent criticism would be almost equally applicable. Calvin could say to his friend and disciple, John Knox, that while one must fight Satan and the evil, he hoped that the "rigorism" of the Scot could be softened [26]. He could write a Dutch pastor that severity should never win the victory over humanity [27], and, in the last year of his life, write the crown prince of Navarre: "Away with excessive severity which would banish everything agreeable from life" [28]. But when Bullinger charged him with a lack of moderation and humanity, Calvin believed the accusation exaggerated and unjustified [29].

---

25) CE I, 408 ff.
26) CG II, 350.
27) CG II, 263.
28) CG II, 452.
29) CE II, 318.

Calvin's confidence in his own understanding of the Gospel and of the direction of the Supreme Commander led him to many successes, but at the same time blinded him to many of his own faults in a way which should serve as a warning to all Christian theologians and churchmen. His confidence, which Calvin identified with the Christian assurance of victory, never diminished from its early height but, rather, increased. He trusted his conscience as a co-knower of God's truth and so could write to his accuser Caroli: "We have a ministry in no wise separated from Christ; if you doubt it, we have the sufficiently sure and faithful testimony of conscience" [30]. When Louis du Tillet, a friend of his youth who was travelling the road back to Roman Catholicism, admonished him that the opposition in Geneva signalled the disapproval of God, Calvin replied: "I beg you to allow me to follow the rule of my conscience, which I know to be surer than yours" [31].

Calvin was not, however, unaware that in a sense every man is his own worst enemy. One of the subtlest and most devastating aspects of the spiritual warfare is the struggle between the new man and the old. Calvin often expressed his recognition of the fact that the Biblical opposition of "flesh" and "spirit" is not identical with the dualism between mind or spirit and matter in Idealist philosophies. But when he came to apply these facts to himself, he had an overwhelming tendency to connect any evil involving him with the body which caused him so much suffering. John Calvin was a chronically sick man. Constitutionally frail, he neglected his health as a student and, as his attention was increasingly demanded by the tasks which the Reformation thrust upon him, diseases progressively overwhelmed his tortured frame. In his thirties, he was already speaking of the successor who must come when he should become too weak to carry the load any further. At his death at fifty-five he bore the marks of the wizened octogenarian. Days before his death he sent a roster of his ills to the consulting physicians of Montpelier, saying of his diseases: "Like a horde all these enemies assault me at once" [32]. Of the foes which bore him to earth he enumerated migraine and gout as well as numerous related respiratory disorders, asthma and pulmonary tuberculosis with the symptomatic fevers and hemorrhages, dysentery and gall stones. One could hardly

---

30) CE I, 173.
31) CE I, 73.
32) CG II, 474.

expect that a prolonged struggle with such a formidable array would leave a man's work, and particularly his attitude toward life, unmarked. To an amazing degree Calvin was victorious over these enemies and transcended the struggle with them. The occasions on which he left his sick bed to mount the pulpit or to attend to some other duty were too numerous to mention. He had the leisure required for the reorganization and definitive formulation of the *Institutes* in 1559 because his health did not permit leaving his bed to carry out his usual responsibilities. Calvin's indomitable spirit refused to yield to the limitations of his tortured body but literally drove it to the brink of the grave.

Yet in a very real sense Calvin's illnesses won a subtle victory. They unquestionably played their part in shaping his *operative* anthropology. Thus, while denying on principle that the old man and the new are anything different than the whole man — body and soul — considered in Adam or in Christ, Calvin came to identify the old man who should undergo *mortification* with the "stinking prison" of his body, and to identify God's man with his "higher" nature. This led to two very dangerous consequences: first, unwavering confidence that the decisions of his understanding and will coincided with the will of God and, second, the tendency to consider man *in* the flesh as the man *of* the flesh. One might, in fact, study Calvin's theology as an analogy of his health and point out "diseased" elements in various doctrines, elements which prove foreign to the Christian faith when measured in the light of the Biblical witness to Jesus Christ. Such an approach would, however, be misleading, because a study of his limitations could only legitimately correct a prior consideration of his achievements[33].

In this introduction we intend, therefore, to understand Calvin's *total* activity from the standpoint of the fact that he considered himself a warrior of God. If this introduction stood alone it would scarcely be a novelty, for sections such as "Calvin als Streiter Christi", (Chapter V of F. Buesser, *Calvins Urteil über sich selbst*) are

---

[33] There is a long history of attempts to understand Luther from his illnesses and abnormalities, and the errors produced by this now largely discredited method are as obvious there as in its corresponding applications to Calvin. (For example, H. Weber, *Die Theologie Calvin, Ihre innere Systematik im Lichte strukturpsychologischer Forschungsmethode*, 1930, A. Lang, "Calvin Schizoid?" *Reformierte Kirchenzeitung* [81], 1931, and H. Weber, "Calvin 'Schizoid'? Eine Erwiderung auf die Ausführungen A. Langs", RKZ [81], 1931.)

not infrequent in the Calvin literature. In the present study, however, it represents the first step in viewing Calvin's entire theological and practical work from the standpoint of the spiritual warfare. This introduction is not simply a waiting room in which we enjoy a diversion until we enter the business offices of Calvin's theology. Instead it is an entrance hall leading directly into the heart of the working area, for Calvin did not consider his warfare a private quarrel. Instead it was part and parcel of the stupendous cosmic conflict into which the whole of creation has been plunged by the revolt of Satan, and above all man, against God.

In portraying Calvin the warrior we have shown a wholehearted and successful soldier of God — perhaps the most successful of the whole Protestant Reformation. "Calvin is the man one needs in times of combat. He is the tireless organizer, the man of the second generation, the disciple and epigone lacking the creative genius of Luther, but much more capable of defending what has been won and providing it with a protective form" [34]. Precisely these final words of De Quervain suggest an informative parable drawn from medieval warfare: *The theology of John Calvin is like a suit of armor.* Its strength and toughness enabled him and his followers to advance through the raining enemy blows to triumphs of great scope. Unfortunately, however, the armor which kept out opponents' thrusts was equally impervious in the opposite direction. The Gospel of Jesus Christ is somewhat cramped within this armor and its operation hampered. The effectiveness of the action of Christ for, upon and in men is expressed only in a limited way through the action permitted by this inflexible mail. The warmth of God's love scarcely filters through this cold steel.

Within Calvin's conception of spiritual warfare are many genuine elements of the New Testament's witness to the accomplished and continuing victory of Christ over the forces of evil which oppose God and oppress man. We shall have much to learn not only from Calvin's failure to do complete justice to this New Testament witness but also from the elements he discovered there and submitted to his keenly systematic insights. This is by no means to say that we can extricate the "real" Calvin from his armor. Neither are we allowed to cut "desirable" pieces out of the armor and save them while discarding the rest. Nor may we burnish the armor overbright,

---

34) A. De Quervain, *op. cit.,* p. 82.

for as Parker's quite different image suggests: "Doumergue used up all the whitewash when he was busy redecorating Calvin, and there is none left for us" [35]. Calvin must stand before us in the whole armor he chose to put on. We must recognize the authentically evangelical elements in their inextricable fusion with ingredients which weaken the alloy.

With this we have said enough about the career soldier of Christ himself. It is high time to turn to his theology, to a reflection upon the redemptive drama, to the presuppositions, the strategy, the tactics, the goals of that warfare with the Spirit's sword.

35) T. H. L. Parker, *Portrait of Calvin,* pp. 8 f.

PROLOGUE: ORIGINAL INTEGRITY

God, His Creatures and His Purpose

This chapter occupies a unique place and has a character peculiar to itself in Calvin's redemptive drama. It is without action and without dialogue, yet it is integral to the most dynamic of all dramas. It is not unprecedented, however, for the greatest of drama, Greek Tragedy, characteristically began in a quite analogous way: with prologue. The prologue to Tragedy ranged far and wide, gathering in its narrative the presuppositions never seen on stage. It sailed the seas and plumbed the past to set the stage for the dramatic economy which concentrated with burning intensity on the central theme of the play itself. So we, as the curtain rises on a drama of ceaseless struggle, behold a landscape of harmonious perfection and unbroken serenity. And, as in Tragedy, our Prologue is no mere divertimento to ease, for the reading participant in Calvin's drama, the transition from the "real" world of daily business to the surreal world of theatre. In the first place, our Prologue introduces the *dramatis personae* and the motivating forces which we shall later behold in action. And, at the same time, this scene relativizes the ferocious combat which will absorb our whole attention. This warfare, after all, represents only a breaking of God's perfect peace, which is already restored in a sense (Calvin would add "for the elect") by Christ's victory [1] and shall be decisively restored when *the creation itself* will be set free for "the glorious liberty of the children of God" [2].

Pagan tragedy, of course, does not offer our only precedent. Milton's *Paradise Lost* — to choose an example distinguished by its artistic merit as well as by its dependence not only on medieval sources but on Calvin himself — deliciously squanders much of its

---

1) Rom. 5:1.
2) Rom. 8:21.

resources *setting the stage* for Fall and Loss. Yet we need go no further than Calvin's definitive *Institutes* of 1559 to justify our procedure. Our organization is warranted if Parker is correct in concluding that Calvin's choice of the *duplex cognitio* as his structural principle separates Book I from Books II—IV, for Book I is the principal source of our Prologue, while Books II—IV contribute heavily to the dramatic action which follows.

One last vital consideration remains. We called the reader "participant" in the drama, echoing the presuppositions of classic tragedy. Without subscribing specifically to Aristotle's *katharsis* of the emotions through pity and fear, we are thus focusing attention on the *end* of art. Calvin is surer of nothing than that the good warfare with the Spirit's sword is *our* fight. *Heilsgeschichte* and *Heilsdrama* are redemptive history and drama for us because *he and we* participate in the history and drama which redeem. And so our Prologue must begin where all Calvin's thought, in the concreteness of ethics and in the abstraction of theological reflection, begins: with the panergistic, the omni-active, God he finds in the Bible.

The Nature and Attributes of God

What should be known about God [1]? Calvin asserts in the opening lines of his crucial first theological treatise: "That he is infinite wisdom, righteousness, goodness, mercy, truth, power and life [2] and wherever we perceive any of these things, they are of him [3]. Also, all things both in heaven and earth were created to his glory ... In the third place, he is a righteous judge, sternly punishing those who swerve from his laws and do not entirely perform his will, who think, speak and act in another way than that which pertains to his glory. Fourthly, he is mercy and gentleness, receiving kindly the wretched and poor who flee to his clemency and

---

1) We must emphasize that in asking the question "What?", which dominates our whole discussion of the nature and attributes of God, we are somewhat artificially divorcing it from the questions "Where?" and "How?" concerning our knowledge of God, although they are inextricably connected with our question "What?" by Calvin himself. However, our purpose is best served by this methodological distinction which places the question "What?" over the whole of this discussion of God's nature.

2) Baruch 3; James 1.

3) Prov. 16.

33

entrust themselves to his faithfulness"[4]. It is important to note the order, typical for Calvin's doctrine of God throughout his career, in which he tabulates what should be known about him: 1) his attributes; 2) that the end of creation is his glory; 3) his judgment; 4) his mercy. With respect to all of these matters, Calvin intends not to refer to an abstract knowledge but one "conducing to his glory and our benefit"[5]. Further, Calvin emphasizes that the very nature of God's self-revelation *limits* our knowledge of him. "God clothes himself with a form that he may be seen and known. Yet, that he clothes himself means that he also hides himself by that which he puts on, as the nakedness of a man is hidden by his clothes"[6]. Therefore, although our knowledge is limited in this way, God reveals *himself*. We may say, then, that we can know God truly, although we do not know him completely.

Calvin's primordial concern for the Divine attributes leads us to ask whether his conception of God is, after all, of speculative rather than Biblical derivation. Calvin did indeed make liberal use of the philosophical terminology universally applied to the doctrine of God in his day. (Particularly striking is the fact that in our opening quotation in this section God is, metaphorically *identified with* his attributes.) Yet Calvin finds "a brief comprehension of *all* that it was *possible* for men to know concerning God" in Exodus 34:6, where he sees an enumeration of God's perfections, "clemency, goodness, mercy, justice, judgment and truth"[7]. This indicates Calvin's clear intention to break with the path of the Scholastic theologians: whereas they attempted to develop their conception of God from philosophical considerations, Calvin's teaching, invariably proceeds exegetically. The very reason these attributes are revealed in Scripture is "that our knowledge of him may consist rather in a lively perception, than in vain and airy speculations"[8]. In specific cases, however, Calvin's "Biblical" God wears the rigid armor forged by logical rigor. For example, Calvin chafes under the Old Testament's application of the verb *naḥam,* to repent, to God. He attributes to God an "immutability" (connoting an emo-

---

4) CR XXIX, 27 f. (Trans. in T. H. L. Parker, *The Doctrine of the Knowledge of God,* p. 3.)

5) I, ii, 1.

6) See Parker, *Knowledge of God,* p. 52.

7) I, x, 2. e. a.

8) *Ibid.*

tional impassivity reminiscent of Aristotle's Unmoved Mover [9]) so inflexible that "with regard to repentance, we must not admit that it can happen to God, any more than ignorance, or error, or impotence" [10]. Calvin softens the threat posed to God's freedom by inviolable immutability through his principle of God's self-accommodation to our frail understanding [11]; but the grace of God fully revealed in his compassionate gift of Jesus Christ is certainly a more *fitting* exegetical key than Calvin's to *naḥam*.

This raises a more serious question about the stress Calvin places on the attributes of God. Does it prevent him from approaching his whole understanding of God from the point at which God reveals himself most fully and decisively, namely, in Jesus Christ? In Book I of the 1559 *Institutes,* Calvin comes to the conclusion that the Bible is the sole definitive source of our knowledge about God, because there God speaks in such a clear way that man (under the guidance of the Spirit) cannot make the radical misunderstanding that he has made of God's revelation in nature and in man [12]. Calvin proceeds to show that not only is Jesus Christ the center of the New Testament, but also that "the end of the Old Testament was always Christ and eternal life" [13]. He indicates that this similarity is more basic than the differences between the two Testaments [14]. Yet Calvin's own doctrine of God often appears *not* to *move* and *operate* from this center of the Biblical message. In speaking about the God whom man can know, Calvin can speak of a God known apart from Jesus Christ. From Calvin's own understanding of the center of the Biblical message, we must question his frequent assumption that Christian theology can and should at first forget its decisive knowledge of God in Christ and consider God the Creator as did the Old Testament: apart, at least explicitly, from Jesus Christ. This criticism presupposes a distinction between theology as a *science* and theology as an *art* [15]. As an *art,* interested only in a limited set of symbols, theology is free to begin its story at any point, to ignore many truths, and to a certain extent — as Luther repeatedly proved — even to distort. Like any *science,* however, when theology makes

---

9) See *Comm.* Gen. 6:6; III, xx, 5; and *Comm.* Rom. 1:18, p. 25.
10) I, xvii, 12, Allen.
11) e. g., I, xvii, 13.
12) chs. iv and vi.
13) II, x, 4.
14) II, xi, 1.
15) See chapters II, III and V of *The Common Quest.*

generalized statements it must not only operate with perfect logical rigor but take great pains to define its presuppositions from the best possible starting point and with reference to all pertinent data. It is in considering *theology as a science* that we insist on using the central fact of Christianity, the Christ event, as this starting point for understanding God, man, sin, redemption, eschatology and even — with John 1, Colossians 1, and Hebrews 1 — creation.

The second thing that Calvin wishes us to know about the God whose will creates the *Heilsgeschichte* with its spiritual warfare is that the end of his creation is his glory. The word glory is perhaps the clearest expression of the centrality of God in Calvin's theology. If the first element of our knowledge of God consists of his attributes, we are probably justified in saying that Calvin thinks of the glory of God as a sort of primary or central attribute, of which others are partial descriptions [16]. "His essence indeed is incomprehensible, so that his majesty is not perceived by the human sense: but on all his works he has inscribed his glory" [17]. The angels [18], the world [19], man — as the *imago dei* [20] — all display God's *gloria*. God's purpose, the manifestation of his glory, also clearly underlies every facet of Calvin's all-embracing doctrine of providence [21].

Although this "panergism" of God's glory has met violent opposition from the first, let us clearly understand the depth of Cal-

---

16) Note II, viii, 25, where Calvin says that God can find nothing higher by which to swear than his glory. Parker thinks that when Calvin's God exercizes his glory a host of his other attributes are revealed (*Knowledge of God,* p. 54).

17) I, v, 1, Allen.

18) I, xiv, 5.

19) I, v, 5.

20) I, xv, 4.

21) Negative evaluations of Calvin seize upon his use of *gloria dei.* Otto Ritschl, *Die reformierte Theologie des 16. u. 17. Jahrhundert,* pp. 171 f. (followed in more primitive form by Herman Wendorf, *Calvins Bedeutung für die protestantische Welt,* p. 13) finds nothing else than the French nationalistic ambition reflected in Calvin's *gloria.* Heinz Otten, *Calvins theologische Anschauung von der Prädestination,* on the other hand, believes that the *gloria dei* consists in his gracious condescension to sinful man (pp. 38 ff. and 72 ff.). Kolfhaus emphasizes the convergence of God's glory and man's salvation, and finds the two united in Christ (*op. cit.,* pp. 518 f.). It is especially important to his purpose to note that the *gloria dei* is the highest ethical motive for Calvin (see also Doumergue, *op. cit.,* p. 283, and Karlfried Fröhlich, *Gottesreich, Welt und Kirche bei Calvin,* p. 40).

vin's concern for the glory of God and the unblinking rigor of his rationale. Calvin assumes that God is omnipotent and that God is everywhere at work. Calvin also assumes that evil exists and that God is just and good. Logical consistency demands, therefore, a double destiny for men — salvation and damnation — and Calvin concludes that God exercises his power and works for his own ends (his glory) even in evil and damnation. If we fail to comprehend how this is just, he calls it the failure of our understanding and not of God's justice, for "the Divine will . . . is only another name for the highest justice" [22].

The incongruity of Calvin's opposing conceptions of God's glory is still more clearly visible when applied to the third and fourth things we should know about God: his judgment and his mercy, for the God of "terrible majesty" and "dreadful glory" is radically contrasted with the God of grace: "For as soon as God's terrible majesty (*horribilis dei majestas*) comes to mind, we cannot but tremble and be driven far way (from him) by a recognition of our own unworthiness until Christ comes forward as the Mediator, *to change the throne of dreadful glory into the throne of grace*" [23]. Thus the criticism which we must make of Calvin's concept of God's glory is not that it gives an improper emphasis to the power of God, but that it is not *centered* in the New Testament concept that the glory (and power) of God is above all and primarily to be seen in the face of Jesus Christ, his gracious gift.

There is one area, however, in which Calvin's doctrine of God bears an explicitly New Testament rather than an Old Testament character, namely, his formal systematic statement of the Trinity. At the beginning of his career, Calvin was accused of Trinitarian heresy by Peter Caroli because Calvin refused to subscribe to the symbols of the ancient church. Calvin apparently meant thereby to reject any authority other that the Bible. It seems clear, however, from all other indications that Calvin's doctrine of the Trinity was thoroughly orthodox and basic to his whole conception of the form and content of Christian faith.

At this point we must make explicit the implications of our repeated distinction between a *theoretical* or *systematic* formulation of a doctrine and the form of that same conception actually *operative* in a given theology. A thinker may include a formulation in

---

22) III, xxiii, 5, Allen.
23) III, xx, 17, part. reten. Allen.

his theology because it is orthodox and traditional or because the shape and balance of his system may require it. When his theology goes into *operation,* however, the concept in question may not work, may not mesh with the other elements of his thought. Then he may be driven to use a different formulation — for example, of anthropology, of law, or of grace — the implications of which he may not like, because with it the system functions better as a whole. First-rate thinkers who desire to be true to the classic Christian faith often recognize such weak *systematic* concepts — usually in part as a result of contemporary critism — and attempt to compensate for it. Thus Calvin takes great care to answer the charges that his immutable, panergistic, foreordaining Deity is "worse than the devil" and destroys human dignity and freedom. Lutherans, similarly, are at great pains to qualify and repair Luther's powerful dualistic tendencies. Such covering efforts tend to obscure the weakness of a formal *systematic* statement, but they merely camouflage an *inoperative* doctrine, so that a too-innocent orthodoxy may actually be the clue to a flaw. Thus, we may use Calvin's orthodox Trinity as a preliminary working hypothesis for understanding the nature of the God who moves in Calvin's drama. Ultimately, however, we may well be operationally dependent not upon the God of grace who is the Father, and the Son, and the Holy Spirit, but upon the law-giving God of glory to initiate the great drama of spiritual warfare, give it its character, and bring it to a victorious end.

God's Creation

We turn now for two reasons to the creation of the sovereign God. First, with Calvin we would "let the world become our school if we desire rightly to know God" [1]. The very work of creation distinguishes this God from all other gods we could imagine and gives us knowledge of him. In the second place, this whole creation in its perfect state sets the stage and provides most of the *dramatis personae* for the greatest of all dramas: the approaching spiritual warfare.

The primary theological significance of the creation is that it is a vast theatre erected for displaying God's glory [2]. Its every feature

---

1) *Introduction* to *Gen. Comm.* I, 60.
2) See I, v, 8, n. 27.

leads us to consider not only it but also — and first of all — its Maker. What gives the creation this peculiar property? It bears the *imago dei*! Many discussions of the *imago* in Calvin's thought deal exclusively with anthropology, with questions about which "part", ability or activity of man images God, and about the fate of the *imago* in the course of the *Heilsgeschichte*. That the cosmos is in the *imago dei,* however, teaches us that the concept of imagery has a broader connotation for Calvin, so that Parker can say of *imago*: "It is the fundamental concept in (Calvin's) doctrine of revelation" [3]. Calvin apparently found the physics of light and optics peculiarly suited to the metaphorical explication of the Christian faith. Thus, the universe is a mirror in which we can see the *effigies dei* (the portrait of God). Calvin uses precisely the same terminology concerning Jesus Christ, but this time in its most proper sense: "It (the universe) is the *imago dei* because it is the *speculum dei* — and not conversely . . . He (Jesus) reflects the *effigies dei* because he is himself God . . . The term *imago* is not made use of in respect to essence, but with reference to us. For Christ is called the *imago* of God on this ground, that he makes God, in a manner, visible to us" [4]. Calvin chooses three Latin words, *effigies, speculum* and *imago,* any of which can be translated image. In Cavin's usage, however, *effigies* clearly means portrait or reflection, and *speculum* means mirror. The word *imago* seems to be based on the root IM, which also underlies *imitor,* to imitate. *Imago,* then, apparently refers to the *act* of imitation. T. F. Torrance is so impressed by this conception that he ignores Calvin's sometime mixing of the metaphor to say that the *imago dei* is stamped or engraved on the creature, and claims: "There is no doubt that Calvin always thinks of the *imago* in terms of a mirror. Only while the mirror actually reflects an object does it have the image of that object" [5]. "Mirroring" is dynamic as contrasted with the static "engraved" or "stamped" and thus preserves the active character of God's grace. God is therefore not only the continuing source but also the *primary* beholder of the *imago dei* [6].

The concept of the Word of God is also necessary to an understanding of the *imago dei* for Calvin, for "the Word itself, however

3) Parker, *Knowledge of God,* p. 75.
4) *Comm.* Col. 1:15, pp. 149 f.
5) T. F. Torrance, *Calvin's Doctrine of Man,* p. 36.
6) II, xii, 6. See also *Sermon* on Job 10:7 f.

it be imparted to us, is like a mirror in which faith may contemplate God"[7]. Thus, in his commentary on Psalm 19:1—9, Calvin calls the heaven "a lively image of God", in such a way that the *imago* is a "visible language", a visual equivalent of God's spoken Word[8]. But what is reflected or spoken in the *imago dei,* the imaging of God in creation? The *imago relates* the image and its divine subject-object, but the *imago* also *distinguishes* Creator and creature, thus excluding any possibility of pantheism. Further, no creature may be exalted to a point at which it is exempted from complete subordination to God's sovereign glory so as to become a second independent center from which dualism could spring. This must be made explicit, first of all, to avoid Manicheism. It is symptomatic of Calvin's Biblical mentality that although Satan as the head of the empire of wickedness[9] appears in almost every strategic briefing of the troops he scarcely makes an appearance in our Prologue. Since the devil was created by God, his malice "comes not from his creation but from his perversion". We have no more metaphysical information than the "hint" of the Johannine Christ that since Satan "abode not in the truth"[10] "he was once in it". Though acknowledging this to be brief and unclear, Calvin finds it "more than enough to clear God's majesty of all slander"[11]. Calvin further wishes, in the face of Scholasticism's Angelic Doctor, Thomas Aquinas, to avoid all speculation regarding even the obedient angels lest they usurp something of God's glory[12]. Consistently, then, Calvin asserts that God's so-called creation is not the work of an artisan who merely forms or shapes the already existent, but the work of the *creator ex nihilo*[13].

The place of creation in our Prologue is assured by the fact that it is not a remote, completed action by a "momentary Creator"[14]. Instead, Calvin considers the doctrine of providence, which is the driving force of our entire drama, to be an indispensable exposition of God's status as Creator. In providence we learn first of God's perfections, particularly his power; second, that God has a purpose

---

7) III, ii, 6. Again, God not only *speaks* through the Bible but is himself *reflected* there, CR LIV, 281.

8) *loc. cit.,* I, 308 and 313.

9) I, xiv, 14.

10) John 8:44 KJV.

11) All quotes I, xiv, 16.

12) I, xiv, 10.

13) *Comm.* Gen. 1:1, I, 70.

14) I, xvi, 1.

in all his actions; third of God's love to men. The statement that God "regulates all things" in such a manner that "nothing happens except what is knowingly and willingly decreed by him" [15] stands at the center of Calvin's doctrine of providence. We may say that it represents the real *skandalon* of Calvin's own theology, rather than the related doctrine of predestination made so unpopular by his successors. Calvin is willing to extend this thesis to include in the counsel of God even the occurrence of evil events and the actions of evil spiritual forces. He can go so far as to say that God arms for the conflict both the devil and wicked men [16], and that whatever our enemies have criminally committed against us has been permitted and directed by his righteous dispensation. This last statement indicates the connection between God's purposiveness in providence and his love for men, for Calvin denies that God makes capricious use of absolute power, "as though God amused himself with tossing men about like tennis balls (pila)" [17]; rather, God sits as judge of the games "to exercise our patience" [18] or otherwise to discipline men. Ultimately, from providence flows nothing but right, although the reasons have been hidden from us" [19], "nor would his *goodness* permit the perpetration of any evil unless his *omnipotence* were able even from that evil to educe good" [20]. Calvin's argument for the value and necessity of a strong doctrine of providence reaches its climax in the question: "Unless Christ had been crucified according to God's will whence would we have our redemption" [21]?

The second of Calvin's perspectives on creation is still more intimately connected with our drama: the cosmos is not only the mirror of God's glory, it is a potential theatre of war. He does not lay out an *independent* scheme showing how "this very beautiful theatre of the world", which was designed to reveal God's glory, became the setting for the warfare between God and those who rebelled against him. Rather, Calvin shows how *the fall of man* under the temptation of the evil one brought about the corruption of the whole creation. Calvin repeatedly asserts that God's interest

---

15) I, xvi, 3.
16) I, xvii, 8.
17) I, xvii, 1, Allen.
18) I, xvii, 8.
19) I, xvii, 2.
20) I, xviii, 3, Allen. Calvin here follows Augustine, see LCC *loc. cit.*, n. 7.
21) I, xviii, 3.

in creation is anthropocentric. Not only is man the peak of creation, but "in the very order of the creation, the paternal solicitude of God for man is conspicuous, because he furnished the world with all things needful, and even with an immense profusion of wealth, before he formed man. Thus man was rich before he was born" [22]. Although Calvin lived in the age of the Copernican revolution, he reasserts the faith of Psalm 8:3—8 that God has graciously bestowed the dominion over all creation upon man, insignificant and undeserving though he may be. This magnificent creation, then, like man its overlord made to mirror the glory of God, is included with him in the sentence, "all things are subject to corruption" [23]. Unlike man, however, the terrestrial creation is not spiritual and therefore neither independent nor responsible for its fall. Rather, the fall of the world from its right relation with God is due to the fact that God has bound its fate to man's [24]. Genesis 3 leads Calvin to the conclusion that Satan can, with God's permission, draw the good but non-spiritual creation into the spiritual warfare and use it there regardless of man. He believes that the serpent was not Satan but a good creature and that God "on this occasion allowed Satan the use of an animal which otherwise would never have obeyed him" [25]. Once the serpent is under the active control of Satan, Calvin can say that Adam and Eve "saw the serpent an apostate from his Creator" [26]. Thus we see that the creation not only furnishes the background for the spiritual warfare but is itself involved in it. Calvin thinks "the condition of the world itself varies with respect to men, according as God is angry with them, or shows them his favor" [27]. This means that while the control of God over all elements of nature remains unbroken even after the fall, he now uses his power — his very *creative* power — in vengeance against man. In this way, for instance, Calvin accounts for deformity and noxious insects [28].

Although the creation in its original design reflected the perfections of its Creator, it was made in such a way that it could be-

---

22) *Comm.* Gen. 1:26, I, 96.
23) I, xiv, 20.
24) *Comm.* Gen. 3:1, I, 139.
25) *Comm.* Gen. 3:1, I, 143.
26) *Ibid.,* p. 142.
27) *Comm.* Gen. 3:17, I, 173.
28) *Comm.* Gen. 2:2, I, 104.

come "subject to futility" and under the "bondage of corruption" [29]. Later we must learn the extent to which Calvin goes on like Paul to emphasize that the creation shall share in man's redemption. Here, we have shown that the whole creation was by its very nature capable of becoming embroiled in the spiritual struggle which flared up at the moment of man's rebellion against God. Just as a landscape does not merely provide a background for war but is itself damaged, so the whole creation is not merely the setting for the spiritual warfare but itself suffers participation in that struggle which centers in God's highest creature: man.

Man's Original Nature

The name of John Calvin is popularly linked with the word pessimism, more precisely, pessimism about man. According to Calvin's stated intentions, however, the truth of this opinion is limited to corrupt man, man the rebel and sinner. Calvin claims to conceive of man before the fall and of man in vital connection with Jesus Christ quite positively. "Man" in our prologue, therefore, should be far removed from pessimism. What, then, is the nature of this creature for whose sake the rest of the creation is ordered? Who is this man, who after all, writes theology and to whom theology is addressed? For all of his concern with God's glory, even Calvin is, in a sense, primarily concerned with man. In fact, the basic problems of the 1559 *Institutes* are how and what man should know and *what* he should *do* on the basis of this knowledge.

It is well for us to begin with Calvin's comment on the order of the creation of man: "Three gradations, indeed, are to be noted in the creation of man; that his dead body was formed out of the dust of the earth; that it was endued with a soul when it was time for it to receive vital motion; and that on this soul God engraved *[sic!]* his own image, to which immortality is annexed" [1]. Already here we see the *tendency* in Calvin's anthropology to regard man

---

29) Rom. 8:20 and 21.

1) This statement represents Calvin's brief synthesis of the first two chapters of Genesis: the three stages or gradations of which he speaks are 1) Gen. 2:7a: "man was formed out of the dust of the earth"; 2) Gen. 2:7b: "man became a living soul"; 3) Gen. 1:27: "God created man in his own image."

not as a unity but as a being made up of separate parts. The basic Biblical conception is that man was created whole and good, and — although created for fellowship with God — created for life on this earth. In contrast to this, the anthropological conception which dominated the thought of classical philosophy held that man was made up of two basically incompatible elements, the one earthly and material, the other transcendent and spiritual: *pneuma* or *nous*. This separation was not overcome in ancient or medieval Christian thought, in spite of the Neo-Thomists' attempt to assert that Aristotelian-Thomistic psychology entails no real division [2]. Although the Reformers attempted to return to a Biblical view of man, Calvin — like Luther and all other theologians emerging from the conceptual world of the Middle Ages — still assumed uncritically that the philsophical anthropology with its faculty psychology (derived from the Platonic-Aristotelian tradition) is congruous with the Biblical conception of man. As Emil Brunner points out: "Psychology as a whole is one of the gates through which ancient thought entered into Christian doctrine. As such, it is all the more important, since its influence was exerted more or less unconsciously, and was not supervised at all" [3]. With regard to the faculty psychology, Calvin felt that although philosophers draw fine distinctions unnecessary to theologians, they are basically quite correct [4]. This is a statement no Protestant theologian would be likely to make today. On the one hand, the faculty psychology is considered basically incompatible with Biblical thought about man. On the other hand, theologians anxious that their thought conform to modern science would have to echo the negative judgment of modern "scientific" psychology [5] upon the "faculties".

It is often clear that Calvin follows the Biblical rather than the classical understanding of man when the two are in open contradiction. The crucial example is his use of "flesh" and "body". He often uses the Stoic phrase "the prison" of the body or the flesh. The ancient slogan *sōma sēma* denoted that the pure, spiritual, rational and immortal *part* of man is tied down to the material and

---

2) See, for example, Etienne Gilson, *The Spirit of Medieval Philosophy*, 1936, pp. 176 and 187 f.; also R. E. Brennan, *Thomistic Psychology*, 1941, especially pp. 64 f. in the chapter, "Man: The Integer."

3) H. E. Brunner, *Man in Revolt*, p. 215.

4) I, xv, 6.

5) See, for example, the critique of C. R. Griffith, *Principles of Systematic Psychology*, pp. 497 ff.

evil *part*. Calvin, however, *intends* the phrase to say that the *whole* and regenerate — in Pauline terminology, the new — man is in this life never free from the sinful old man who, like the other, is characterized by *both* mind and body. This tendency of Calvin to separate the soul and body of man is not isolated in such a way as to limit this dangerous separation to anthropology. It comes to a head in Calvin's Christology, where the relation of the divine and human natures of Christ are compared at one point with the human soul and body. The tendency toward a split between the "parts" of man is reflected in a tendency toward the separation of the two natures of Christ [6]. This trend appears again in Calvin's "spiritual" interpretation of the Lord's Supper, and in eschatology.

Calvin has relatively little interest in the first of his three stages or "gradations" of man's creation, which he referred to as man's "dead body (which) was formed out of the dust of the earth". Certainly he considered that this body is a part of the good creation and as such reveals God's perfections. He explicitly says that there was no part of him (man), *not even the body,* which was not adorned with some rays of its (the *imago's*) glory [7]. Calvin is invariably reluctant to praise the body in the concrete, however, and displays a fundamental distrust of it, "for nothing is more absurd than for those who not only inhabit a cottage of clay [8], but who are themselves composed partly of dust and ashes to boast of their own excellence" [9]. Thus, we cannot deny that Calvin introduces an element of fundamental distrust toward *man* — not as sinner, but *as man* — even into the picture of man's original righteousness. We shall not be surprised, therefore, if man's body proves the weakest soldier in the *militia Christi,* the most vulnerable to the attacks of the forces of evil.

Calvin enunciates a basically dichotomous theory in I, xv, his definitive treatment of the soul. He sometimes distinguishes between soul and spirit in man, but he usually employs the word "soul" to indicate the whole of man's "essential part". "*By the soul*", Calvin tells us, "*I understand an immortal, yet created essence, which is man's nobler part*" [10]. Calvin's emphasis on *immortal* in this defini-

---

6) See pp. 73—6 below.
7) *Comm.* Gen. 1:26, I, 95.
8) Job 4:19.
9) I, xv, 1, part. reten Allen.
10) II, xv, 2.

tion is extremely important, for he repeats at every stage of the redemptive drama that the soul does not share the fate of the body, sinking into oblivion [11] but remains ultimately separate from the mortal body of which it is the immortal governor. Since the soul is, further, an "immortal yet *created* essence" it draws its immortality from the purpose of the Creator it images but from whom it does not emanate as a part [12].

Calvin postulates the soul's organization into various faculties. His terminology may seem artificial and unnecessarily elaborate to our modern minds, but Calvin's use of faculties is brilliantly clear and simple compared with that of Thomists, medieval and modern, which sometimes becomes labyrinthine. Calvin intends only to outline the psychology useful in theology and leaves the philosophers "to discuss these faculties in their subtle way" [13]. He considers it essential to distinguish the *sensory* system, the *intellective* system and the appetitive or *voluntary* one. We might think of the sensory system as a radio receiving set which "picks up" energy from all directions and relays it to a common tuning and amplifying circuit, for Calvin speaks of "five senses . . . by which all objects are conveyed into a common sensory [LCC has "presented to common sense"], as into a general repository". These "objects" (modern psychology still uses the term "sense perceptions") are then sorted and evaluated by the three intellectual faculties: the fantasy, reason or universal judgment, and the understanding. Of the third system, the voluntary, Calvin says: "Similarly, to . . . the three cognitive faculties of the soul correspond three appetitive faculties: will, . . the irascible faculty (capacity for anger), . . . and the concuscible faculty (capacity to desire inordinately)" [14]. To avoid a complex formulation which can lead to obscurity and be dangerous, Calvin proposes, as appropriate to human nature in its primal integrity, to hold "that the human soul consists of two faculties, understanding and will . . . The understanding is, as it were, the leader and governor of the soul; . . . the will always respects its authority and waits for its judgment in its desires" [15].

---

11) For various aspects of Calvin's attitude toward the soul's immortality, see I, xv, 3; I, xv, 6; the whole of III, xxv, 7 and III, xxv, 6.

12) A theory revived by Servetus: see I, xv, 5.

13) I, xv, 6.

14) All quotes *Ibid.,* part. reten. Allen.

15) I, xv, 7, part. reten. Allen.

This organization of the faculties makes an important difference between Calvin and his Roman Catholic opponents, one evident in discussions about sin. In general, they think that *sense* is more or less subject to the inevitably sinful material body and through it sin enters into man. Sinful sense and pure untainted reason struggle for the control of the will. For Calvin, on the other hand, mind, reason, intellect, are by no means necessarily allies of God in the arena of spiritual warfare. He considers *sense as part of the understanding,* the reasonable faculty. When man sins it is because his *reason* (which Scholastic thought usually considers incorrupt, even though weakened by the fall so as to be vulnerable to defeat by sense) is *corrupt* since the fall [16]. Because it completely controls the will, this corrupt reason leads man to a sinful decision.

The conscience is an element (almost another intellectual faculty) of man's psychic makeup which plays a far greater role in Calvin's thought than scholars often recognize [17]. Calvin's definitive statement about the conscience provides the basis for understanding the two kinds of government (the court of conscience and the political one) to which man is subject: "When men grasp the conception of things with the mind and understanding, they are then said (*scire*) 'to know', from which is derived the word (*scientia,* 'science' or) 'knowledge'. In like manner when men have an awareness of Divine justice ... this awareness is called (*conscientia*) 'conscience'" [18]. Calvin conceives of the conscience as a genuine source of the knowledge of right and wrong which survives man's fall, and over which man does not possess control. Calvin's repeated reference to the captivity and liberation of the conscience stresses its role as weapon and prize of spiritual warfare.

Thus, Calvin defines conscience in functional or dynamic terms: the conscience is "knowledge" or "apprehension". But we must ask what the content of this knowledge is in order to understand the

---

16) *Ibid.*

17) A notable exception is E. A. Dowey, *The Knowledge of God in Calvin's Theology,* pp. 56—72.

18) Unaccountably, no one (not even the editors of LCC) seems to recognize that most of IV, x, 3 is lifted word for word from III, xix, 15 (between the two translations we have chosen that from IV, x, 3). This should be a clue sufficient to suggest the need for a much more careful study of the relation between Calvin's concepts of conscience and natural law, on the one hand, and conscience and the work of the Holy Spirit in man on the other. See the useful material in LCC, III, xix, 3 n. 24 and IV, x, 3 n. 8.

function of conscience. On the one hand, God through the conscience places men before his tribunal, for "conscience is a thousand witnesses" [19]. On the other hand, our study of the pertinent texts discloses that for Calvin it is the conscience to which God addresses the *testimonium spiritus sancti internum*. We could infer this from the familiar passages in the *Institutes,* but it is directly affirmed in the statement: "The true conviction which believers have of the Word of God . . . spring(s) . . . from the sealing of the Spirit, who imparts to their consciences such certainty as to remove all doubts" [20].

Calvin considers the conscience to be the possessor of knowledge not from man's side but only from God's side. It receives only the specific knowledge which God is pleased to give to man, and man is not capable of controlling this knowledge or of obtaining further knowledge by it; rather, *this knowledge determines him.*

The conscience, which alone retains its integrity in fallen man, points us back to the *perfection* of human faculties in the original state. Calvin believes that man's perfection *principally* refers to the soul in all its parts — even the senses [21]. The most striking aspect of his doctrine of man's original perfection comes when we find Calvin, whose name is usually linked with the doctrine of the bondage of man's will, maintaining that man was *endowed with* free *will:* "In this integrity man by free will had the power, if he so willed, to attain eternal life" [22]. Finally, despising the physical, earthly "part" of man, Calvin finds the decisive evidence of primal perfection when "the terrestrial origin of his body was almost obliterated" [23]. The peak of perfection comes in Calvin's insistence that there was no death before man had sinned because there was no weakness of the body. Thus death can no more be a friend to natural man than can his deadly enemy, sin.

The true importance of man's original perfection for Calvin becomes clear when he *equates it with the* imago dei *in man,* generally

---

19) III, xix, 3, see n. 25. Also IV, x, 3.

20) *Comm.* on Eph. 1:14, p. 208. See also I, vii, 4 and III, iii, 22.

21) *Comm.* Gen. 1:26, I, 95.

22) I, xv, 8. — The concept of freedom, in fact, is extremely important to Calvin, who devoted to it the entire chapter from which come the definitions of conscience (III, xix, "Christian Freedom"). See also Louis Goumaz, "Calvinisme et Liberté", *Les Cahiers de "Foi et Verité",* Geneva 1951.

23) *Comm.* Gen. 3:10, I, 180.

regarded as the center of Calvin's anthropology [24]. In defining the *imago* we have already subscribed to the thesis that Calvin understands the *imago dei* primarily in terms of the metaphor of light and the mirror. At all points in a discussion of the *imago dei* in Calvin, the Word of God (as Emil Brunner emphasizes) plays an important role, "the Word itself ... is like a mirror in which faith may contemplate God" [25]. Although we must regard it as a mixture of metaphors, the fact remains that Calvin unites the concepts of the Word and the *imago* in man, and man is no longer the mirror which is to *reflect;* he is now the hearer who is to *respond.* When man, who is created in the *imago dei,* hears and responds to the Word of God, Calvin understands that he perceives and receives and reflects again the *reflection* of God, whose Word is also his *imago.* This fits in with Calvin's idea of the indispensability of Scripture in relation to man's true and solid knowledge. Yet the true meeting point of the doctrines of the Word of God and the image of God is not in the Scripture but in Jesus Christ, for "Christ is not only the image of God, in so far as he is the eternal Word of God, but even on his human nature, which he has in common with us, the likeness of the glory of the Father has been engraved *[sic]* so as to form his members to the resemblance of it" [26]. However we understand the way in which man images God, we must come back to Calvin's idea of the soundness and orderliness of man's original psychic makeup when we speak of what being in the image of God means for the nature of man. As T. F. Torrance has shown, "The image of God is the uncorrupted excellence of human nature", and is equivalent for Calvin to the terms *integritas, rectitudo* and *ordo* [27], which taken together explicate the fact that "it was the spiritual life of Adam to remain united and bound to his Maker" [28].

For man to reflect the glory of God, to be in the imago dei, *then, really means for man to live wholly in accordance with the order of God, in right relationship with God and all of creation.* Here is the indispensable starting point for the redemptive drama which consists

---

24) See *Comm.* Gen. 1:26, I, 93 & I, 13, 4.

25) III, ii, 6.

26) *Comm.* John 17:22, II, 185. Peter Barth, therefore, places the entire *imago dei* question under Calvin's assertion: "We may judge from its restoration what the original has been" ("Das Problem der natürlichen Theologie bei Calvin").

27) Torrance, *op. cit.,* p. 35.

28) II, i, 5.

in warfare with the Spirit's sword. Here is the theological analogy to the serene summer of 1914 shattered by the guns of August heralding the war which bulked cosmic in scope. Before the curtain can rise on our drama, however, we must meet the force which shall decide its course and denouement.

God's Eternal Purpose to Save

In a manner possible only with a dynamic conception of the *imago,* Calvin gives a history of the *imago dei* in man which is, in fact, a complete outline of God's *Heilsgeschichte:* "The image of God is the uncorrupted excellence of human nature, which shone in Adam before his defection, but was afterwards so vitiated, and almost obliterated, that nothing remains from the ruin but what is confused, mutilated, and disease-ridden. Therefore, it is now partly visible in the elect, inasmuch as they are reborn in the Spirit, but it will obtain its full glory in heaven" [1]. We can not deny the fact that Calvin attempts to preserve God's sovereignty unsullied by teaching that God's glory is also shown in the accomplishment of his purpose *not* to save some men. But it would be incorrect to say that Calvin is principally or even equally interested in the damnation of those he calls *reprobi.* Calvin is vitally concerned with the repair of the "vitiated, almost obliterated, confused, mutilated and disease-ridden" image of God in man, not with its final destruction.

Calvin's goal in discussing God's eternal decrees is always to preserve the initiative of God in man's salvation. In order to do so he goes to extreme lengths to stamp out every spark of human initiative *in this area* which might flare up to challenge it. Ephesians 1:4 ff. is most appropriate to our Prologue and to Calvin's purpose, for it asserts that God "chose us in him (Christ) before the foundation of the world". This means to Calvin that God's determination to save man was already present when man is still in his state of original righteousness, in fact, *at a time* when we did not even exist [2]. Lest we forget that God's primary and ultimate purpose in man's election is his *own glory* Calvin adds: "The essential end

---

1) I, xv, 4, part. reten. Allen.

2) *Comm.* Eph. 1:5, p. 200. Calvin's emphasis on temporal priority here asserts a pre-destination not subject to *praescientia* (pre-science or foreknowledge). See III, xxii, 8; III, xxi, 5; III, xxiii, 6 and 7.

(of election) is ... the glorification of God, to which our sanctification appears subordinated"[3]. This invites the traditional charge that Calvin destroys man's freedom and makes him into an automaton that is no longer man.

There is indeed a plentiful supply of texts in which Calvin makes man's election rest upon what seems to be God's *capricious* choice. For, in his own words, "what basis is there for discriminating between those who yet had no existence, and whose condition was to be the same in Adam"[4]. "It isn't fair!" Calvin himself expresses our natural reaction in his famous passage about the *decretum horribile:* "The decree is dreadful indeed, I confess. Yet no one can deny that God foreknew the future final fate of man before he created him, and that he did foreknow it because he so ordained it by his own decree"[5].

We must defend Calvin's inexorable unfolding of his presuppositions and even defend the presuppositions themselves against all emotional criticism which falls short of his exegetical energy and logical rigor. This is not to say that Calvin's doctrine of predestination is invulnerable. We must, in fact, level a twofold criticism against this doctrine, both prongs of which grow out of the internal criterion of the Christian faith, out of theological truth central for Calvin himself. The first part of our objection is that Calvin's insistence on a rigid system of double predestination seriously cripples realities which he wishes to protect: God's freedom, and even his power, completely to overcome evil. While it is true that God's choice of some *logically implies*[6] that he does not choose others, logic is not so holy as to compel us to draw this inference with a force that defeats God's freedom to save men[7].

The second prong of our criticism concerns the heart of Christian theology. Within the actual unfolding of the *Heilsgeschichte* Calvin

---

3) K. Froehlich understands the question concerning God's grace as the basic one for the entire Reformation. Corresponding to and contrasting with Luther's form of it, "How do I apprehend a gracious God?", Froehlich formulates Calvin's, "How does God's glory become powerful through me?" (*Die Reichsgottesidee,* pp. 15 f.).

4) III, xxii, 2, part. reten. Allen.

5) III, xxv, 7, part. reten. Allen.

6) III, xxiii, 1.

7) Though Calvin makes it a rule in writing theology to include experience in a role subordinate to scripture and reflection upon it (CG I, 174), he frequently (e. g. III, xxii, 2 and III, xxi, 1 and 7) begins his argument on

sees Christ as the content of the Scriptures, the center who draws the Old and New Testaments together into one; but beyond human history, Calvin assumes that he can speak of God without speaking of Christ. This means that the decree of God precedes, temporally but also in importance, his grace in Christ, so that Calvin relegates Christ to the role of the *means* of accomplishing God's purpose: The proper effective cause (of our election) is the pleasure of the Divine will. The means is Christ, the goal is the praise of grace [8]. Calvin can say, on the other hand, that our assurance of election rests not in ourselves, and "not even in God the Father, if we conceive him as severed from his Son" [9]. The very real weakness in Calvin's formulation of predestination, however, is manifest in the lifeless but formidable thing his followers made of it, finding it increasingly easy to bypass Christ and depend solely on the hidden *electio patris* [10].

This weakness becomes most acute, then, at the juncture of the two prongs of our objection. In his tendency toward a doctrine of limited atonement, Calvin limits God's power to win victory precisely where it is most intense and significant — in Jesus Christ. In the exegesis of such passages as I Corinthians 15:22 and Romans 5:18, Calvin (in the company of almost all of the church's great theologians, to be sure) gladly seizes upon the phrase *all men* in its strictest sense when Paul refers it to condemnation and death in Adam, but retreats and "explains away" the same expression when it refers to decisively new life in Christ. Even so, Calvin's use of the Biblical motif of election against the serious and ever-recurring Pelagian limitations upon God puts Christian theology deeply in his debt.

Consideration of his purpose has brought our Prologue full circle: back to God. Although the stage is now fully set, Calvin's respect for the power of that purpose to drive the redemptive drama forces

---

predestination from experience — not, however, in a manner to justify Weber's definition of the Protestant ethic". See LCC III, xxii, 1 n. 4 and III, xxiv, 4 n. 7. Further, R. W. Greenlaw, ed., *Protestantism and Capitalism: The Weber Thesis and Its Critics.*

8) *Comm.* Eph. 1:5, p. 200 (see also II, xxii, 2).

9) III, xxiv, 5.

10) A decisive difference remains between them, however. Whereas God's decrees seem as transparent to them as the multiplication tables, Calvin will not probe "too presumptuously" into the "*mystery* of predestination", II, i, iv.

us to pause one last instant before raising the curtain upon it: "When God created man, he certainly foresaw that he would not long remain in an undamaged condition. So, according to his wonderful wisdom and goodness, God foreordained Christ as the Redeemer who should rescue the corrupt human race from its destruction. Precisely here God's incomparable goodness shines most brightly, that he came *beforehand* with means of salvation of his grace ready for our trouble, that he foreordained the restoration of life *even before the first man fell into death*" [11].

---

11) *Comm.* I Pet. 1:20, p. 52 (author's transl.).

ACT I: THE LION ON A LEASH

Satan and Man: Rebellion and Servitude

"Your adversary the devil prowls around like a roaring lion, seeking someone to devour". I Peter 5:8.

What masks shall the actors wear? What metaphors will the theological dramatist choose? What parts shall God and Man and Christ and Satan — the permanent members of the theological company — play in this particular drama on the constant themes of innocence and sin, ethics and redemption? The answers are by no means obvious, for the metaphorical treasury of the art of Christian theology is practically inexhaustible. Calvin himself uses many casts of characters to fill out the redemptive drama of the *Heilsgeschichte.* To choose just one such family of symbols, his definition of the *munus triplex Christi* (the God-man's roles as prophet, priest and king) gives Calvin material for three dramas: he could, for example, write of man's fall from innocence to ignorance cured by the prophet's revelation of truth; of man's impurity sullying his own untainted origin and requiring the ministrations of the sacrificial priest to wash him clean; of man's laziness and disobedience to Divine sovereignty undone by the inspiring power of the obedient, humble prince. And we must emphasize here, once for all, our recognition that our choice to isolate one form of the drama of Calvin's theology is legitimate, and we believe vitally important, but represents a radical reduction of the whole.

As we concentrate now on what we have defined as First Act, however, that climactic pivot of Milton's *Paradise Lost,* the Fall, three questions arise — each essential to the clear definition of the drama. First, who bears the responsibility for man's fall? Is it Satan alone, as the Manicheans claim? Or man alone as the Pelagians answer? Second, in what did man's sin essentially consist? Is it a transgression of the law which would require the Redeemer who appears in Act II to be a legal *advocate* or a *bondsman* who brings the price of man's ransom? Is it impurity or ignorance or a rebellion which requires a *mediator* to reconcile the warring parties? Third, how serious is man's sin? Is the damage from the Fall a sprain, a crippling injury, or a fatal one? Is Satan an accomplice in man's sin, or a seductive conspirator, or a tyrannical robber-baron impressing helpless serfs into his army? These are the questions of this chapter which must now be answered by Calvin the soldier-dramatist in terms of the spiritual warfare.

An Historical-Theological Background of Demonology

The sixteenth century was the devil's golden age. He who was later to be rationalized out of existence was then in the prime of life. He cavorts across the painter's canvas and the writer's page. His name was on the tip of the popular tongue. Demonology, like the rest of angelology, had played a very significant role in medieval thought. The mind of that long and mysterious era between his death and high Scholasticism had been dominated by the gigantic figure of Augustine of Hippo. He was prevented from radically rejecting the concept of evil and of Satan drawn from his pre-Christian Manicheism by his opposition to the "Invictus"-like Pelagian denial of importance to forces outside of man. Roman Catholic theology considers Augustine's conception the last great safe outpost this side of Manicheism, and moves between this pole and the relatively tame conception of Thomas Aquinas [1]. While we here characterize the magnificent intellectualism of the Scholastics as mild in its treatment of evil, we must bear in mind the virile militancy of the Christian mind which had preceded the Scholastic period. This more characteristically Romanesque ferocity persisted in the popular mind during the era which saw cathedrals — both of Gothic architecture and of Scholastic intellect — arise to tower above the plain.

To fix the place of Satan and of the doctrine of evil in medieval Catholic thought, we shall begin with Anselm of Canterbury, whose

---

1) See *Satan*, ed. Pere Bruno de Jesus-Marie, a work by French Carmelites on the history of demonism in Western culture.

De casu diaboli was probably written in 1077—79. He represents the first pinnacle of Scholasticism, and his thought in this area, as in so many others, did much to determine the character of the subsequent period. Anselm's concern for the fundamental goodness of all being gives a temper to the doctrine of evil and a color to the picture of Satan which is completely foreign to that we shall find in the Reformers, for Anselm and Scholasticism in general can find a place for Satan in the irrevocably good structure of being. In comparison with the titanic struggle of the insidious rebel pictured by the Reformers, Anselm's *Fall of the Devil* seems like a slight misunderstanding in the family of God. Whereas the Reformers are to describe Satan's actions with violent verbs — he rebels and attempts to overthrow God, he plots to undermine God's order by the seduction of man, he enslaves man, he is cast out and conquered by Jesus Christ — the character of Anselm's interest in Satan is evident in verbs such as: he could, if he would, but he should not.

For Anselm evil is negative, evil is — in the Idealist tradition — absence of being, of good. "All reality has arisen from God's creative will, and is therefore worthy. Insofar as the devil is, really is, worthiness is attributed to him, that *bonitas essendi* which is given to all beings as such" [2]. This view puts Anselm in the Catholic tradition, for Allers finds it strongly represented in the writings of Ireneus, Basil, Chrysostom, Gregory of Nazianzus and Augustine, who — in addition to preserving residual traces of Manicheism — "baptized" once for all the Neo-Platonic concept of the non-substantiality of evil. This Neo-Platonism is suggested by a magnificent minature in a manuscript (dating from about 880) of Gregory of Nazianzus, which presents Satan as a nobly dressed graceful youth whose angelic appearance is qualified only by mauve coloration in contrast to the healthy (being-full) pink glow of his angelic fellows. How then is God, with whom the positive content even of Satan's evil will originates, to be freed from responsibility for it? Such a question as "Whence is evil if righteousness is the original?" [3] is inadmissible because it treats the negative as a positive, unrighteousness as being as real as righteousness. Evil is an accidental, not a substantial phenomenon [4]. Wherein, then, does Satan's sin consist? There are only two things which one can will: the right and

---

2) R. Allers, *Anselm von Canterbury*, 1936.
3) *De casu diaboli*, XXVII.
4) F. R. Hasse, *Anselm von Canterbury*, II, 436.

the pleasant. Satan "sinned in requiring something pleasant, which he did not have and should not have at that time, but which could increase his happiness . . . He required this in a *disorderly* way, and thus extended his will beyond righteousness" [5]. As to ultimate responsibility for this act of Satan's will, Hasse says that Anselm will not hear of a necessity of evil. The origin of evil is for him, in one word, the purely *arbitrary*. As far as God is concerned in this responsibility, Anselm uses the term "permission", so that "evil occurs not without God, but also not through God" [6].

The whole section on foreknowledge is interesting because it reveals Satan *not* as the furious mutineer who seeks to overthrow God's authority and replace it with his own. He is assumed to know that his sin will not overthrow God's order and appears more like a small boy who is about to steal some of his mother's cookies. The idea of a fixed number of the blessed further demonstrates the peculiarities of the medieval Catholic conception of Satan [7]. The *number* of pure spirits being once fixed by God, it cannot be changed. It will not do, then, that the original number of goods spirits should forever remain reduced by the badness of the devil [8], but the demons, according to Anselm, are "incapable of redemption" [9]. Therefore God must replace fallen angels with exalted men. Thus, Anselm's doctrines of Satan, good and evil have sacrificed much of the *antithetic* character found in the New Testament and have become practically pure *thesis*.

In turning from Anselm to Thomas Aquinas we pass from Scholasticism's first bloom to its full flower, and in the *Summa Theologica* find the dialectic method in its full-blown Aristotelian formality. Aquinas has made exhaustively explicit the hierarchy of being, which reaches its fantastic effulgence in the ontological realm *between* that of God and that of the earthly creatures. There we find Satan in his place in the angelic hierarchy, that meticulously graded staircase which gave Thomas his title: Angelic Doctor.

After the first 43 questions of the Summa, concerning God, the next 20 questions deal with creation in general and the angelic world. Questions 44—48 deal with the procession of things from

---

5) *De casu*, IV. e. a.
6) F. R. Hasse, *Anselm von Canterbury*, II, pp. 427 and 439 f.
7) See *Cur deus homo?*, I, XVI.
8) Allers, *op. cit.*, p. 123.
9) *Cur deus homo*, II, XXI.

God and their distinction among themselves. Question 49 investigates the cause of evil, Article 1 asking whether good can cause evil. The provisional answer is no, although Augustine had argued that there is no possible cause outside of God. Aquinas concludes that since a being as such is good, the material cause of evil is good. But evil has no formal cause, since it is rather a *privatio formae;* it has no final cause, but it rather is a *privatio ordinis ad finem;* it does have a cause of agency, not through itself but *per accidens.* Thus God is the author of the evil that is punishment, but not of the guilty evil (*malum culpae*). Article 3 asks whether there is a Highest Evil (*summum malum*), which is the cause of all evil. This must be answered in the negative, ultimately because although beings are good through participation in the good, no being is evil through participation but through *privationem participationem.* Interestingly, Aquinas says that it is only among men that evil is to be seen in the majority of cases. He concludes that evil results from a good cause *per accidens.* In Question 63, article 3, Thomas asks: Did the devil desire to be like God? Here he develops the idea which appears in Anselm's *De casu diaboli,* VI. He wishes to say that there is a sense in which the desire to be like God is good, and also that it was impossible for Satan to do what he *knows* is wrong (since to *know* the good is to do it); but the fact of evil *must* be reckoned with. Article 7 asks: Was the highest of the sinning angels the highest of all? Although this is *inconveniens,* Aquinas finally admits that since the highest of all the angels had the most pride, it is most likely that he should fall. Question 64 deals with the punishment of the evil spirits. It is not primarily eschatological but concerns the results of their fall before the human *Heilsgeschichte* began to unfold. Though their natural knowledge remains undiminished, purely contemplative knowledge *(speculativa)* is diminished but not totally withdrawn; affective knowledge, which produces love of God, is completely taken away. Although he would assert the opposite with respect to man, Aquinas represents the *fides catholica* as holding that the will of the evil angels is hardened in evil (*obstinata*).

Thus in eleventh century Anselm and thirteenth century Aquinas we see the intellectual form of the unified medieval culture which suppresses chaos within its powerful will to order. When this order began to shatter on all fronts of life, however, it was not their conception of evil, but rather the vigorous and radical one introduced by the Protestant Reformers, which made possible a deeper understanding of the seriousness of this evil and the necessity of opposing it strenuously. It was, then, in the pungent words of Martin Luther, one determinative type of sixteenth century man, that Satan and his works came to vivid expression. Luther found Satan everywhere in both the physical and spiritual worlds, lurking not only in men's minds but rustling through the monastery at night. Convinced that this latter activity of Satan is merely a product of contemporary superstition, the main line of Lutheran scholarship has ignored or rejected Luther's use of the devil [10]. Some, however — for example, Harmannus Obendiek and the Ludensian school — believe that Luther made extremely significant theological use of the conception of Satan. The name of Calvin, on the other hand, is not *usually* connected with that of Satan (although it is reported that Luther once referred to him as a devil). Satan is a frequent factor in Calvin's writings, but they reflect remarkably little of the currently popular conception of devils. That atmosphere is best studied through the figure of the Saxon titan who had such a definitive effect on the whole of the Reformation, including Calvin.

There have been many attempts to understand Luther's conception of the devil in terms of the history of culture or in the categories of modern abnormal psychology [11]. One of the most interesting studies in these areas is that of Max Osborn, "Die Teufelliteratur

10) Julius Köstlin, *Martin Luther, Sein Leben und seine Schriften,* claims that the concept of the devil bears no relationship to the central psychological phenomenon in Luther's theology, namely, *Anfechtung* or temptation. Heinrich Boehmer, *Der Junge Luther,* who finds Luther delivered up defenceless to the superstition of his time and culture, leads the "child of his time" school, which had included Otto Scheel, *Martin Luther, vom Katholizismus zur Reformation,* and Adolf Hausrath, *Luthers Leben* (following Ellinger), to which Erich Klingner, *Luther und der deutsche Volksaberglaube,* partly subscribed.

11) From the Roman Catholic side, H. Denifle and A. M. Weiss, *Luther psychologie als Schlüssel zur Lutherlegende* and *Luther und Luthertum in der ersten Entwicklung,* give a devastatingly revealing systematization of Luther's conception of the devil, and H. Grisar, *Luther,* underwrites that judgment when he speaks of Luther's "demonology and demon-mania". Early psychiatric and psychoanalytic investigations made his belief in devils the decisive symptom of a sick Luther (Friedrich Küchenmeister, *Dr. Martin Luthers Krankheitsgeschichte;* Wilhelm Ebstein, *Dr. Martin Luthers Krankheiten und deren Einfluß auf seinen körperlichen und geistigen Zustand;* Preserved Smith, "Luther's Early Development in the Light of Psychoanalysis", *American Journal of Psychology* XXIV (1913). All such explanations are rejected by Emil Mattiessen, *Der jenseitige Mensch, eine Einführung in die Metapsychologie der*

des XVI Jahrhunderts". This work is proof of the author's contention — as true for aesthetics as it is fatal for theology — that if angelology is, as Schelling claims, the most boring of all subject, the study of demons is the most interesting. The German *Teufelliteratur* of the sixteenth century was composed primarily by Lutheran ministers, and therefore certainly had a Biblical core. In its myriads of offshoots, however, this literature unquestionably made far greater use of other sources. Historically, figures from Greek and Roman myths brought back by Rome's conquerors were added to the ancient Germanic myths to form one gigantic pandemonium. When the German people were converted to Christianity the Catholic missionaries and theologians were able, in large measure, to banish the entire group from the positive conception of deity. But the suppressed pantheon simply went underground to emerge again as "Christian" demons. Osborn says: "The devil took possession of the whole mighty heritage. He absorbed the inimical powers and sinister beings of the heathen tradition, the wild giants, the devastating storm and water demons, the figures of the kingdom of the dead in the imperial hellish court; but besides, also the incalculable horde of smaller, more harmless brownies, water-sprites, dwarfs and goblins" [12]. To these were added the conceptions which had grown up within the church. This tradition includes motifs from patristic literature, the secular and religious literature of the Carolingian era and the theological writings of the eleventh and twelfth centuries, which developed detailed descriptions of the opposing armies, their camps, the battle lines, the banners, the open battles and sieges. Then, from the international Latin works, the allegorical warfare of the virtues and vices passed into the national literatures. German, Italian and English literature were greatly affected, but the most highly developed form appeared in the French *moralités* and *diableries* [13]. This trend influenced the development of the whole of European drama, for which the devil became indispensable soon after the insertion of "Devils-scenes" in Vienna in the thirteenth century. Another form in which Satan appeared was the devil's

---

mystischen Erfahrung). Martin Rade, *Zum Teufelglaube Martin Luthers,* 1931, gives a more balanced treatment, while Vittorio Macchioro, *Martin Luther, ein Held des Glaubens,* thinks Luther's conception of Satan shows his soul as the battleground of two periods of history.

12) Osborn, *op. cit.,* p. 2.

13) See F. Mone, *Schauspiele des Mittelalters,* II, 27.

epistles — a literary type familiar to us through C. S. Lewis' *Screwtape Letters*. This form is documented as early as the twelfth century and reached its peak of fame and circulation in the *epistola luciferi* by Heinrich von Langenstein in 1351. These motifs were preserved and embroidered in the popular mind and when the collapse of medieval culture created a vacuum in the field of literature, the devils leaped in with a vengeance. From the Roman Catholic point of view the sixteenth century is a period of abysmal decadence involving the complete breakdown of morality, learning, science, as well as of the whole social economic and political order. The Reformation was the product and the summation of this degeneration. "An elite alone escaped the general chaos, and their will to reform was the way that led to the council of Trent" [14].

"The century of the Reformation became the golden age for Satan's literary significance, when poetry, like all the plastic arts, was, in the words of Goethe, 'able to present all of the necessary and accidental evils of the world in the person of the grotesque devil'. Here the religious influence which was exerted on literature as on everyone and everything else in Germany during this theological age, added a tremendous impetus to the growing power of popular poetry. And above all, the devil found a powerful advancement through the mighty personality which took such a definitive hold upon the entire development of its time: that of Martin Luther" [15]. Luther was the son of peasant stock. His father left the farm for the mines, and although he became the owner of half a dozen foundries the atmosphere of the family remained that of the peasantry. For these untutored folk, "the woods and winds and water were peopled by elves, gnomes, fairies, mermen and mermaids, sprites and witches. Sinister spirits would release storms, floods and pestilence, and would seduce mankind to sin and melancholia. Luther's mother believed that they played such minor pranks as stealing eggs, milk and butter; and Luther himself was never emancipated from such beliefs. 'Many regions are inhabited', said he, 'by devils. Prussia is full of them, and Lapland of witches. In my native country on the top of a high mountain called the Pubelsberg is a lake into which if a stone be thrown, a tempest will

---

14) *Satan,* ed. Pere Bruno, p. 311.

15) Osborn, *op. cit.,* pp. 4 f. — The testimony of non-Germanic Roland Bainton is well-calculated to underline the extent of Luther's influence: *Here I Stand,* pp. 300 f.

arise over the whole region because the waters are the abode of captive demons'" [16].

Under the influence of Luther and their common Germanic heritage, Lutheran ministers composed a great number of writings in which the devil was the sole central character. These Goedeke calls *Teufelliteratur,* for they characteristically gave "demonic personification to all vices and objectionable customs" [17]. These widely-circulated tracts were intended to edify while entertaining, and for a long time performed a popular and important literary function [18]. The early devils-books [19] still had a theological flavor. But when the books began to roam into every area of public and private life they lost all of the restraining influences of the Biblical witness. Osborn classifies these writings according to subject: sin and vice devils (miserly and luxury devils, envy devils, flattery devils, lying devils, care devils, melancholy devils); devils from tavern life (drinking devils, gambling devils, dancing devils, cursing devils, laziness devils); fashion devils (pantaloon devils, hair curling devils, clothing devils, naughtiness devils); marriage and family devils (marriage devils, ten wives devils, house devils, whoring devils, domestic devils); religious devils (devils for saints, wise and educated men, sabbath devils, the evil seven in the devil's *Karnoeffelspiel* — a card game, sacraments' devils, clergy-mishandling devils); devils of public life (brawling devils, court devils, devils of the hunt, law-court devils, oath devils, begging and mendicant devils, plague devils). Satan, for these authors, "is the frightening enemy of the human race, who has, to be sure, not lost the last remnants of the old popularity and amiability, but is no longer by any means the old, *easy to overcome Satan of Catholicism, comic in his ineptness.* He is, according to a favorite Biblical passage [20], a roaring lion who prowls around seeking someone to devour. He is, as in the Faust saga, the tempter, and he is, finally, the chosen tool of the revenge of the angry Deity. In spite of this, however, Gustav Roskoff *(Geschichte des Teufels)* is right when he thinks that already 'under Pro-

---

16) Bainton, *op. cit.,* p. 19.
17) Goedke, *Grundriss,* 2nd edn., II, 479 ff.
18) Osborn, *op. cit.,* p. 7.
19) J. Hocker, *Teufel selbst,* 1566 and *Wider den Bannteufel,* 1564; L. Milchius, *Der Zauber Teufel,* 1563; Andreas Musculus, *Von der Teufels Tyranney,* post 1566.
20) I Pet. 5:8.

testant hands the devil begins to pale'. *The writers of our tracts are no longer as serious as was Luther in his struggle with a personal devil.* Only with the earliest, the court devil, the drinking devil, the pantaloon devil, the marriage devil, are they relatively logical in carrying out a consistent conception of the devil. Already Musculus' swearing devil deviates from the style" [21]. By 1588, tracts appeared in which the name of Satan was not even to be found on the title page. By the beginning of the seventeenth century the whole of the demonic apparatus had been subsumed into the Faust plays [22].

Obendiek is certainly correct to insist that the theological conception which Luther had of the "ancient foe" of God and man is to be divorced from that of *some* of his followers. They exaggerated it so ridiculously that they robbed his teaching of all theological usefulness. It would require a surgeon of incomparable deftness, however, to extricate the Christian elements from the surrounding popular superstition even within some of Luther's own literary outpourings. It is no wonder that when the Enlightenment drove the shadows of superstition from men's minds, it swept away openness to the Biblical teaching about Satan along with credulous acceptance of water-sprites, pixies, brownies and elves. Nor is it surprising if scholars are reluctant to mine the dangerous old diggings of Satan's role in the Lutheran tradition — or even in the Christian heritage as a whole.

In view of the situation in Germany, and particularly in view of the dependence of the German tradition upon the French, it is remarkable that there is so little trace of this development in Calvin's teaching about Satan and the demons. An exception can be found in his commentaries on the word "Satyr" in Isaiah 13:21 and 34:14. (The Hebrew word itself in these late passages probably designates a goat-like demon — a strange enough creature to begin with). Calvin comments: "It will not be amiss to explain what follows about Satyrs and Pans, who are called by the French, according to the various dialects of the provinces, sometimes *Luittons,* sometimes *Follets,* and sometimes *Loups-garouz* . . . The devil performs strange tricks by means of Fauns and Satyrs, so that their names are given to him" [23]. Added to this is the sermon which Calvin preached on the occurrence of the remarkable case of the

---

21) Osborn, *op. cit.,* pp. 185 f. e. a.

22) *Ibid.,* pp. 186 and 209.

23) *Comm.* Isa. 13:21, I, 429.

recalcitrant sinner who lived on the outskirts of Geneva. He leaped from his (supposed) death-bed screaming that he was possessed of the devil, raced across the fields and hurdled a high hedge, disappearing without a trace [24]. Calvin also connected the devil with France's extravagant finery, but without mentioning the Lutheran "clothing devil". Finally, we must mention Calvin's less than exemplary conduct in the matter of the witch trials. There may be a limited number of other examples of popular superstition to be found among his sermons, but we must emphasize the fact that his theological utterances about Satan are remarkable free from popular superstition. One might argue a lack of imagination in comparison with Luther. In the light of Calvin's borrowings from the German Reformer, however, it is all the more noteworthy that he rejected the elements of popular superstition. One is ultimately forced to pay tribute to the theological sobriety of Calvin in this entire area.

B. B. Warfield has noted that Calvin's treatment of the devils in the Institutes appears first in the 1543 edition [25], and Calvin claims in 1559 that his sole reason for teaching about devils at all coincides with that of the Bible, which "aims at arousing us to take precautions against their insidious machinations, and to equip ourselves with those weapons which are sufficiently firm and strong to vanquish the most powerful enemies" [26]. Calvin freely admits that the material which Scripture offers is quite insufficient to provide a comprehensive demonology, but uses this very fact as *the criterion for a strict limitation on philosophical speculation:* "It would ill comport with the dignity of the Holy Spirit to feed our curiosity with empty histories to no effect" [27]. *This obviously provides him grounds for rejecting the popular superstitions which plagued the Protestant conception of Satan,* but he explicitly condemns excessive speculation about evil angels more characteristic of Catholic theology: "Let those who are not satisfied with these testimonies have recourse to the Sorbonian theology, which will teach them respecting angels to satiety, so as to precipitate them to hell with the devils" [28]. It is significant that Calvin specifically rejects the remarkably modern-sounding psychological interpreta-

24) See CG I, 275 f.
25) Warfield, *Calvin and Calvinism*, p. 328.
26) I, xiv, 13, part. reten. Allen.
27) I, xiv, 16. part. reten. Allen.
28) *Comm.* II Pet. 2:4, p. 397.

tion which equates the demons with aspects of man's own makeup. He insists that Satan is a personal being, a real actor in the spiritual drama: "We must refute those who babble of devils as nothing but evil emotions or perturbations which come upon us from our flesh. But this may easily be done, because the testimonies of Scripture on this subject are numerous and clear" [29].

This passage forces us to ask whether a twentieth century theologian may permit himself to speak with any degree of seriousness about the devil and demons who so concerned the sixteenth century Reformers. At least we must insist that modern theology can no longer accept the ultimately egotistical Pelagian answer to the problem of evil, namely, that man is the sole creator of it. Without losing sight of the service of Enlightenment, of modern physical and psychological science in driving out the dusty shadows of superstition, we may do well to listen to the Reformers who, of all the Christians after the ancient church, made most of the Biblical words about the victory of God in Jesus Christ over forces of evil which are both personal and cosmic [30].

The Creation of Satan and His Fall

In speaking of what we can and ought to know about Satan's *origin* and *essence,* Calvin — in this area largely in agreement with Anselm and Aquinas, though his method is sharply divergent — is satisfied that "what is useful to us, God has made known, that is, that the devils were at first created that they might serve and obey God" [1]. Calvin asserts that Satan and the demons were not at this time evil, for "it is an impious madness to ascribe to God the creation of any evil and corrupt nature" [2]. The two statements that God created all things and that all he created was good exclude every form of the dualism which Calvin summed up as Manichean: "There are not, however, two adverse principles, such as the Manicheans have imagined; for we know that the devil is not wicked by nature or by creation ... We know also that he is not equal to God, so that he can with equal right or authority contend with

29) I, xiv, 19. part. reten. Allen.
30) See H. E. Brunner, *Dogmatics,* II, 155 ff.
1) *Comm.* II Pet. 2:4, p. 397.
2) *Comm.* Gen. 3:1, I, 142.

him ... John, in the last place, in saying that some were born of God and some of the devil, imagined no traduction [propagation] such as the Manicheans dreamt of" [3]. Consequently, Calvin interprets the phrase "from the beginning" in John 8:44 in light of the words, "he did not remain in the truth": "These words plainly state that there was a change for the worse, and that the reason why Satan was a liar was, that he *revolted from the truth.* That he is a *liar,* arises not from his nature having been always contrary to truth, but because he fell from it by a *voluntary* fall" [4]. Here, we come for the first time upon Calvin's distinction, which he applies particularly to the problem of free will, between necessity and compulsion. Calvin believes that the term necessity leaves room for the term voluntary. For example, most people eat necessarily but also voluntarily. With respect to Satan, Calvin uses this terminology to express the diametrical opposition of the devil against God, but also his complete responsibility for this enmity: "The devil, who can only do evil, yet sins with his will" [5].

The depth of the split between Satan and God's good creation is seen in Calvin's conviction that Satan's rebellion is irrevocable, his awful fate sealed: "The devil ... it is certain, was long ago sentenced and condemned to hell without any hope of deliverance" [6]. Once an irreconcilable enemy of God, Calvin's Satan plots a blow calculated to cast the whole of God's creation into a turmoil so great that it too will be involved in rebellion against God. In a rationale Milton's demon will later follow, Satan, therefore, strikes at the heart of creation, God's highest terrestrial creature: man. Calvin precisely defines Satan's motivation in this attack and outlines his strategy: "Since he was the adversary of God, he attempted to subvert the order established by him, and because he could not drag God from his throne, he assailed man, in whom his image shone" [7]. The offensive against man immediately reveals to Calvin two salients, two arms of a pincers: Satan's attacks on God's truth and upon man's devoutest service to his Creator, his worship of God.

---

3) *Comm.* I John 3:8, p. 211.
4) *Comm. loc. cit.,* I, 351. part. e. a.
5) II, iii, 5.
6) *Comm.* Matt. 25:41, III, 183.
7) *Comm.* Gen. 3:1 ff., I, 146.

The latter thrust presupposes that the whole meaning of man's existence is continual acknowledgment of God's sovereignty and the advancement of his glory, so that the purpose and value of worship is to make explicit his dependence upon God and his gratitude for God's goodness. Calvin senses the strategic import of worship and warns against Satan's subverting it even at the moment it is instituted [8]. Satan's tactics aim at transferring the initiative in worship from God to man, so that man offers not what God requires but what he wishes to give [9]. Calvin finds Satan's attack upon the truth of God no less dangerous, since his idea of truth and his concept of God are inseparably united [10]. The objective of Satan's attack on truth is not only to *injure* God, but also to *destroy* man: "We need not wonder that Satan puts forth such strenuous efforts to extinguish the light of truth; for it is the only life of the soul. So, then, the most important and most deadly wound for killing the soul is falsehood" [11]. The falsehood which Satan chooses to perpetrate first is, of course, a false conception, or many false conceptions, about God. Since Satan's strategy succeeds, Calvin can say that none of the (pre-Christian) philosophers can exculpate themselves from the charge of revolting against God by the corruption of his truth, because their theo-logies were not free of Satan's deceptions [12]. Further, the devil makes a frontal attack on truth at the very focus of its revelation: God's Word. Thus, particularly in his *Commentary on Genesis,* Calvin condemns the extra-Biblical myths (which comparative religious science would call parallel phenomena) as Satanic efforts to discredit the Biblical narrative. This is merely symptomatic, however, for Obendiek finds Calvin's whole teaching about Satan oriented toward the demonic offensive against God's Word: "What is the barricade against which Satan attacks with his might and cunning? Here is the point at which the basic unity of Luther and Calvin makes its appearance. Like Luther, Calvin knew that Satan and God's Word are inimical!" [13]

---

8) *Comm.* Gen. 4:26, I, 223.

9) *Comm.* John 6:15, I, 234.

10) See references to Jesus' assertion, "I am the truth," but also to the giving of the law and the ten commandments, e. g. II, viii, 23.

11) *Comm.* John 8:44, I, 352.

12) I, x, 3.

13) Obendiek, *Der alt böse Feind,* p. 70. Obendiek also considers the Reformers' Biblical *theology* a primary target for Satan.

Though the overthrow of God is the ultimate objective of Calvin's Satan we must turn now to man, for he *is* the principal *battlefield* upon which the spiritual warfare is to be fought. The *Heilsgeschichte* we follow is the history of what happens to him, for his fate will determine the success or failure of Satan's cunning and powerful campaign to overthrow God's good creation.

The Fall of Man

The presupposition underlying every phase of Calvin's teaching about the Fall of humanity is that man's action, like that of Satan, is a voluntary one for which he is held fully responsible. Calvin even uses the doctrine of man's free will before the Fall [1] to seal man's responsibility for the terrible thing which happened to him. The outbreak of spiritual warfare in the realm of the earthly creation is immediately signalled when Calvin uses the term rebellion, and by the very presence of Satan, that rebellious warrior against God. Man's *willing* consent to Satan's revolutionary instigation makes him already a military ally in the struggle against God — and against his own salvation. Calvin follows the strategy of temptation as it develops to a breakthrough when the woman willingly engages in conversation with the rebel. Only then the breach is opened and Satan — speaking through the *persona* or mask of the serpent, the good creature God allows him to use — "leaps to open assault. For he is never wont to engage in open war until we voluntarily expose ourselves to him, naked and unarmed" [2]. In spite of Satan's cunning which calumniates God and induces Adam to revolt, Calvin insists that Adam "willingly bound himself over to the devil's tyranny" [3]. Immediately thereafter, however, man falls under the spell of that revolutionary spirit and becomes a different creature — not a new, but precisely the *old man*: "But after they (Adam and Eve) had given place to Satan's blasphemy, they began, like persons fascinated, to lose reason and judgment; yea, since they were become the slaves of Satan, he held their very senses bound" [4]. Thus, man fell because of his own disobedience, for which he has no excuse

---

1) See II, xv, 8, quoted on p. 35 above, and III, xxiii, 7.
2) *Comm.* Gen. 3:4, I, 149.
3) II, v, 1.
4) *Comm.* Gen. 3:1 ff., I, 154. See also *Ibid.,* p. 139.

but is completely responsible. At the same time this disobedience constitutes a rebellion, instigated by Satan, and the fall was a fall into the hands of Satan — a fall into slavery.

Even here, however, Calvin's greatest actor, his sovereign God, cannot be absent or inactive, even where his highest creation revolts against himself. Yet, faced with the question *why* God determines *this* decisive twist of the dramatic plot-line, Calvin declines to probe into the "mystery of predestination" by being "too presumptuously curious" [5]. Whatever the *ultimate* dramatic rationale for it may be, the fact is that the fall of man *immediately* causes a serious disturbance of God's good, ordered cosmos, a chasm rending the very center of creation and spreading itself into faults running into every area of it. Since the fate of the cosmos is tied to the one appointed to have dominion over it, when man sinned the earth, which would otherwise have remained a perfect paradise, was cursed for man's sake [6]. Further, the creation, provided for the purpose of nourishing man, now turns against him and the earth, together with previously good creatures, makes man's lot a miserable one [7]. Thus, man's revolt against God forces the whole of God's creation: 1) to pass from order to chaos; 2) to become corrupt and produce corrupt and evil beings; 3) to pass out of man's intended dominion and become his enemy. The convulsive shudder of this reaction actually threatens the sovereignty of Calvin's God, for the rest of creation passes out of his direct control since man stands so firmly between Creator and cosmos that God can, at best, operate on it *through him.* Calvin allows the rebellion of man, in effect, to negate all of the goodness of God's creation.

More dreadful than the disfiguring of earth's fair face, however, is the corruption and slavery into which man has cast *himself* by his revolt against his Creator. Following Augustine, Calvin describes the damage in terms of original sin. Original sin appears to Calvin to be an *inherited crookedness and corruption of our nature* diffused through *all the parts of the soul* [8]. He hastens to make clear that this does not destroy our responsibility [9], for we might say — in line with his distinction between necessity and compulsion — that

---

5) II, i, 10. Allen.
6) *Comm.* Gen. 2:8, I, 114.
7) *Comm.* Gen. 3:19, I, 177; Luke 13:10, II, 154; Luke 4:39, I, 250.
8) II, i, 8. Allen. e. a.
9) *Ibid.*

original sin is not so much a hereditary disease as a hereditary weakness or lack of resistance to the disease of sin. Calvin conceives of the human *nature* as "adorned" with gifts — above all the *imago dei* — in the person of Adam, believes that in Adam "Satan deceived our *nature*", and thinks that after the fall this *nature* is "denuded" or "stripped" of these gifts. Thus Adam bequeaths to his descendants a *nature* which is mutilated, crippled, and in this way under the curse. It is as though the mold from which were cast all subsequent human natures were made from the distorted, atrophied nature of the fallen Adam [10]. Calvin assesses the damage from the Fall as so great that no more than traces or remnants (*reliquii*) of the *imago* remain [11]. The *imago* is described as "vitiated and maimed" [12], even occasionally as "obliterated" [13]. But perhaps the most terrible description speaks of the *image of Satan* into which the impious have degenerated [14]. With his usual directness Luther says: "Man *must* be an image either of God or of the devil". And after the Fall, "*Aus dem Bild Gottes wurde ein Bild des Teufels*" [15]. Thus man undergoes a spiritual process similar to the degeneration of handsome Dorian Gray into a copy of his own hideous portrait: Man's greatest gift, his reflecting of the gracious Creator, becomes man's greatest curse — he now presents the likeness of God's enemy. Calvin relentlessly explicates the result of original sin in the doctrine of the total depravity of man's nature. This doctrine does not so much designate the permeation of every cell of body and soul with corruption as the fact that this curse rests on *each of the faculties* of man's *soul* [16]. The main thrust of Calvin's concept is, in contradistinction to the usual Scholastic idea, that man's *mind* is included under the curse [17]. Actually, Calvin, who had received training from Renaissance humanists, has a high regard for the abilities and accomplishments of the human intellect in the "natural" realm. This is particularly plain in his remarkable misunder-

---

10) See II, i, 6 and 17.

11) II, ii, 17.

12) *Comm.* Gen. 1:26, I, 95.

13) *Comm.* Gen. 3:1, I, 139.

14) I, xiv, 18.

15) See Obendiek, *Der alt böse Feind,* p. 70. Obendiek also considers the Reformers' Biblical theology a primary target for Satan.

16) Calvin says in II, i, 8 that we are *vitiati perversique* in all parts of our *nature.*

17) See *Comms.* Eph. 4:17, p. 289 and Rom. 12:2, p. 454.

standing of the term "light" in John 1. That light, which for the Johannine Prologue is the preincarnate Christ, Calvin's Stoic mentality reads as universal reason available to all men. In the "spiritual" realm, however: "In short, natural reason never will direct men to Christ; and as to their being endued with prudence for regulating their lives, or born to cultivate the liberal arts and sciences, all this passes away without yielding any advantage" [18]. In fact, it is precisely the mind, man's most precious, certainly his proudest, possession that Satan seizes in order to drag man into his service in the spiritual warfare against God [19]. Calvin is, however, not satisfied to say that the understanding (mind plus senses) is captive; he must show that the will is in itself corrupt and enslaved (Jacobs uses the term "willing necessity") [20] so that its evil choices are not simply due to the fact that the understanding has become a bad "guide and governor of the soul" [21].

Man's enslavement forces Calvin to describe the army of evil into which he has been impressed. Satan's transition from his pose as the mentor offering to help men "to be as gods" to his role as man's captor and tormentor occurs as soon as man succumbs. The realization of Satan's dominion over men may be gradual but it is inexorable and complete [22], not avoidable or reversible as men like to believe. The path to innocence is barred, and man's alternatives now are the bondage to Satan into which he has fallen, and the kingdom of Christ which lies ahead [23].

Calvin believes that in his enslavement of man Satan has efficient lieutenants and powerful allies. The first of these is *sin* not simply as an isolated act displeasing to God, or even as the root (original sin) which produces these fruits, but as a cosmic power which holds sway over fallen man. Individual sins have the power to divide or separate man from God [24]. Also the root of separation from God in original sin can only result in man's enslavement by God's spiritual enemies, for "all who derive the contagion of sin from corrupted

---

18) *Comm.* John 1:5, I, 34.

19) *Comm.* I Cor. 12:2, I, 396.

20) Paul Jacobs, *Prädestination und Verantwortlichkeit bei Calvin*, p. 136.

21) See II, 2 and II, 5.

22) *Comms.* Amos 5:15, II, 275, Gen. 8:21, I, 284 and Ezek. 16:50, II, 159.

23) See *Comm.* I John 3:8, p. 211.

24) III, xx, 21. Calvin can also use the favorite expressions of modern existentialism, "estrangement," II, i, 5, and "alienation" I, xv, 4.

nature are slaves from their birth" [25]. But when sin becomes a cosmic power, it is a terrifying slaveholder who cruelly domineers over men; or, again, a veritable monstrosity: "(The Psalmist) understood only too well how vast is the abyss of our sins, how many are the faces of our crimes, how many heads this monster bore, and the long tail it dragged after it" [26]. Calvin warns of this formidable foe that "sin is the foundation of Satan's kingdom" [27]; but there is another member of the unholy alliance with which sin is even more closely related: *death,* for "where sin reigns, we shall find nothing but the wrath of God which draws death along with it" [28]. Interestingly, Calvin does not treat death as an independent tyrant, a full member of the evil entente. Instead, he speaks of it more often as the result of sin and as a tool or weapon of Satan and sin in their tyrannical domination over men. Calvin makes the familiar Biblical distinction between death as a natural occurrence and as a spiritual reality [29], and considers sin responsible for both the character and the existence not only of the second death, but also of the first. Therefore, "We must consider what it was that he (Christ) feared; why was it that he dreaded death except that he saw in it the curse of God, and that he had to wrestle with the guilt of all iniquities, and also with hell itself" [30].

We must remember that the sixteenth century European was so concerned about spiritual death partly because of the dread imminence of physical death [31], about which Calvin can use similar terminology: "Human life is ... threatened with a thousand deaths", and is even "involved in death" [32]. Though he makes "estrangement" (from God) the *death* of man's soul [33] Calvin, unlike modern existentialists, does not consider death the reality which defines man. Death is, however, a dread warrior, an active personal enemy and conqueror: "He (Christ) surrendered himself to death to be subdued, not that he might be overwhelmed by its power, but rather that he might overthrow that which threatened

25) III, xi, 21. Allen.
26) III, iv, 16. part. reten. Allen.
27) II, iv, 1.
28) *Comm.* John 3:16, I, 123.
29) *Comm.* Heb. 2:15, p. 73.
30) *Comm.* Heb. 5:7, p. 123.
31) See the whole of I, xvii, 10.
32) *Ibid.*
33) II, i, 5.

us, which indeed had already overcome, and was triumphing over us"[34]. Nevertheless, Calvin would rather express the relation between death and man's spiritual slavery by saying: "Sin, the cause of death, reigns in us"[35].

The power of death is demonstrated by the remedy which extends, Calvin insists, beyond the *bodily part* of man: "Man must be born again, because he *is* flesh"[36]. This flesh is not, however, simply identical with man; it is man's enemy and an ally of the forces which enslave him. Calvin does not expressly go as far as O. Cullmann, who believes that in Romans 7, for example, flesh is a transcendental power which tyrannizes over men, but the flesh, ironically, "frees us so from God, that it makes us the bond-slaves of the devil"[37].

Calvin speaks of the law more positively than any other Reformer[38], but considers that the law of itself (ceremonial as well as moral[39]) can only accuse, condemn, and destroy, and in spite of its creation for a good purpose, it now "becomes an occasion of sin and death"[40]. God's law is then intimately related with man's other enemies, especially the flesh and sin.

It must strike us as strange that God's law finds itself in partnership with Satan, sin, death and the flesh, and in enmity against God's creature. This results from man's rebellion in which our carnal and corrupt nature contends violently against God's law, which must then "arm God's wrath" against the sinner[41]. Therefore, when the law becomes man's enemy, it is not simply a tool which has been wrested from God's hand by Satan for his own purpose. Instead, the law remains God's law, the weapon of his wrath against man.

This brings us to face the reality most terrible for fallen man. It certainly would seem enough that he was to be crushed beneath the powerful hand of God's enemies, but the final unbearable blow is that God himself makes war upon his rebellious creature. God remains primarily "the enemy of iniquity", but he is undeniably

---

34) II, xvi, 7. Allen.
35) *Comm.* Eph. 2:1, p. 220.
36) II, iii, 1. e. a.
37) *Comm.* Rom. 6:20, p. 241.
38) *Comms.* Rom. 7:2, p. 246 and II Cor. 3:17, II, 185 f.
39) II, vii, 17.
40) II, vii, 7.
41) *Ibid.*

"our enemy", and carries on an active warfare against sinful rebels. Although God's hostility against man carries to a disastrous end only those whom Calvin believes never to be delivered by Christ, God's enmity against all men — except as they exist in Christ — is of the same quality [42]. At this point, Calvin seems to be carried away by the logic of his metaphor of spiritual warfare. His omni-active God has sacrificed the initiative in reconciliation. Although God has promised the coming of the Deliverer, this helper must be virtually a *tertium quid,* for the heaviest link in the chain which binds us in our spiritual slavery is the knowledge that God, who made us in love and called us good, is our enemy.

With this statement we have ceased to look at man's predicament as before, externally, in apparently *disinterested* objective analysis. Instead, it warns us that we must now look at man from his own point of view, *existentially,* in terms of our own involvement. It is not only that God is displeased with man, but "that man is an enemy to God" [43]. Sometimes Calvin refers just to the reprobate in these terms [44], but this insane attitude of fallen man toward his Creator is not limited to them, for "we are all the mortal and avowed enemies of our God, till we are justified and received into his friendship" [45]. One of Calvin's favorite metaphors for man's continuing rebellion is that men, like the Giants, assailants of the Olympians of classical mythology, are making war against God. The comparison emphasizes the rebels' foolhardy audacity [46]. Calvin gives many concrete instances — from the Bible, church history and his contemporary scene — of men and institutions which wage war against God, for example, the ancient Babylonian imperialists [47], and the "Romanists in the present day" who are Christ's chief adversaries [48].

The *ambiguous* situation of *fallen* man is epitomized in the pivotal case of the chief priests and Pharisees who attacked Jesus *in the name of God:* "True, they do not openly proclaim that they wish to war with God, but as they cannot extinguish Christ but by

---

42) *Comm.* John 13:27, II, 71.
43) III, xi, 11.
44) *Comm.* Isa. 32:17, II, 423.
45) III, xiv, 6. part. reten. Allen. See also *Comm.* I Cor. 10:22, I, 340 f.
46) See *Comm.* Gen. 11:1 ff., I, 324 and 328.
47) *Comm.* Isa. 47:8, III, 457.
48) IV, ii, 16.

overturning the power of God, they unquestionably fight against that power openly by presumption and sacrilege" [49]. Here man, as a sinner and slave of the forces of evil, is so befuddled that he wars against God and thus he fights against the source of his life and his hope of salvation. This piteous tragedy is the true measure of what has happened to man in the Fall, for in the very act of fighting the Creator, we willingly harden ourselves: we deliberately change our own nature and dupe ourselves about the real situation [50]. The inevitable result of all these exertions of enslaved man is, therefore, spiritual suicide, the ultimate expression of *man's* being *against himself*.

The opposite side of the coin of man's enmity against God and himself is his alliance with Satan; but once man is under the command of Satan, he is not longer treated as an equal whom Satan wishes to recruit as a co-conspirator. Man's relation to Satan is entirely that of a slave to a tyrannical master [51]. Calvin emphasizes "that sin has possessed all the parts [by which Calvin means the faculties] of the soul" [52], thus connecting materially the doctrine of total depravity with man's enslavement. Most important, under Satan's tyranny man loses all ability to *understand* rightly: he has no basis within himself for love toward God or resistance toward Satan [53]. Satan's control of the human mind leads immediately to the concept of demon possession, so that Calvin says in reference to ancient times: "Demoniacs is a name given in Scripture, not to all indiscriminately who are tormented by the devil, but to those who, by a secret vengeance of God, are given up to Satan, so that he holds possession of their minds and of their bodily senses" [54]. The freedom of the will is a ludicrous and empty construct in this context: "The philosophers thought that any man is a slave by his own choice, and that by the same choice he returns to freedom. But Christ maintains that all who derive the contagion of sin from corrupted nature are slaves from their birth ... Yet this slavery is voluntary so that they who necessarily sin are not compelled to sin" [55]. This conviction of Calvin's that we are responsible for all

49) *Comm.* John 11:47, I, 449.
50) *Comm.* Isa. 59:4, IV, 249 and III, ii, 10.
51) *Comm.* Gen. 3:15, I, 169.
52) II, i, 9.
53) *Comm.* II Tim. 2:26, p. 235.
54) *Comms.* Matt. 4:23, I, 245 and Acts 19:16, II, 218.
55) *Comm.* John 8:34, I, 344.

our misfortunes regardless of the overbearing power bending our wills is vividly expressed in the picture of man's will as a horse which either God or Satan can ride [56]. Luther, too, borrowed this illustration from Augustine. The related Biblical suggestion that sinful men are or become children of the devil points to the decay, deformation or remolding of the *imago dei* in man into the image of Satan [57]. Even worse, the human slaves of Satan whom no horror can arouse "are surely far inferior to the devils" [58].

The clear distinction between the children of God and the children of Satan forcibly confronts us with the separation between the elect and those whom Calvin calls *reprobi*. He says that by the righteous vengeance of God, David was *for a time* delivered to Satan, although *ultimately* God abandons to Satan's governance only the impious and unbelievers [59]. To be sure, the reprobate are *ultimately* the most miserable of men because God "delivers them unreservedly to Satan" [60]. The condition of the reprobate and the sons of God "in the present life is commonly one and the same" however, "except that the sons of God have by far the worst of it" [61], for when a person is fully under the control of Satan, he offers less resistance and requires less Satanic attention. Calvin claims, in his *direct and systematic* statements, to be pessimistic only about *fallen* man, *apart from Christ*. He will even insist that "the unbelievers deserve our sympathy rather than that we should let ourselves be led away from our concern for them" [62], for "Paul does not abandon hope of pardon, even if men are ensnared in the devil's net" [63].

Yet after this has been said, we are still left with the overwhelming weight of passages indicating that man's slavery is so devastating as to deny God's constant mercy and to cancel the goodness of God's creation as the determinative fact about man. Calvin seems in danger of losing by his severity the definitive things learned about God and man from the reconciliation effected in Jesus Christ,

---

56) II, iv, 1, see n. 3.
57) I, xiv, 18.
58) III, ii, 10.
59) I, xiv, 18.
60) *Comm.* John 13:27 ff., II, 71. e. a.
61) *Comm.* Gen. 15:15, I, 417.
62) CG II, 7.
63) I, xiv, 18.

namely, that God wills to redeem *man as such,* for man is his own beloved creature.

In considering fallen man's negative relationships with God, himself and Satan, we have reached the low ebb of man's condition. In his corruption and enslavement man seems to have no hope. But if servitude represents his nadir it marks the zenith of Satan's power, because the success of his strategy for robbing God of his creation has resulted in the erection of a vast kingdom of evil — with Satan as its head.

The Kingdom of Satan

In order to comprehend what Satan has won, Calvin says that the devil is now called "the prince of this world", because under the term *world* is included the whole human race" [1]. Not only men but also angels are subjects in Satan's kingdom, "for though all the *devils* are apostate angels, yet many passages of Scripture assign the highest authority to one who assembles under him, as in one body, all the wicked" [2]. Here we see that Calvin takes seriously the Biblical conception of an organic continuity of beings which the individually-oriented modern mind can only conceive of as distinct. Above all, he believes that the Pauline metaphor of head and body designates a *real* organic union between Christ and the elect, and therefore reasons analogically: "For as the church and society of saints have Christ as head, so the faction of the impious and impiety itself are represented to us with their prince, who holds supreme sway over them" [3]. This union of Satan and the wicked allows Calvin to extend to them the activity attributed in Scripture to him.

The extent of Satan's dominion is better shown in Calvin's use of Biblical metaphors such as "prince of darkness", or "prince" or "god" of this world [4]. When Satan is called the "prince of the power of the air", Calvin can say that Satan "rules in the air and holds the world in subjection under his feet" [5]. While forced to deal

---

1) *Comm.* John 14:30, II, 104.
2) *Comm.* Matt. 25:43, III, 182 f.
3) I, xiv, 14.
4) See *Comms.* Luke 12:51, I, 469 and Gen. 3:15, I, 169.
5) *Comm.* Luke 10:18, II, 33.

with the incipient *Weltbild* problem, he insistently denies that this Pauline conception is inextricably bound with the ancient cosmography, as the "the devil has formed, and keeps for himself, the middle region of the air"[6]. Calvin, in contrast to the milder Scholastic view, thinks that in his own mind Satan is "robbing God of the government of the world, and claiming it for himself"[7]. However, although his power over the reprobate is very real his power over the elect is temporary and limited: "They (unclean spirits) wear out believers with fighting, ambush them, harrass them with raids, beset them in combat, and frequently fatigue them, throw them into confusion, terrify them, and sometimes wound them, yet never vanquish or crush them"[8]. Nonetheless, Calvin has placed Satan in a very exalted position among the enemies who enslave man. It is true that in the Gospels Satan's dominion over man is particularly stressed. In the rest of the New Testament, however, especially in the Pauline corpus, sin as an objective power, death, the flesh, the law, etc., are more commonly mentioned tyrants over men. A present-day attempt to deal with the problem of evil by writing a theology of spiritual warfare would probably have to consider these as at least equal partners in the evil entente. The fact that Calvin elevates Satanic majesty to a truly royal status above the other enemies of man shows Calvin, after all, more a child of sixteenth century Satanology and the medieval tradition behind it than his criterion of dependence on the Biblical would admit. Finally, however, Calvin's Satan is not the independent and self-sustained lord of this world, for "the devil is called the *prince of this world,* not because he has a kingdom separated from God (as the Manicheans imagined), but because, by God's permission, he exercises his tyranny over the world"[9]. Thus Calvin carefully restrains his teaching about Satan in the theological context determined by his doctrine of God. Satan's power, then, can only be defined by a discussion of the relation between his kingship and God's.

---

6) *Comm.* Eph. 6:12, p. 337. As Wendel shows, *op. cit.,* p. 36, Calvin was by no means as scientifically sophisticated as Melanchthon.

7) *Comm.* Matt. 4:9, I, 220.

8) I, xiv, 18. part. reten. Allen.

9) *Comm.* John 14:30, II, 104.

It has been said that when developing the relationship between the providence of God and his election, Thomas Aquinas subsumes predestination under providence; Calvin, on the other hand, takes predestination as God's ultimate purpose, which is served by his providential activity. Let us make this statement a working hypothesis, a possible key for understanding the dominion of Satan over fallen man.

In spite of Satan's stature as the conqueror of man, when Calvin compares him with God as an opponent he shrinks to such dimensions that the believer can have no ultimate terror before him. Calvin believes the author of the eschatological picture of Isa. 27 in using Leviathan "speaks allegorically of Satan and of his whole kingdom, describing him under the figure of some monstrous animal" with whom we have to do as with a wild beast who with his helpers would *sink* our ship and us *if God* did not limit his power [1]. Since this is true Satan is actually nothing worse than a dragon on a chain, a lion on a leash from which he can never break loose. He has power to harm those whom God permits to enter his bailiwick, but his activity is limited in every dimension by the providence of God [2]. This concept of Satan (as an enchained dragon or as a raging lion on a leash) does not imply to Calvin a pointless whim of God. Instead, he says that God's purpose is to use Satan in the execution of his providential government. To be sure, God primarily uses the obedient angels for the execution of his commands. Their proper function is to "dispense to us God's benefits for our salvation" [3], but sometimes God "has celestial angels, when it pleases him, as *executioners* of his vengeance" [4]. However, God also uses the work of the devil and his angels in this latter activity. How can we account for this, in view of the fact that "it would be absurd to attribute to devils the honor of presiding over the judgments of God, since they do not yield him voluntary obedience" [5]? One possible answer lies in the awful conception of Satan's work of punishing the reprobate to the ultimate. The job of God's *exe-*

---

1) *Comm.* Isa. 27:1, II, 246 f.
2) See I, xvii, 11 and *Comm.* Joel 2:11, 54.
3) *Comm.* II Cor. 4:4, II, 194.
4) *Comm.* Zech. 1:7—11, V, 36. e. a.
5) *Comm.* Gen. 19:13, I, 504.

cutioner [6] is no work for the elect angels, even though it be *God's* judgment which is executed.

At this point we observe a fundamental distinction between Calvin and Luther. In spite of all formal and systematic attempts by Lutheran theologians — indeed by Luther himself — to patch over the dualistic split in the Lutheran deity, the separation of a *deus absconditus* from the *deus revelatus* introduces a Manichean tendency *operative* in Lutheran theology. Calvin, on the other hand, prefers a monism which subsumes evil — even the deadly operations of Satan [7] — under the glorification of God, and this endangers the goodness and the very holiness of God Calvin tries so assiduously to protect.

Within the limits of his role as the executor of God's judgment, Satan's dominion over man remains firm [8]. When we inquire about the quality and extent of Satan's dominion over particular individuals, however, we squarely encounter the doctrine of election which is here — as throughout Calvin's conception of God's providence — the great watershed determining the character of the treatment men receive. Calvin has certain favorite examples [9] which he employs repeatedly to make this distinction clear. However, the classic figure of the elect in Satan's power is Job. Calvin considers that although "holy Job" was not deserving of such treatment (as was King Saul), he was "troubled and vexed by Satan" [10], because God gives Satan a certain limited power over the elect — as sinners — apart from their redemption and for his own purposes of testing them. In the case of the reprobate Satan's dominion means something quite different, as Calvin delights to explain of Pharaoh's hardened heart [11], of the evil spirit from the Lord which troubled Saul [12], of the "lying spirit" in the mouths of Ahab's prophets [13]

---

6) *Comms.* on Isa. 19:14, II, 65 and Acts 12:23, I, 492.

7) Calvin considers that the church fathers "sometimes shrink too scrupulously" from the truth that God uses Satan to execute his judgments (I, xiv, 3, part. reten. Allen).

8) *Comm.* Matt. 12:29, II, 71.

9) Such as David's temporary deliverance into the hands of the devil, e. g. I, xiv, 18.

10) *Comm.* Acts 12:23, I, 492. See also I, xiv, 7, I, xviii, 1 and I, xvii, 7 and 8.

11) II, iv, 4.

12) *Comm.* Ps. 35:4—6, I, 578 and II, 4 f.

13) *Comm.* Isa. 41:22, III, 272.

and of certain New Testament characters, notably Judas [14]. Although Calvin believes that Satan no longer fights against those who are securely enslaved, his tyranny over them is far from light, for those under this bondage are considered already dead [15]. At the same time, these concrete examples, clarifying the distinction between those delivered to Satan for testing and those delivered for punishment, force Calvin to parcel out with care the responsibility involved in God's delivery of men to Satan. The key to his solution might be termed the principle of co-action — which here connotes co-operation rather than coercion — in Calvin's entire doctrine of providence. In one action it is possible for God, the elect, wicked men and Satan all to work simultaneously — each with his own design and authority and his responsibility corresponding to these [16]. The crux of the matter lies, for Calvin, in the question: "For how should not the truth of God stand which the chiefest enemies are enforced to fulfill? Yet wisdom is necessary here, lest we join God and Satan together" [17]. The supreme example of Calvin's use of coaction is, of course, the crucifixion of Jesus: "The Jews are not therefore excusable, because they fulfilled the Scriptures; because we must consider their wicked will, and not the event, which they did not look for, which ought, in fact, to be counted a miracle. If we look into their work by itself it is quite contrary to God; but as God, in the sun and other planets, by wonderful cunning, tempers contrary motions, and such as strive among themselves, so he directs the perverse endeavors of the wicked by his secret power, unto another end than they thought, which he desires" [18]. This method of reckoning is genuinely sophisticated, as is demonstrated in the analogous mathematical operation of the calculus, in which one seeks techniques by which to hold constant all but one variable in a complex function, so as to study its effect on the whole. Calvin, therefore, earns the satisfaction he expresses: "Therefore we see no inconsistency in assigning the same deed to God, Satan, and man; but the distinction in purpose and manner causes God's righteousness to

---

14) *Comm.* John 13:27, II, 70 f.

15) *Comm.* Gen. 2:17, I, 127.

16) See *Comms.* Ezek. 9:3, I, 303; Gen. 50:20, II, 487; Rom. 1:24, p. 76. — This method did not, of course, originate with Calvin. See, for example, Augustine's superb hypothetical story of the bad and good sons, cited in I, xviii, 3.

17) *Comm.* Acts 13:27, I, 528.

18) *Ibid.*

shine forth blameless there, while the wickedness of Satan and of man betrays itself by its own disgrace" [19].

The election of God is, then, the decisive factor in man's treatment even within the kingdom of Satan; but in its primary significance God's predestination gives man hope and assurance for deliverance from this slavery to sin and death [20]. Calvin finds God's *promise* to redeem the elect out of Satan's power spoken at the very beginning of Satan's dominion, applying Gen. 3:15 to Christ and his body, the church, for "that God might revive the fainting minds of men, and restore them when oppressed by despair, it became necessary to promise them, in their posterity, victory over Satan, through whose wiles they had been ruined" [21]. Thus, man's only *possibility* of escape from Satan's prison lies in God's *purpose* [22] and *promise* to deliver him through the "Lamb slain from the foundation of the world" [23]. The *power* of God alone can break the control of the forces of evil over man, for as Augustine says: "When God makes sheep out of wolves, he reforms them by a more powerful grace to conquer their hardness" [24].

In this Act we have caught a glimpse of the scope of Calvin's vision, of the Copernicus-like awareness that as vast and numerous as are our earth and its inhabitants the cosmic powers "above" it and us overwhelm our imaginations. In saying that man is no match in the spiritual warfare for Satan, who in turn is no match for God, Calvin does not intend to bring on to his stage a smaller man than any fellow theological dramatist — but a greater God. Therefore, those who put their trust in God may, in hope, rise up from the prison of Satan and turn their eyes toward the dawn, the appearance of the Son of God, Invader, Conqueror, Restorer, who is to deliver them from their slavery into the "glorious liberty of the sons of God".

---

19) II, iv, 2.

20) II, iii, 2.

21) *Comm. loc. cit.,* I, 169. See also *Comm.* John 10:8, I, 400.

22) "That they who were the slaves of Satan may submit and devote themselves unreservedly to God," *Comm.* Isa. 41:8, III, 255.

23) II, v, 3.

24) III, xxiii, 1, part. reten. Allen.

ACT II: THE DIVINE INVADER

Christus: Invader, Victor and Restorer

"For some centuries during which everything was submerged in profound darkness, when the prince of this world made sport and jest of almost all mortals, like another Sardanapalus Satan lay idle and luxuriated in utter peace. For what else had he to do but sport and jest, in tranquil and peaceable possession of his kingdom? Yet when the light shining from on high in a measure shattered his darkness — when that Mighty One alarmed and assaulted his kingdom [1] — then he began to shake off his accustomed torpor and to hurry on his armour".

Prefatory Address to King Francis I of France, 7, August 23, 1535,   (part. reten. Allen)

Thus opens the climactic scene of the drama of salvation. Thus Calvin defines the area common to our metaphor of spiritual warfare and to technical Christology: Jesus Christ is the light shining into the darkness of Satan's kingdom; he is the Mighty One (the "strong man" of Luke 11:22) who comes for the purpose of assaulting the fortress of evil. With the straightforward and energetic economy of these words Calvin expressed what to him is the most important thing about the incarnation of God the Son in the man Jesus, called Christ. For Calvin, the basic issue in the incarnation is that the power and purity of God the Son truly and effectively enter into humanity, so that he will be able to redeem man's nature, at least that of the elect, from the miserable condition into which it has fallen. Translated into the language of spiritual warfare, this means that *the Mighty One* invades the kingdom of Satan by firmly establishing himself on and within the struggle's decisive battleground: man.

---

1) See Luke 11:22.

The Christus Victor motif in soteriology corresponds to a Christology of the Divine Invader. In response to our term "Invader Christology" one distinguished scholar has suggested that all orthodox Christology, at least beginning with Athanasius, could be so designated. This fact plus Aulen's historical treatment of the Christus Victor theme obviates an extensive consideration of the historically familiar.

Calvin believes the strategic importance of Christ's being both God and man to be so great that Satan has, from the first, exerted every effort to suppress the knowledge of one of Christ's natures, "that either he might not have the full power to save us, or we might not have the ready access to Him" [2]. Calvin himself is overwhelmingly impressed with the difference which being God the Son makes between this man and other men, "because not one of the ordinary rank of men could have been found, who was competent to perform so great undertakings; that is, to reconcile the Father to us, to atone for the sins of the world, to abolish death, to destroy the kingdom of Satan, to bring us to true righteousness and salvation" [3].

Calvin uses two New Testament passages to express the Invader Christology, the first of which is I John 3:8: "The reason the Son of God appeared was to destroy the works of the devil".The other passage, Heb. 2:14, forms the heart of his argument on the necessity for Christ to assume real humanity. Against all forms of the Docetic conception of Christ, Calvin maintains that Christ "took flesh and blood, 'that through death he might destroy him that had the power of death'" [4]. Calvin is concerned that the Son of God *fully* enter into humanity in order to undergo man's deepest fate, to take upon himself man's heaviest burden, death, so that having thus entered the crucial sector of the battle-ground his power could be brought to bear on the host of God's enemies [5].

Thus, the Invader concept touches Calvin's Christology at the center from which that doctrine begins and to which it always returns. The implications of the concept of the Invader only become clear, however, when we set it within the context of Calvin's

---

2) *Comm.* Matt. 22:42, III, 67.
3) *Comm.* John 20:31, II, 282.
4) II, xii, 1.
5) See *Comm.* Heb. 2:14, p. 71.

complete representation of Christology in II, xii-xiv[6]. His central concern is immediately visible in the title of Chapter xii, in which Christology is explictly rooted in Calvin's soteriological answer to the classic Christological question formulated by Anselm as *Cur deus homo?*: "Christ had to become man in order to fulfill the office of Mediator". The first paragraph expresses Calvin's tendency to say not merely *peccator non capax dei* (the sinner cannot reach God) but even *finitum non capax infiniti*: "Even if man had remained immaculately innocent, his condition would have been too lowly for him to reach God without a Mediator"[7]. The primary and actual problem of man is his sin, his corruption, his rebellion which puts distance between him and the God of glory and of holy purity. As we would expect from Calvin's exceedingly strong emphasis on the majestic sovereignty of God, however, the qualitative difference between Creator and creature presents — in theory, to be sure — a sufficiently insurmountable obstacle to obstruct man's union and communion with God, even apart from sin. Because of sin, however, the incarnation of the Son of God was needed in order that man might reach God. Christ becomes *one with us* so that, for the sake of "the wondrous exchange", we might be *one with him*[8]. Christ does what we cannot: he obeys God, he obtains victory over death. He must be man to die and God to conquer death. We must be content with this Christ who has been given to us as the price of our redemption and not speculate (as had one Lutheran theologian, Andreas Osiander) as to whether or not he would have come if man had not sinned[9]. Against all Docetism, ancient and con-

---

6) Egbert Emmen has provided the monographic treatment of Calvin's Christology, *De christologie van Calvijn,* Amsterdam, 1935. (We shall speak further of J. S. Witte's section, "Die Christologie Calvins", in Vol. III, pp. 487—529 of *Das Konzil von Chalkedon.*) Calvin's Christology is solidly rooted, not in static speculation on essences but in dynamic soteriology. Therefore, we find much of his Christology operative in his *munus triplex Christi* (threefold office) discussed in II, xii—xiv. Henrik Schroten, *Christus, De Middelaar bij Calvin,* offers an extensive section on the threefold office, pp. 482 ff., preferable to J. F. Jansen's, *Calvin's Doctrine of the Work of Christ,* with its questionable thesis of an inoperative prophetic office. (See, further, LCC I, xv, 1, n. 2.)

7) II, xii, 1, part. reten. Allen.

8) II, xii, 2.

9) Calvin is repeatedly anxious to refute Osiander (see I, xv, 3 especially), since he was accused of holding the same doctrine. Note the apparent conflict between Calvin's statement from II, xii, 1 (quoted in our text immediately

temporary, Calvin argues in II, xiii that Christ took our flesh because it was necessary that our sins be expiated in that very flesh. *Our* universal *fallenness* suggests that "human" and "sinless" are mutually exclusive. Calvin does not attempt to solve this problem through his affirmation that Christ is the son of David through Mary; rather, Christ was sanctified by the Spirit in such a way that he is true man, yet free from all fault and corruption.

These formulations of the *necessity* for *both* natures and the full authenticity of Christ's *humanity* [10] in II, xii undergo their dogmatic test in Calvin's attempt to define the *relation* between the two natures of Christ in II, xiv. He begins with the symbol, excellent for stressing the union of two *different* natures, of the Virgin's womb housing Christ's human nature representing a temple within which the Son of God dwelt, so that "he who was the Son of God became also the son of man — not by confusion of substance, but by unity of person" [11]. Much less happy is Calvin's choice of the makeup of man as a symbol to illuminate and stress this *union* of two different natures. Calvin considers that Christ, like man, is made up of two different parts or substances — in the one case divine and human nature, in the other soul and body. These two different substances can be spoken of separately, or as a whole, or the properties of one may be attributed to the other. At all times, he states systematically, however, here is one whole made up of two distinct parts [12]. What on the surface appears such a neat analogy, making use of the terms of classical Christology, is shown to be extremely dangerous by the fact that any inadequacy of Calvin's anthropology is inevitably reflected in the Christology which he binds to it. We are tempted to suggest that the analogy could become very fruitful if a sounder theological anthropology were used, but the weakness of the analogy itself is exposed by Karl Barth's statement that Calvin does not appear to realize that the Son of God does not *require* a human nature as the soul needs the body [13]. Calvin's failure to recognize this danger is due to his tendency to

---

above) and his denial of Osiander's straightforward assertion that Christ positively would have come if man had not sinned.

10) "The eternal deity of the Son" had occupied sections 7—13 of xii, the trinitarian chapter of "The Knowledge of God the Creator", Book I.

11) II, xiv, 1, part. reten. Allen.

12) All ideas, *ibid.*

13) K. Barth, *op. cit.,* IV, 2, p. 58.

regard the body as qualitatively less essential to man's being than the soul.

This same tendency appears in the use to which Calvin puts the analogy. His ultimate separation of man's soul and body in practice plainly sets the face of Calvinistic Christology in the direction of the Nestorian separation of the two natures of Christ. This is particularly clear when he attempts to apply certain Biblical passages concerning Jesus to his divine nature, others to his human nature, some to both natures, and holds that still others refer to the communication of properties *(communicatio idiomatum)* between the two [14]. Calvin exerts considerable effort to reject the confused, almost pantheistic [15] — and therefore monophysite — Christology of Servetus, and on the other hand to define and defend his formulation against the charge of Nestorianism [16]. He attempts here to steer a course between the Scylla of Nestorius and the Charybdis of Eutyches. His view of the ultimate fate of Christ's human nature, however, makes it clear which of the perils threatens to sink his Christological ship and its precious cargo. One scarcely dares to ask what happens to man whose only hope is based on the union of some men with the glorified *humanity* of Christ. How shall we "see God as he is" when on the basis of Calvin's assumption, Christ ceases to "join us with the Father", *ceases to be man,* "the ambassador of the Father", having discharged the office of Mediator (the "correct" center of Calvin's Christology) so that God ceases to be the Head of Christ [17].

J. T. McNeill's loyal Calvinist claim that "Calvin adheres strictly to the line of Chalcedonian orthodoxy" [18] could apply *strictly* only to the center of Calvin's Christology, when Jesus Christ is actually playing the soteriological role of the Mediator: "Let this then be our key to right understanding: those things which apply to the office of the Mediator are not spoken simply either of the divine nature or of the human" [19]. However, Calvin's other three "Christs",

---

14) See II, xiv, 1 f., and esp. n. 4.

15) II, xiv, 8.

16) II, xiv, 5—8. It is significant that his rejection of Nestorious is flat and categorical, the condemnation of a right strawy opponent, without the subtle insights customary in Calvin's historical dogmatics.

17) All II, xiv, 3. See also *Comm.* I Cor. 15:24, II, p. 24 f.

18) I, xiv, 1, n. 1. Roman Catholic scholarship, see Witte below, does not give him the unambiguous support this note implies.

19) I, xiv, 3.

the Docetic-appearing (divine only), the Ebionite-appearing (human only) and the attempt (which had even originally been monophysite-tinged) to unite them by a *communicatio idiomatum* are imperfect expressions of the *unio personalis* and not *strictly* Chalcedonian. Not only these fringes of his thought, however, betray Calvin's inner impatience with Chalcedonian orthodoxy, for in the dimension of time he is anxious to release the Christ even from his role of Mediator. Ultimately only God-ness is to Calvin good enough for the Christ; being-human is so unworthy that Calvin is restless to rid him of it. Thus Emmen is correct in asserting about the Mediator-in-action, the general who displays no flaws while discharging his militant duty, that Calvin felt no need for developing a more systematic exposition of the *munus triplex* because for him their paradoxical unity is guaranteed by the paradoxical union of the two natures of Christ "that no rationalism can ever put asunder" [20]. The work of Christ is a personal work, therefore it must be a unitary work: *"Officium Christi est, recta nos ad patrem manu ducere"*. The limitations of generals often emerge, however, in peacetime so that we must admit that some of Witte's criticisms of Calvin's Nestorian tendencies squarely hit their mark: "Calvin believes he perceives a certain parallelism in the action of the God-man, and in his representation of this action it seems as though each of the two natures appears on the scene as an autonomous totality" [21]. If Calvin were willing to draw the logical conclusions, "the consequences of such autonomy lead to *two persons* in Christ" [22]. This, of course, would be too much to ask even consistent-minded Calvin to do. As Witte later admits, Calvin intended only to emphasize certain elements of Antiochene Christology: especially the claims that the two natures are *unmixed* and that both are involved in our salvation [23]. Like the Antiochenes themselves, who were driven toward Nestorianism by the strength of the monophysite tendencies of the Alexandrine Christology they opposed, however, Calvin's opposition to the monophysite elements in certain Lutherans confirmed his own Nestorian bent [24]. Luther's affirmation of the Real

20) E. Emmen, *op. cit.*, p. 51.

21) Johannes L. Witte, "Die Christologie Calvins", *Das Konzil von Chalkedon*, III, 508.

22) *Ibid.*, p. 511.

23) See *ibid.*, pp. 528 ff.

24) Wendel sees this danger most clearly. See *op. cit.*, pp. 229 f.

Presence in the Lord's Supper led to the acceptance of the ubiquity of the body of Jesus, sometimes expressed in the theory of consubstantiation [25]. The express, systematic, formal denial that *ubiquitas* means the transferal of the omnipresence of God the Son to the human nature through a *communication idiomatum* by the Formula of Concord did not negate the *operative* monophysite tendencies which Calvin fought in Lutheranism, especially in Joachim Westphal [26]. Small wonder, then, if, as Witte says, the *incarnation* means *only* the humiliation of the Son of God for Calvin [27], and he looks forward to its ultimate reversal. How much more consistent with Calvin's own concern for man's union with God which consists in the person of Christ, and operates only there, is Barth's statement affirming the *continuing unity* of Christ's natures: "Jesus Christ has forever ceased to be *only* God . . . throughout eternity he retains *also* his human nature [28].

From this perspective we can evaluate the concept of the Invader as related to Calvin's Christology at its center. Perhaps the simile of medieval armor may prove useful again, but only if used as a parable — a different parable than in our Introduction — which makes a single point applicable precisely as limited here. Calvin conceives of the Son of God as of a warrior whose task is to liberate captives from prison. To do so, he must enter this prison, which he can only do in the form, the costume or disguise, of a captive [29]. But when *he* assumes this "form of a captive", it also becomes a suit of armor which he wears to do battle with the jailors tyrannizing over the captives. This suit of armor, Christ's humanity, is quite a useful thing. It is not a suit of armor in the sense that it protects the divine nature within; on the contrary, this armor would be at best an ineffective museum-piece if it were cast off by its Divine Wearer. It is simply the prescribed equipment for doing battle with the enemies of God. During his earthly life, his death, his resurrection and session at the right hand of God *until* the enemies are finally completely overcome, the Divine Warrior never removes his

---

25) See IV, xvii, 22, n. 73.

26) See IV, xvii, 20—34, and especially n. 67. IV, xvii, 16, n. 54 asserts Luther's limited responsiblity for this development.

27) Johannes L. Witte, "Die Christologie Calvins", *Das Konzil von Chalkedon,* III, 516.

28) K. Barth, *op. cit.,* IV, 2, p. 111.

29) Calvin often speaks of Christ as "clothed in our humanity," or says that "he allowed his divinity to be hidden by a 'veil of flesh'." II, xiii, 2.

armor. Although it remains something different from him, he maintains it in constant connection with himself until his mighty work is done. But when all of the enemies have been decisively disposed of, the Divine Warrior removes his now needless armor: he sheds his human nature, he is "content with that glory which he enjoyed before the creation of the world" [30].

We could wish that Calvin had unequivocally understood the two natures of Christ from the *unio personalis* which is their relation, so that at all points in the history of his action we would be presented with the one Son of God, who, as the man he was and is and shall be, accomplishes the salvation of men and their reconciliation with God. Then Christ's human nature would not be a lifeless and ultimately dispensable suit of armor, but a living reality in such a union with the life of God the Son that neither its life nor that of men united with it could be extinguished. Instead, the life itself would then overcome death and darkness and devil, and all the weakness and malice that can ever separate us from each other and from God.

Jesus Christ: The Conqueror

In his *Christus Victor,* the book which made the Western theological world conscious of the work of Christ as a mighty victory over the forces of evil, Gustav Aulen ignores Calvin's doctrine of the atonement. There is also relatively little recognition of the Christus Victor element in Calvin's thought among Calvin scholars, but T. H. L. Parker devotes one chapter in his study of Calvin's preaching to the Gospel which Calvin preached. There he says that Calvin expressed his view of the work of Christ in five ways: 1) Christ was a sacrifice; 2) His death was a satisfaction for sin; 3) Christ's death was also an obedience, to cover up our wickedness and make an atonement for sin; 4) The atonement is also a cleansing from sin, which is a pollution of the human soul in the eyes of God; and 5) The death of our Lord is a victory. "Men are enslaved in their wills by the devil, and are unable to love and serve God. Christ gains the victory over the devil, sin and death ... by dying on the cross and voluntarily suffering pain of body and soul" [1]. In this section on Christ as Conqueror we shall concentrate on the last-

---

30) II, xiv, 3.
1) T. H. L. Parker, *The Oracles of God,* pp. 87 f.

named way of understanding the work of Christ. We have already seen that the Advent of Jesus, his very entrance upon the stage of history, has a decisive significance because of the coming of deliverance implicit in that event. As Calvin reads the Gospel accounts, however, Jesus bursts forth as conqueror throughout his life, as well as in his death and resurrection.

a. The Historical Consideration of Christ's Victory

The first such major revelation of the Victor comes at the time of the temptations by Satan following Jesus' baptism. (Significantly, Puritanism, with its Calvinistic emphasis on spiritual warfare, sees the victory over the *tempter* as Christ's decisive act. Milton's *Paradise Regained* deals exclusively with it.) Calvin's interest in maintaining unsullied the purity of Christ's divine nature forces him to ask immediately how the sinless Christ could be genuinely tempted without being affected by sin? He answers that this is possible since Adam's nature was liable to temptation while it was still innocent and reflected the *imago dei.* Further, Satan's temptations did not even mark Jesus with the "slight wound" which they always inflict upon us [1].

Calvin describes the course of the temptations in consistently military terminology. When the Lukan Christ is described as full of the Holy Ghost it is for the battles which he had to fight [2]. Christ's defensive strategy confounds the enemy: "Christ was not an unskillful gladiator, as not to know how he might ward off the strokes of his adversary, or idly to present his shield on the left hand when he was attacked on the right" [3]. Christ's struggle and victory are significant for us in two ways: on the one hand, Christ won an objective triumph, fighting "in single combat with the devil, that by his victory he might obtain a triumph for us" [4]. On the other hand, Christ won a subjective victory, so that he may be called the universal model of all the godly [5]. Calvin considers the recorded temptations not an isolated incident but an essential element of his whole work, since these temptations are, first, the intensified climax of what Calvin believes to have been a siege lasting forty days. He

---

1) *Comm.* Matt. 4:1 ff., I, 212.
2) *Ibid.,* p. 211.
3) *Ibid.,* p. 213.
4) *Ibid., p. 210.*
5) *Comm.* Matt. 4:6, I, 218.

thinks that Jesus was also subject to similar attacks of the tempter in subsequent events throughout his historical existence, although this moment marks the one occasion on which God lifted his restraining hand to permit his Christ to bear the full brunt of Satan's power to tempt [6].

Further, since Calvin holds that prayer is the principal exercise of faith, and the principal weapon in the arsenal of God's soldier [7], he consistently emphasizes that in his *prayers* to the Father Christ carried on the warfare against evil. First, Calvin underlines the role of prayer in preparing Christ's victory in the temptations [8]. In commenting on Jesus' second crucial prayer, taught to his disciples, Calvin makes several allusions to the spiritual warfare. Most significant is his judgment that whether the petition for deliverance from evil refers to sin or to the evil one himself, the ultimate enemy is Satan [9]. Finally, Calvin thinks that as a result of Jesus' decisive prayer in the garden of Gethsemane "he was furnished with new arms" for the gigantic struggle ahead [10].

The most significant phase of Christ's spiritual warfare before the Passion is probably made up of the miracles of exorcism and healing, in which he not only gave a living sign of the coming victory over the forces of evil, but already constituted the vanguard of victory during his earthly life. Calvin understands demon possession as Satan's seizure, with God's permission, of the faculties of a human soul so that he controls and tyrannizes over the body of that person [11]. Calvin classifies diseases as God's heralds, by whom he executes his judgments [12].Thus, Calvin's overarching doctrine of providence, which in turn serves the election of God, subsumes these evils which afflict men under God's purpose — while still asserting man's responsibility for the fact of his servitude, if not its specific form. Christ's relation to the occupying powers and the men they "possess" is defined by Calvin's belief that Christ has been *sanctified* for a *purpose* — the purpose of delivering men from

---

6) *Comm*. Matt. 4:11, p. 221 f.

7) This is strongly emphasized throughout W. Stuermann's *Calvin's Concept of Faith,* especially, p. 314.

8) *Comm*. Luke 3:21, I, 203.

9) *Comm*. Matt. 6:13, I, 329.

10) *Comm*. Matt. 26:46, III, 239.

11) *Comm*. Luke 4:33, I, 248.

12) *Comm*. Luke 4:39, I, 250 f.

the tyranny of the devil and overturning his kingdom [13]. The *power* with which Christ did this is mightily displayed when the Gadarene worships Christ even though still dominated by demons: "The whole of Satan's kingdom is subject to the authority of Christ. For the devils, when Christ summons them to appear before him, are no more at their own disposal than were the wretched men whom their tyranny was wont to drive about in every direction" [14]. The parable of the strong man cast out of his house is Jesus' own explanation that his exocisims and healing miracles are not evidence of an *alliance* with Satan, but an expression of God's powerful opposition to him. This passage demonstrates to Calvin that Jesus' exorcism are not a theatrical sham in which Satan pretends to be defeated in order to vanquish the complacent more easily, but rather: "Christ attacked Satan in open combat, threw him down, and . . . stripped him completely of all his armor . . . Everybody knew that Christ had driven Satan from his possession, and nothing was plainer than *all his miracles tended to this object;* and hence it was easy to conclude, that his power, which was so opposed to Satan, was divine" [15].

The positive side of Calvin's understanding of the exorcisms is that precisely through them the kingdom of God is established. Satan's kingship must be and has been broken by Christ's action in order for that of God to be proclaimed. Calvin's anthropological dualism again plays its role here, for he says that the exorcism's rescuing of men's *bodily senses* proclaimed Christ as Deliverer from the devil's spiritual tyranny over their *souls* [16], rather than that the deliverance of whole men from Satan's tyranny was the forerunner and first fruits of the total deliverance from the entire occupying alliance brought by Christ's death and resurrection. Although Calvin has said that men are responsible for their slavery and that Satan is God's instrument in punishing the rebels, he does not think of Satan as having a *right* over men. Satan remains the usurper, who has no rights, to whom nothing is due. Christ does not bring him payment, but subdues him by a violent struggle and wrenches men from his control by main force [17]. Thus, viewing Christ as the

---

13) *Comm.* Mark 1:21 and Luke 4:31, I, 247.

14) *Comm.* Mark 5:6, I, 430.

15) *Comm.* Matt. 12:25 ff. and parallels, II, 68. e. a.

16) *Comm.* Matt. 12:28, II, 71.

Conqueror emphasizes the power of God, just as the sacrificial work of Christ emphasizes the holiness and justice of God, the prophetic work of Christ emphasizes the nature of God as truth, and the concept of reconciliation, which embraces all forms of the work of Christ, emphasizes the loving will of God to save men.

Finally, the success of the disciples (specifically the seventy in Luke) reveals that not only is Christ mighty in his own brief ministry in Palestine, but he is also able to communicate this victory and power throughout the whole of human history by the living *Word of witness* — of which he as the eternal Word of God is the content — to his mighty acts. To Jesus' assertion, "I beheld Satan fall like lightning", Calvin adds: "From the one instance, Christ leads them to the whole class; for he commanded his Gospel to be published for the very purpose of overturning Satan's kingdom. So then, while the disciples rested solely on that demonstration which they had obtained from experience, Christ reminds them, that the power and efficacy of their doctrine extends further, and that *its tendency is to extirpate the tyranny which Satan exercises over the whole human race* ... We ought also to attend to the comparison which he employs, that the thunder of the Gospel makes Satan fall like lightning; for it expresses the divine and astonishing power of the doctrine which throws down, in a manner so sudden and violent, the prince of the world armed with such abundant forces" [18]. But what would have been the consequence if Calvin had followed out the implications which bristle from the statement made in the height of his enthusiasm for Christ's mighty victory? What other conclusion could he draw from the overthrow of the one Satan, who exercises tyranny over the *whole* human race, than that all men have been objectively freed by Christ's conquest? In addition, the scientific picture which Calvin here attempts to use symbolically has very interesting theological implications. Within the framework of his scientific understanding he assumes that the thunder of the disciples' proclamation caused the lightning of Satan's fall. But Jesus says: "I saw Satan fall like lightning from heaven. Behold, I have given you authority ... over all the power of the enemy". If the simile may be pressed as Calvin does, it would seem rather to say that the power of God in Christ is what makes Satan fall like lightning, and

---

17) *Ibid.* It was Origen who had held that Christ saved by his death paid as a ransom to the devil for the release of men.

18) *Comm.* Luke 10:18, II, 33. e. a.

the thunder of proclamation which rolls down through the centuries is the *result* of that lightning.

Between the exorcisms and healings at the beginning of Jesus' ministry and the crucial last events of his Passion, Calvin interprets only isolated events in terms of his warfare with the forces of evil. He compares Sabbath legalists who would prohibit Jesus' healing with the "Papists", who consider themselves sole possessors of Christianity and true heirs of the Church Fathers, just as the Pharisees considered themselves "the intimate friends of God" and true heirs of Moses whom they actually used as a shield in opposing Christ [19]. When Calvin shows how Jesus turned Moses against his attackers, it is surprising that he does not picture Christ using the words of Moses as a *sword,* in fact as the sword of the Spirit, the Word of God [20], particularly when he describes Christ's action as similar to foiling the Papists "with their own weapons", the Church Fathers [21].

Calvin thinks Jesus overcame a very dangerous obstacle when, during his Galilean victory procession, he refused the people's enthusiastic clamor to make him a king [22]; "If he had permitted himself to be now made a king, his *spiritual* kingdom would have been ruined, the Gospel would have been stamped with everlasting infamy, and the hope of salvation would have been utterly destroyed" [23]. Protruding through the obvious truth of this statement is Calvin's qualitative separation between "spiritual" and this-worldly. He is convinced that "my kingdom is not of this world" refers not only to origin and authority but means that Christ's kingship does not *now* objectively prevail *in* this world. This has sinister consequences for all persons and institutions not expressly "spiritual" and therefore considered enemies of God. Finally, Calvin puts an unusual construction on the sorrow of Jesus at the threshold of Lazarus' tomb: "Christ does not approach the sepulchre as an idle spectator, but as a champion who prepares for a contest; and therefore we need not wonder that he again groans; for the violent

---

19) *Comm.* John 5:45, I, 223.

20) Eph. 6:17, Heb. 4:12.

21) *Comm.* John 5:45, I, 224.

22) John 6:15.

23) *Comm.* John 6:15, I, 234. See also *Comm.* Luke 13:31, II, 158 for a related Satanic strategem.

tyranny of death, which he had to conquer, is placed before his eyes" [24].

During the first stage of the Passion week itself, Calvin believes that Jesus' prediction of the coming events shows us the Son of God already victorious over death as he advances with "cheerfulness and courage" to meet it [25]. In Gethsemane, however, we no longer behold this cheerful courage. Instead, Calvin speaks of Christ's fear of death. This teaches us the strenuousness of his struggle, for he was not "victorious without fighting" [26]. So impressive is the picture of Christ's battle in prayer there, that Calvin understands Hebrews 5:7 not as saying "He was heard on account of his reverent awe", but, "he was heard [that is, he received deliverance] from what he feared", even though the original word for fear is *eulabeia*, reverentia, rather than *phobos,* terror or dread. Calvin thinks that Jesus dreaded death because in it he saw the great enemies of man, the curse of God, the guilt of all iniquities, hell itself. He obtained what he prayed for, "sustained by the saving hand of the Father, when after a short conflict he gained a glorious victory over Satan, sin, and hell" [27].

Calvin also sees Jesus' arrest in the garden fraught with dangers. That Peter succumbs to the militancy *of this world* results from a strategem of Satan in *his spiritual* warfare. He wishes "to involve the Gospel in eternal disgrace, as if Christ had kept company with assassins and seditious persons for revolutionary purposes" [28], but Christ defeats his strategy by refusing to become embroiled. Instead, Christ, (in the Johannine account) follows the victorious course of commanding Peter to put away his sword, and himself submits to being bound. In a remarkable statement combining the concept of substitution with the metaphor of deliverance from the enemy, Calvin describes Christ's victory: "the *body* of the Son of God was *bound,* that our *souls* might be *loosed* from the cords of sin and Satan" [29]. As Jesus moves purposefully on, Calvin is careful to asserts that he fulfills the requirements of both halves of the two-part anthropology, that he drinks to the full the cup of suffering in

24) *Comm.* John 11:38, I, 442.
25) *Comm.* Matt. 26:1—13, III, 185.
26) *Comm.* Matt. 26:39, III, 234.
27) *Comm.* Heb. 5:7, p. 123.
28) *Comm.* Luke 22:51, III, 248.
29) *Comm.* John 18:12, II, 197. e. a.

body *and* in soul, for "if his soul had experienced no punishment, he would have been only a Redeemer for the body" [30]. Conscious of the necessity of this combat, Calvin's moves resolutely to Golgotha, the ignominy and infamy of which did not prevent him from "erecting there a splendid trophy of his victory" [31].

At various points during the actual crucifixion, Calvin points out elements of God's victory shining through the darkness of Christ's apparent defeat and exermination. In Jesus' cry, "Why hast Thou forsaken me?" Calvin sees that he bears the full weight of what we have described as the most terrible aspect of man's slavery — the enmity of God himself. Calvin calls this "his chief conflict . . harder than all the other tortures", and says that in enduring this, Jesus was seized by a horror sufficient to "swallow up a hundred times all the men in the world". Nevertheless, he who suffered our condemnation, both in his body and in his soul, maintained a "struggle with the sorrows of death, as if an offended God had thrown him into a whirlpool of afflictions", and by the amazing power of the Spirit achieved the victory" [32]. As soon as Jesus "yielded up his spirit ... the graves were opened" which leads Calvin immediately to the conclusion: "This was also a striking miracle, by which God declared that his Son entered into the prison of death, not to continue to be shut up there, but to bring out *all* [*sic!*] who were held captive. For at the very time when the despicable weakness of the flesh was beheld in the person of Christ, the magnificent and divine energy of his death penetrated even to hell" [33]. The burial of Jesus did not, for Calvin, have the same purpose as an ordinary human interment; rather it was a dramatic device whose purpose is to heighten the subjective effectiveness of the drama of salvation; it was added principally as a sort of preparation to set off what God was shortly to do, namely "exalt gloriously above the heavens his Son, the conqueror of death" [34]. Consequently, Calvin thinks of the death as a definite period or phase [35] in the history of the Son of God.

---

30) II, xvi, 12.

31) *Comm.* Matt. 27:33, III, 296.

32) All quotes from *Comm.* Matt. 27:46, III, 318 f.

33) *Comm.* Matt. 27:52, III, 324. e. a.

34) *Comm.* Matt. 27:57—61, III, 331.

35) Of three days, see *Comm.* Mark. 9:31, II, 330.

Calvin's well-known interpretation of Christ's descent into hell makes it part of his *exinanitio* (humiliation) rather than his *exaltatio* [36]. Calvin's unusual emphasis makes the descent *figurative,* part of the *inner* agony [*agon* means struggle] "in the sight of God", in his soul, unseen "in the sight of men" [37]. From the standpoint of the metaphor of spiritual warfare, Calvin sees this period of Christ's work as a fearful but victorious struggle against the forces of evil, because "he must also grapple hand-to-hand with the armies of hell and the dread of everlasting death" [38]. What Christ did in his descent into hell was to absorb all of the punishment of death and to conquer every aspect of it for his own people. "Therefore, by his wrestling hand-to-hand with the devil's power, with the dread of death, and with the pains of hell, he was victorious, and triumphed over them, that in death we may no longer dread those things which our Prince has swallowed up" [39]. It is precisely here, at the depths of Christ's struggle, that we learn the *cost* [40] of our salvation, for nothing is as costly as war — no price [41] so high as the price of victory!

Whatever may be claimed for the death of Christ as in itself victorious, we are left with Paul's statement, "If Christ has not been raised, then our preaching is in vain and your faith is in vain" for, Calvin adds, "He cannot be the author of salvation to others, who has been altogether vanquished by death" [42]. Calvin believes that the Prophet of the Suffering Servant, among others, already knew that *this* death is not the *finis* of the Christ [43]. It is still imperative, however, that the order be preserved, through suffering and death to glory and victory [44]. Christ is arisen — the Christ who has, at least metaphorically, descended even to the depths of hell seeking out his own among the lowliest captives [45]. What, then, was accomplished in this resurrection? Symbolically, it is the confirma-

---

36) See II, xvi, 8—12, esp. n. 23 for the history of the interpretation of this article of the Creed.
37) II, xvi, 10. See n. 25.
38) II, xvi, 10.
39) II, xvi, 11.
40) II, xvi, 12.
41) II, xvi, 10.
42) *Comm.* I Cor. 15:14, II, 19. See also II, xvi, 12.
43) *Comm.* Isa. 53:8, IV, 120.
44) *Comm.* Isa. 53:3, IV, 114.
45) II, xvi, 9.

tion and seal of the beneficial effect of the death of Christ, for "it is by rising from the dead that he obtained the palm of victory" [46]. Substantially, Christ's resurrection is itself a conquest, in fact, the resurrection may be thought of as *the* victory which includes in itself the triumph of Christ's passion and death: "For although our redemption and satisfaction was accomplished by his death, by which we are reconciled to God, yet the victory against sin, death and Satan, was gotten by his resurrection. Hence, also, came righteousness, newness of life, and the hope of blessed immortality. And, therefore, oftentimes resurrection only is set before us for our confidence of salvation, not that it should lead us away from his death, but because it testifieth the effect and fruit of his death; to be brief, *his resurrection contains in it his death*" [47].

Calvin assigns a place in the *Heilsgeschichte* to the appearances of Jesus after his resurrection, too. They are not independent victories. Calvin knows that they will not satisfy sceptics as to the truth of the resurrection because they definitely were not "splendid tropies of his victory" set up before Pilate, the priests and all the inhabitants of Jerusalem [48]. The guards, and Pilate who zealously sent them to watch the tomb, were in facts heralds of the resurrection by their very silence or their falsehood [49]. The primary purpose of the appearances, however, was to confirm the victory which had taken place in the resurrection, and to create faith *in his own people,* although Calvin does *not* make this an opportunity to represent the creation of faith as a victory over unbelief and the forces of the Father of lies, who seeks to maintain it.

The final event which Calvin places here is Jesus' ascension. He applauds Paul's interpretation of God's ascension in Psalm 68:18 to mean Jesus' entry into the heavens: "The noblest triumph which God ever gained [Calvin soon adds: "No ascension of God more triumphant or memorable will ever occur"] was when Christ, after subduing sin, conquering death, and putting Satan to flight, rose majestically to heaven, that he might exercise his glorious reign over the church" [50]. Christ's present exalted place provides three

---

46) II, xvi, 13.

47) *Comm.* Rom. 10:9 f., pp. 392 f. e. a. See also *Comm.* I Cor. 15:17, II, 20; II, xvi, 13; and *Comm.* Acts 1:21, I, 66 f.

48) III, xxv, 3.

49) *Ibid.*

50) *Comm.* Eph. 4:8, p. 272. e. a.

direct benefits for men. The first two are not explicitly connected with the metaphor of spiritual warfare, although they could be and are in fact essential to Christ's victory. (First, he who suffered and died in our nature also rose and entered heaven in our nature, so that "we do not await heaven with a bare hope, but in our Head *already possess it*" [51]. In this solidarity with his own, Christ brings into the presence of God their nature — in a real sense brings them — as a prize of victory, a vital bit of booty. Secondly, Christ intercedes for his own as their protector.) Third, and directly related to spiritual warfare, he gives them apprehension of his might, "in which reposes our strength ... our victory over hell", and which shall "restrain the raging enemies of his cross and of our salvation" [52].

b. The Systematic Consideration of Christ's Victory

The systematic writings of Calvin are as inevitably filled with echoes of the victory of God in Christ as the Epistles of the New Testament find their center in the work of Christ consumated in the death and resurrection recorded in the Gospels. Calvin does not look upon this victory as a heroic triumph of Jesus *qua homo,* a prize then offered to God: a human consumation of God's kingdom. Instead, it is the victory *of God* won on the battlefield of human history and in the human nature of the Son of God — in that sense *qua homo* — for the glory of God and the salvation of men. When Isaiah 59:17 speaks of God as donning pieces of armor, Calvin assures us that this was not to deprive Christ of his armor and role as Redeemer, but to underline the fact that God borrowed nothing extrinsic to himself and had no *merely* creaturely assistance in the work of our redemption [1].

This emphasis on *God's role* in Christ's victory stresses the continuity of deliverance: the promised, fulfilled and remembered deliverances of Israel in the Old Testament are continuous with the deliverance of Israel and all of Abraham's seed in Christ. By virtue of his conviction that Jesus Christ is the content of the Old Testament as well as the New, Calvin is able to see the intertwining of

---

51) II, xvi, 16. e. a.
52) *Ibid.* part. reten. Allen.
1) III, xi, 12. See also *Comm.* Isa. 49:25, IV, 44; I, v, 7; and *Comm.* Isa. 35:10, III, 73.

God's deliverance from the inimical spiritual powers [2], which hold God's people bound through their sins, and from their human agents who hold Israel in political bondage. In two eras of Israel's history the connection between God's political and spiritual deliverances are particularly striking: the corporeal servitude of Israel in Egypt is the "type" of the spiritual captivity suffered by all men. As God rescued Israel from Pharaoh's tyranny, our "heavenly Vindicator having freed us by the power of his arm . . . from the devil's deadly power . . . leads us into the Kingdom of freedom" [3]. Here at the point at which soteriology and sanctification meet, at the seam of the saving historical life of Christ and the life of the Christian, we realize that liberation implies liberty. The Christian freedom which Calvin, in the spirit of the Reformation, prizes so highly grows out of redemptive freeing. As his argument runs at the heart of his chapter on Christian freedom, freedom from constraint makes us capable of joyous obedience, since being emancipated by grace, believers need not fear the remnants of sin [4].

Interestingly, Calvin understands the return from Babylon as surpassing the deliverance from Egypt, because he sees it in *direct* connection with the victory of Christ, not merely as a type of it [5] — Calvin complains that Jews limit the promised deliverance to the return from Babylon, while Christians improperly restrict the meaning to the spiritual redemption wrought in Christ. In reality, he says, "we must begin with the deliverance which was wrought under Cyrus [6] and bring it down to our own time" [7], for the promised scope of God's victory was only fulfilled when "Christ achieved a conquest and illustrious triumph over Satan, sin and death" [8].

Calvin works out the dimensions of deliverance in such a complete way that we can march once again down the line of his enemies

---

2) Calvin does not realize that this apocalyptic motif is a relatively late addition to the stream of Biblical thought.

3) II, viii, 15.

4) III, xix, 5—6.

5) *Comm.* Isa. 43:19, III, 342. — Some probably authentic passages by Isaiah of Jerusalem do, of course, connect the liberation of God's people from Assyria or Babylon with a Messianic figure.

6) II Chron. 36:22 f.

7) *Comm.* Isa. 52:11, IV, 103.

8) *Comm.* Isa. 59:19, IV, 267. See also *Comm.* Col. 2:15, p. 190. This complex of passages bears the indelible imprint of the *Heilsgeschichte* as formative for Calvin's thought.

and ours and observe no longer their power over man, but their subjection by and to God in Jesus Christ. In considering man's slavery, we began with Satan as the enemy who contrived the fall of man and went on to describe the captivity under Satan's allies. Man's condition followed a descending line which reached the depths in the enmity of God himself against him; but now that we can consider the broken power of these foes, we shall encounter them in the reverse order. The aspect of Christ's victory which represents *the decisive turning point of the entire spiritual warfare* is the reconciliation of man to God, which, paradoxically, appears to be no part of that dramatic struggle. From this center the effect of victory spreads all along the whole battle-line of man's enemies until the conquest of his allies and the destruction of his weapons means the defeat of Satan himself. In his study of the atonement, Aulen lists the two ideas of reconciliation and Christus Victor under the single heading of the classic view. He attempts to coordinate the two as equal factors, but as the very title of the English version indicates, the former is practically subsumed under the latter. Actually, *reconciliation* is the more comprehensive term, indicating the goal of Christ's work — however that work is expressed. As Aulen himself says, connection with the concept of reconciliation makes of Christus Victor more than a concept of slavation. The whole is now a doctrine of the atonement.

Considering II Cor. 5:19, the *locus classicus* of the concept of reconciliation, Calvin says: "For what purpose, then, has God appeared to men in Christ? For the purpose of reconciliation — that, hostilities being removed, those who were aliens, might be adopted as sons"[9]. With these few simple words Calvin accomplishes what Christus Victor theology chronically fails to do — the systematic need for which Aulen rather futilely asserts — namely, to connect the motif of victory with the central theme of soteriology: reconciliation. Necessarily, Calvin thinks *from* a reconciliation context appropriate to victory. He does not use the alienated husband-wife metaphor with which Hosea begins Biblical reconciliation theology. Instead, he chooses Hosea's subordinate theme, reconciliation between Father and son[10], or youth eligible for adoption[11].

---

9) *Comm.* II Cor. 5:19, II, 237.

10) Hos. 11.

11) Rom. 8 etc.

In this context our Act I becomes an Absolom-like rebellion of man against his Davidic Father. That Absolom must die rather than receive the gracious acceptance accorded the returning Prodigal is not due to a lack of paternal affection (note David's indulgence of this emotion, e. g. II Sam. 13:59; 14:1; 18:5, 33 etc.). The Father's love is ineffectual in direct approach to Absolom, but the crucial failure arises from the fact that Joab is *only a mighty warrior,* not the Mediator. In the less allegorical terms of our second chapter, the epitome of man's slavery is that the enmity of God himself oppresses him. The epitome of God's victory in Christ, then, is that God reconciles men to himself by conquering the enmity which oppressed man [12]. "God's enmity" gives Calvin a very useful device for linking the metaphors of salvation and atonement: specifically, substitution, victory, reconciliation. The Mediator substituted for our disobedience the obedience which characterized the whole course of his life, climaxed and summarized in his obedient death [13]. By this way of living and dying he abolished our sins, destroyed the enmity between God and us, and thus established the reconciliation [14]. The victory over the divine enmity which oppressed man and the reconciliation of man to God are from this point of view actually the reverse sides of the same action of God in Christ.

The "enmity" of God, however, also introduces certain ominous elements into Calvin's theology. Scrutiny of this concept reminds us that Calvin's holy God of glory is separated by a virtually infinite gulf from his earth-bound bodily creation "man", now, worse, "sinner". This allows Calvin's God to build up a righteous indignation until it grows into an enmity in which that Deity virtually despises man. It is significant that whereas the Biblical God, whose *love* is *prior to his holiness* invariably *initiates* the reconciliation of the rebel *to himself* Calvin's God, whose holiness tends to be prior to his love, often [15] needs to *be* reconciled to his *unworthy* creature. This complex of ideas teaches us why the concept of the Mediator is so important to Reformed thinking (see, for example, Emil Brunner, *The Mediator,* and Heinrich Schroten, *Christus, de Middelaar bij Calvijn*) and just what it is the Mediator does. The Mediator is not only the *priest* whose sacrifice restores the religious rela-

---

12) III, ii, 28.
13) Phil. 2:7.
14) II, xvi, 5.
15) e. g. II, xii, 4; II, xvi, 2, and II, xvii, 2.

tionship between God and man, and is not only the *prophetic* Advocate who by wisdom settles a labor dispute, in either role reestablishing the covenant. The Mediator primarily mediates re conciliation, ends enmity, unites persons. Theologically, this Act is totally congruous with the *unio personalis* of the Mediator. Cal vin's Nestorian-tinged Christological difficulty, therefore, distorts the reconciliation and this in turn exerts a reaction detrimental to Christology. Calvin's God and man are so far apart, in every sense, that the Mediator almost becomes a *tertium quid,* a thing neither fully true God nor fully true man, but "a degree midway between God and us" [16]. Calvin would, of course, be horrified to recognize the Gnostics' intermediary being, which he systematically rejects [17], operative in his own theology. For Calvin, we may consider God's ordinance the first cause of Christ's merit [18] so that our faith in Christ follows this as second and proximate cause with Christ him self somewhere in between as "means" of reconciliation but more than "only a formal cause" [19]. In the context of God's *plan,* then, the Mediator is little more than its instrument. In the *act* of re conciliation where the Mediator is dramatically dynamic, on the other hand, God the wounded partner plays a strangely (for Calvin) passive role. We must emphasize finally, however, that it is the very magnificence of Calvin's conception of the Mediator who fulfills the whole *munus triplex* which drives us beyond it to this critique.

Another way of expressing this connection between victory and reconciliation grows out of the fact that when he considers its mighty efficacy, Calvin breaks into joyous exultation in praise of the cross, which the victory of Christ has transformed from an instrument of torture and death into a *triumphal chariot* in which he celebrates his conquests, and by which he shall raise all men along with himself to his Father [20]. As an explanation of *how* victory becomes reconciliation this magnificent *tour de force* is too sketchy, so that the process by which the cross of Christ receives

---

16) II, xiv, 3.

17) IV, xvii, 30.

18) I, xvii, 1.

19) All terminology from I, xvii, 2.

20) *Comm.* John 12:32, II, 37 and repeatedly, on the basis of Col. 2:15, in the *Comms.* but apparently only once (II, xvi, 6) in the 1559 *Institutes.* Jansen, *op. cit.,* p. 54, refers to this metaphor as "one of Calvin's favorite expressions".

this power must be described in terms of its role in Christ's conquest of the enemies of God and man.

In the connected series of victories which make up the earthly history of Jesus, the decisive event which is the sum of all previous conquests and the necessary precondition of those that follow is his suffering and death on the cross. What is accomplished in this decisive event? The central answer lies in the fact that there man's *sin* has been dealt with, atoned for, washed away, forgiven; and thus, to put the whole in terms of the spiritual warfare, the *power* of sin over men's lives has been broken [21]. As to the way in which Christ's death caused the dissolution of sin's might, "the Father destroyed the force of sin, when the curse of it was transferred to Christ's flesh" [22]. The suffering and obedience of Christ are two factors which help explain the effect of the cross, but ultimately, Calvin emphasizes, "Christ *by dying, put sin to flight*" [23]. Since God condemned sin in the flesh, it means not only that individuals are free from their own sin, but even that the very "kingdom of sin, by which we were oppressed, was abrogated" [24]. This means that sin's allies, the law and its curse and judgment, have been dealt with, and "We are freed from the bondage of the law of the Lord" [25]. Therefore, the devils who accuse us before God were disarmed when the indictment against us was destroyed on the cross [26]. Calvin actually paints Christ as opposing himself to the "ire and judgment of God", bearing the curse due to us, and emerging as conqueror [27].

When Christ breaks the power of sin by his death, he consequently vanquishes the sinful *nature* of man which is the *willing* servant of sin [28]. Calvin thinks that what Paul terms "the old man" means the whole of our sinful nature, which must perish if we are to be restored to true life. "This old man" of ours dies when he "is fastened to the cross of Christ, because through his strength it is slain" [29]. Where Paul speaks of the warfare between the flesh and

---

21) II, xii, 3.

22) II, xvi, 6.

23) *Comms.* Rom. 6:10, p. 227. e. a. and John 12:14, II, 23.

24) *Comm.* Rom. 8:3, p. 282 (author's transl.). See also IV, xi, 1.

25) *Comm.* Rom. 6:14 f., p. 233. See also *Comm.* Rom. 7:4, pp. 247 f.

26) *Comm.* Col. 2:13—15, p. 190.

27) *Comm.* Rom. 4:25, p. 185.

28) I, v, 7.

29) *Comm.* Rom. 6:6, p. 224. See also *Comms.* Rom. 6:4, p. 221 and Rom. 5:10, pp. 197 f.

the Spirit, "what else does the flesh mean but 'the old man?'" [30]. This is the power, the principle which is characterized "by enmity against God" [31]. On the cross Christ *has* won the decisive battle over this transcendental power "flesh". Only remnants (*reliquii*) of the flesh survive in the Christian, so that although "the flesh has not yet fully died out, it no longer exercises lordship but bows to the Spirit" [32]. Further, Christ's death represents the death of death: in the death of Christ, all of death's fatal poison was expended upon him. Or, to use Calvin's picture, "Christ by dying has swallowed up death" [33].

The word "swallow", repeatedly restored in such contexts by F. L. Battles in the LCC where Allen uses words such as "destroyed", reintroduces ancient and rather barbarous yet powerfully pictorial metaphors. Our sophisticated sensibilities are so quick to reject the fish-hook theory of saving victory held by the Church Fathers that we are not even conscious of the stark purity of its artistic convention: Satan (or death), that killer shark, is lured by the strategy of the Great Fisherman into snapping up the bait of Christ's human nature, thus impaling himself on the killing hook of Christ's deathless divinity. Another metaphor of combat identifies the suffering servant with Christus Victor, the lamb of God who takes away the sin of the world with the lion who devours the devil-lion seeking some one to devour [34]. Calvin's image of evil as the swallower who is swallowed, the devourer who is devoured recalls the dark submarine world in which Darwinian-Spencerian survival of the fittest best applies. No doubt, the Jonah-whale picture used by the Gospels themselves is the source of some of this. Calvin says Christ "let himself be swallowed up by death, as it were, not to be engulfed in its abyss, but rather to engulf it [35] that must soon have engulfed us" [36]. The squeamishness which will not hear of a sacrificial theory of the atonement (the lamb) because it

---

30) *Comm.* Gal. 5:17, p. 163

31) Rom. 8:7.

32) *Comm.* Gal. 5:25, p. 169.

33) *Comm.* Rom. 10:6, p. 389 (author's transl.). See also II, xvi, 7 and 11.

34) I Pet. 5:8. — Augustine utilizes Hosea 13:8 in his sermon, "The lion and the lamb," while Calvin says, "the lion is the lamb" of Rev. 5:9 f. in his first sermon on Isa. 53, CR LXIII, p. 602. See L. Nixon, *The Gospel according to Isaiah,* p. 20.

35) See I Pet. 5:22 vg.

36) II, xvi, 7.

is "slaughter-house religion" will no doubt continue to find the fish-hook, the lion and the shark or whale unpalatable substitutes for the symbol "Christ". But it must also deny itself most of Shakespeare and Greek Tragedy as well as almost all creative modern theatre, much of which is vulgar and none of which is neat.

We must remember how important this victory over death is to Calvin, for his rejoicing in Christ's victory over death reflects his deep-rooted concern for the immortality of the soul and the assurance of a future life where *justice* should be done and there would be *no more pain*. The union of the two natures in Christ is necessary precisely so that death can be vanquished: he who had to be man to die had to be God to conquer death [37]. This, then, is the glorious victory which allows Calvin to place that bit of eschatology, "The Final Resurrection", at the summit of Book III of the 1559 *Institutes*.

Reversing the scale which we descended in following man's enslavement after his fall, we have heard the ascending crescendo of Christ's victory trumpets till their full-throated soaring climax heralds his overthrow of Satan, the sovereign of the kingdom of evil. We have witnessed Satan's empire melting around him before the onslaughts of the Mighty One. He awaits defeat like some chessking whose forces are inexorably swept away. His fate was sealed when God, who ultimately controls Calvin's Satan, reconciled men, his rebellious creatures, to himself. We have seen the devil's allies and weapons, through which he held man enslaved, defeated and destroyed. Now the downfall of the prince of evil himself is at hand.

For Calvin, this victory comes as no happenstance explosion, but as the fulfillment of the promise made to the first woman: as Christ is Abraham's true seed [38] so is he the woman's true seed who shall bruise the serpent's head [39]. Calvin not only utilizes Jesus' pictures of lightning from heaven and the defeat of the strong armed man but also generalizes Jesus' exorcisms into the defeat of Satan for the benefit of all God's elect: "Whenever God draws near us, and, above all, when he approaches us in the person of his son, the design is, to rescue us from the tyranny of the devil, and to receive us into his favor" [40]. Calvin imaginatively interprets the Messianic

---

37) See II, xii, 3, *Comm*. Rom. 3:28, p. 85 and II, xii, 2.
38) Gal. 3:16.
39) *Comm*. Gen. 3:15, I, 170; I, xiv, 18 and II, xiii, 2.
40) *Comms*. Matt. 12:43, II, 83 and Matt. 12:29, II, 71.

prophecy, "and the government shall be upon his shoulder", to mean that on his shoulder Christ carried the cross by which he gains his splendid triumph over the prince of this world [41]. The cruel cross on which Jesus suffers in weakness and succumbs to death is most difficult to paint as a triumph. The clarion call of victory can be heard by all who listen to the resurrection trumpets but in this defeat, considered alone and for itself, where is God's victory? Calvin must call upon other conceptions than that of the warrior's mighty arm to show how God wins victory in Jesus' weakness. When the Johannine Jesus says, "It is finished", just before he expires, Calvin believes the endurance of substitutionary suffering achieves victory [42]. Commenting on the Johannine farewell address, Calvin calls into play first, the decree of God, then, the obedience of Christ despite the scorn God allows Satan to heap upon him [43]. This "despite" points to the fact that Satan is made the means of his own defeat. As Paul implies in I Cor. 2:8, Satan's part in bringing about the death of Christ, which atones for sins and thus destroys the power of his allies and tools, sin and death, is decisive in the overthrow of his own kingdom. Calvin's portrayal of the progressive overthrow of Satan's kingdom springs from "if I be lifted up ...": "Christ concludes that he will obtain a *glorious* triumph by his death ... and this too was accomplished; for the death of the cross, which Christ suffered, is so far from obscuring his high rank, that in that death his high rank is chiefly displayed, since there his love to mankind, his infinite righteousness in atoning for sin and death, subduing Satan, and at length, opening heaven, blazed with full brightness" [44]. This conquest has also decided the character of the life of the Christian, for "The victorious death of Christ ... shall not last only for a small time, but shall go beyond all number of years" [45]. Although we shall have to do in the Christian life with these same enemies, they shall not be the same, for they are defeated and broken. Victory has been decisively and permanently denied them by the mighty Invader who has become the Conqueror — Jesus Christ.

---

41) *Comm.* Isa. 9:6, I, 308. See also *Comm.* John 14:30, II, 104.
42) *Comm.* John 19:30, II, 237.
43) *Comm.* John 14:31, II, 106.
44) *Comm.* John 12:32, II, 74.
45) *Comm.* Acts 8:33, I, 358.

It would be a mistake to underestimate the importance of what Calvin has said here. The grandeur of the victory of Christ, of the objective establishment of his kingship "in heaven and on earth and under the earth" [46] is scarcely matched by any other concept of theology. It catches the cosmic scope and the intense power of God's salvation in a unique way. As almost everywhere in theology, however, it will be necessary even here to explore the limitations inherent in the formulation. In the first place, the concept of Christ's victory is *in itself* incomplete. The classic view of the atonement is more than a doctrine of salvation only because and insofar as it is connected with the more comprehensive concept of the reconciliation and the view of Christ as Restorer it implies. Secondly, Calvin's own theology is at one crucial point poorly adapted to the concept of Christ's victory. Calvin's tendency toward a doctrine of limited atonement — driven to its ultimate consequences only by his successors — *limits* the effectiveness of Christ's work *from God's side*. Operatively, that that light from on high hymned in the opening words of this Act "in a measure shattered his (Satan's) darkness", probably signifies *only* "in a measure". We shall have to ask in Acts III and IV, to what extent is Christ's victory actually operative in Calvin's theology? Assuming as Calvin does, however, the objective character and solidarity of the enemies: assuming the existence of the kingdom of evil with Satan as its head: if Christ's victory objectively destroys Satan's kingship then it destroys *all* objective slavery to him and his allies — as Calvin, in enthusiasm for Christ's triumph, occasionally seems close to confessing.

Jesus Christ: The Restorer

Calvin is aware that more is needed by man than the defeat of his enemies. He can, therefore, point beyond the scene of battle to reconstruction of the vanquished: "He (Christ) has not only gained a complete victory over the devil, sin, and death, and all the power of hell — *but out of rebels he daily shapes a willing people*" [1]. It is not enough that rebellious man has been set free from the inimical forces outside him and even from the rebellion within him: we must investigate how this freedom is given positive

---

46) Phil. 2:10.
1) *Comm.* Eph. 4:8, p. 273. e. a.

content, and what that content is. The objective military triumphs of Christ continue for us in the Christian life and are apprehended by faith, since Christ has ascended the throne of power, after spoiling his enemies and enriching his people, in order to exercise his lordship by pouring his spirit, which is his power, upon his own and by protecting them from the ferocious enemies he shall finally lay low when he completes the building of the church [2]. Liberation and protection from enemies, concepts freely used by Calvin at this point, do not provide a sufficient basis for a lasting positive relation between liberator and liberated — as hard political experience has shown us once more since World War II. The Christian, the new man, is not to be defined as a soldier-of-fortune who simply follows the leader emerging victorious from the decisive battle. Therefore, however glorious and sweeping Christ's conquests, the positive content of the connection between God and man — as well as the Christological concepts on which it depends — must be expressed with the help of symbols other than those of the spiritual warfare.

The central soteriological metaphor of reconciliation through the Mediator goes far to provide a key for the solution of this problem [3]. But it is our conviction that Calvin describes the uniting of God and men in Christ primarily by using the concepts of *substitution* and *incorporation*. In *God in our Place, the Substitutionary Character of Calvin's Doctrine of Reconciliation,* Paul van Buren makes a strong case for this thesis that "substitution" is central for the whole of Calvin's Christology and soteriology. The term substitution is understood as meaning "in our place" and "for us". We shall utilize this aspect of Calvin's thought just where it merges with the concept of Christ as Conqueror. Perhaps the most perfect expression of substitution is given by the apostle Paul: "For our sake he who had done no sin was made to be sin by the Father, so that in him we might be made the righteousness of God" [4]. First of all, the statement implies that Christ takes upon himself the form of a servant, and is made in the likeness of man [5], in order that he may receive the burdens of sin for our sakes *and* in our place, and

---

2) I, xvi, 16. See also II, xvi, 13.

3) See *Comm.* II Cor. 5:19, II, 237.

4) II Cor. 5:21, a passage which appears eleven times in the 1559 *Institutes,* here given in a synthesis of Calvin's paraphrases there — which the RSV now approaches.

5) Phil. 2:7.

we in exchange may receive what is his, the righteousness of God. Christ's solidarity with us in human nature is the presupposition of both halves of the transaction. On one side of the equation, when Christ died in the due course of the *Heilsgeschichte*, "He was not compelled by Satan" or the victim of his own weakness but rather, in voluntarily submitting to death "he was substituted in our place" [6]. From his side, God "was pleased to bruise" his Suffering Servant, "because he stood in our place, and in no other way than by his death could the justice of God be satisfied" [7]. This statement makes explicit the primary *locus* in which the metaphorical principle of substitution works for man's salvation: the court of God's justice. It is there that we men would stand as debtors and law-breakers, unable to pay or atone for our crimes, except that Christ presents himself in our place, and pays our penalty and brings free pardon so that we are acquitted [8]. This substitution is, however, by no means simply a one-sided transaction in which Christ takes upon himself the load of our curse. After Christ suffers in our nature even unto death, the other side of the equation operates, for in his triumphal procession into the heavens he exalts this same nature in its union with that of the Son of God. The dying Stephen "sees Christ reigning in that flesh wherein he was abased; so that in very fact *the victory consisted in this one thing*" [9]. Because of this conviction, Calvin is careful to explain that Paul's resolve not to know Christ after the flesh does not contradict what "scripture proclaims throughout, that Christ does now as certainly lead a glorious life in our flesh, as he once suffered in it . . . He has opened up for our nature the kingdom of God, from which it had been banished, and has given it a place in the heavenly dwelling" [10]. Since Christ, in the great exchange, imparts his righteousness to men, Calvin can also say that our righteousness is a memorial of his victory [11]. Again coupling the two atonement metaphors of substitution and victory, Calvin asserts that the death of Christ gives us "a fear-

---

6) *Comm.* John 14:30, II, 105.

7) *Comm.* Isa. 53:10, IV, 123.

8) *Comm.* Matt. 1:21, I, 98 f.

9) *Comm.* Acts 7:56, I, 315 e. a.

10) *Comm.* II Cor. 5:16, II, 232. This insofar as the present phase of the *Heilsgeschichte* and the *unio personalis* are concerned — *is* perfect Chalcedonian orthodoxy.

11) *Comm.* John 6:55, I, 267.

less triumph over death, because the Son of God has endured it in our place, and, in his contest with it has been victorious" [12].

In these passages it is clear that the concept of substitution — as represented by "for us" and "in our place" — is an *in*clusive rather than an *ex*clusive one. The fact that it is not we but Christ who suffers the penalty for sins *in our place* does NOT mean that the payment is not valid *for us*. The fact that "we receive the Father's blessing *in his place*" does NOT mean that the blessing is not waiting *for him*. On the contrary, the concept of *substitution* as Calvin uses it paradoxically *means* the church's *participation* in Christ's action. It is the rich concept of in-corporation which enables Calvin to make this connection and to deepen the significance of the wondrous exchange. "Incorporation" roots in the Pauline idea of salvation, which originally concerns the Jews as his people, "is of the church as the body (*corpus*) of Christ, so that the promise extended indiscriminately to all who are incorporated by faith in the 'one body' of the church" [13]. To become a Christian and thus to receive Christ's benefits is to be incorporated as a member of the *corpus Christi* [14]. Finally, Calvin uses "head and body" with full metaphorical strictness, for he thinks of the corporeal union of Christ and Christians as a reality of the highest order — a spiritual reality.

The concept of incorporation controls Calvin's thinking about sanctification and the Christian life to a very great extent, other terminology being subordinated to it. For example, the characteristic Pauline expression "in Christ" is taken to mean "in the body of Christ". Christ is also said to be *in us* in the sense that the Head is thought of as imparting its life to the members of the body. Paul's account of the institution of the Lord's Supper gives Calvin cause to synthesize all these turns of phrase: "Christ is, however, obtained, I affirm, not only when we believe that he was made an offering for us, but when he dwells in us — when he is one with us — when we are *members of his flesh* [15], — when, finally, we are incorporated with him (so to speak) into one life and substance" [16].

12) *Comm.* John 14:30, II, 237.
13) *Comm.* Matt. 10:21, 98 f.
14) See CG I, 304, *Comm.* I Cor. 12:12, I, 405, and *Comm.* I Cor. 12:27, I, 412.
15) Eph. 5:30.
16) *Comm.* I Cor. 11:24, I, 379.

Even the important concept *participatio* is understood in terms of our participation in Christ, in the vital connection of the members of the body with the Head and its life. In praise of our incorporation into the triumphant Head Calvin proclaims that we are *only* received into the number of God's children by being ingrafted into the body of Christ [17]. Therefore, Christ neither fell under the power of death, nor triumphed over it in his resurrection, for himself alone; but all which was begun in the Head *must be* accomplished in all the members" [18]. Since Calvin understands Romans 6:3 to mean that by baptism we are incorporated into Christ, we partake of Christ's victory over sin [19]. Similarly, all who are ingrafted into Christ partake in his victory over *death,* for united with Christ their Head, they cannot be extinguished by it [20]. Ultimately, the union of the Church with Christ means the union of Christians with God: "The union of our soul with God is the true and only life" [21], but the nature of the atonement is such that this union with God takes place only in Christ [22]. This means to Calvin that all God's blessings come only through Christ as Head to the church as his body. Therefore, this "only" accounts for our concern that the humanity of Christ, through which we are joined with him be not dissolved.

The cosmic result of what has occurred is "that *the world* has been brought into a state of good order by the victory of Christ, by which he overturned the authority of Satan" [23]. Christ's restoration of order and unity applies primarily, of course, to man, for "as the ruin of the human race is that it is broken and scattered, the restoration of it consists in its being properly united in one body" [24]. In Christ's body, the love of God restores men to a right relationship with himself, and this means the restoration in Christ of man's intended dominion over creation [25]. This does not, however, mean simply a restoration of man's original nature and possibilities, in-

---

17) *Comm.* Isa. 42:1, III, 284.
18) III, xxv, 3. e. a. See also *Comms.* I Cor. 15:57, II, 65 and II Cor. 2:14, II, 157.
19) *Comm. loc. cit.* p. 220.
20) *Comms.* Isa. 26:19, II, 237 and John 8:52, I, 357.
21) *Comm.* Eph. 2:1, p. 220.
22) See *Comms.* II Cor. 1:20, II, 137 f. and Matt. 12:18, II, 59.
23) *Comm.* John 16:11, II, 141.
24) *Comm.* John 17:21, II, 183.
25) *Comm.* Heb. 2:5, p. 57.

cluding the possibility of falling again, for Calvin insists that those who are united with Christ are given *perseverance in this life*. Yet in view of Calvin's tendency to treat the humanity of Christ as ultimately dispensable, does Christ bring to his body an *eternally* indissoluble union with himself, not simply as a — or even as the only — perfect man, but as God the Son, God himself?

Incorporation portrays Christ's benefits for the church as a corporate whole; but Calvin, often considered a father of modern individualism, is quite interested in the salvation of individuals. Calvin's view of Christ as Restorer, that "out of rebels he daily shapes a willing people", reminds us of his concern for the repentance and conversion of individuals. "Repentance" does not primarily mean a regret of misdeeds and a sorrow for the sad state in which the sinner finds himself; "conversion" does not merely signifiy a sudden urge to get out that state. Rather, both terms denote the point at which the rebel becomes one of God's willing people. They describe a single total attitude in which the Christian begins his pilgrimage or warfare in this life: repentance and conversion mean that the Christian *turns* toward God, consciously turns his back upon all of the enemies of his salvation, and focuses all of his efforts and his attention upon his Savior. Calvin, who speaks in one famous passage of his own "sudden conversion", says: "A man is said to deliver his own soul, who by repentance rescues himself from the snares of the devil, in the same manner as some men are said to save others, when by holy warnings they bring back wanderers into the right way" [26]. Yet even here the initiative remains in God's hand: "Whomsoever God chooses to snatch from death he vivifies by the Spirit of regeneration. Not that repentance, properly speaking, is the cause of salvation, but it is . . . inseparable from faith and from God's mercy" [27]. Here where God's mercy and man's repentance meet we must test concretely whether Calvin limits the power of God exactly at the decisive point — in the action of God in Christ. Calvin attempts the careful definition to guard against this possibility: "The kingdom of Christ extends, no doubt, to all men; but it brings salvation to none but the elect, who with voluntary obedience follow the voice of the shepherd; for the others are compelled by violence to obey him, till at length he utterly bruises them with his iron scepter" [28].

26) James 5:20. — *Comm.* Isa. 44:20, III, 380.
27) III, iii, 21, part. reten. Allen. See also *Comm.* Isa. 49:9, IV, 25.
28) *Comm.* John 17:2, II, 165.

There are those, no doubt, who refuse to obey; but if what Calvin says here is true, we are either wrong in calling God's act in Christ his crucial one, or wrong in designating it entirely salutary. Calvin's statement does preserve the initiative of God; but to protect the holiness and honor of God, Calvin limits the scope of his salvation. In smashing his enemies, Calvin's God smashes also some men, and that means some of his own beloved creatures whom he made to have dominion over his good creation, and to bear his image. He has failed to realize his manifest purpose in creation and failed to overcome completely the enmity between himself and man.

We are not here advocating a universalistic doctrine of salvation. We are saying that the God who wills that all men shall be saved [29] has objectively brought his will to pass in the victory of Jesus Christ. He has *overcome the world* [30] insofar as it is his enemy and Satan is its prince [31] and god [32]; but he has *reconciled the world to himself* [33] and is its Savior [34] insofar as it is his good creation which he loves [35]. As to individual men, since Christ *has* risen victoriously, not those who by God's grace believe in that resurrection, but those who persist in ignorance and denial of Christ's *victory for them* are "of all men most miserable" [36]. Those who suffer from and succumb to diseases which can be diagnosed and cured but refuse this aid are happy by comparison. In view of the grace by which alone he believes in — or knows — the victory of Christ, it is with humility as well as rejoicing that the Christian looks to Christ not only as the Victor over God's enemies, but as the Victor *for him.* Satan has been overcome. The power by which he reigned has been broken so that men (Calvin would limit this to the elect) are *free* to leave his prison, his kingdom.

Yet when we turn our backs upon this "ancient foe" Calvin would not have us carelessly expose ourselves so as to present a vulnerable target. Satan is no foe upon whom one dare turn his back in this sense, for hear what he says about the parable of the outcast unclean spirit who returned: "Above all, when he has been

---

29) I Tim. 2:4.
30) I John 5:4 f.
31) John 14:30.
32) II Cor. 4:4.
33) II Cor. 5:19, John 3:17.
34) John 4:42, I John 4:14.
35) John 3:16.
36) I Cor. 15:12—19.

vanquished and put to flight by Christ, it only tends to whet his rage and keenness to do us injury. Before Christ makes us partakers of his energy, it seems as if it were in sport and amusements that this enemy reigns over us; but when he has been driven out, he conceives resentment at having lost his prey, collects new forces, and arouses all his senses to attack us anew" [37]. This means that the Christian has not only humbly to rejoice but earnestly to strive, since "freedom has its degrees according to the measure of their faith; and therefore Paul, though clearly made free, still groans and longs after perfect freedom" [38].

The phrase "though clearly made free" is Calvin's signal that the victory of Christ is not indecisive or needs human completion. This is stated more positively in his assertion: "In our Head, indeed, this victory always fully existed, for the prince of this world had nothing in him [39]; in us, who are his members, it yet appears only in part" [40]. Therefore, we must with Calvin embark upon the pilgrimage along the road where this "in part" moves toward the completion which already exists in the Head of the body. It is along this road that we shall encounter the body of Christ as the Holy Army (*sancta militia*), the Troop of God (*compagnie de Dieu*).

37) *Comm.* Matt. 12:43, II, 83 ff.
38) Rom. 7:24. — *Comm.* John 8:32, I, 342.
39) John 14:30.
40) I, xiv, 18, part. reten. Allen.

ACT III: THE GOOD FIGHT

The Spiritual Warfare of the Militia Christi

"that . . . you may wage the good warfare". I Tim. 1:18
"Fight the good fight of faith." I Tim. 6:12

The logic of our drama now brings us to the present time and the imperative mood: "Fight!" "Wage the warfare!" You and I are ordered to wield the Spirit's sword. The logic of theological drama has brought us to the Act which must in some form describe actual living here and now, must prescribe ethical conduct. As the most immediate, it may be the most important of all the Acts. It is certainly the fullest. It must be existential for Calvin; but for Calvin it cannot be existentialist, because it cannot stand alone. As Charles Trinkhaus has said: "Calvin's effort to eliminate religious subjectivism ran parallel to the later effort of Galileo to eliminate or control the subjective factors distorting the observation of natural philosophy" [1]. Ethics in the Anglo-Saxon mold, utilitarian, empiricist, pragmatic, existentialist, situational, tends to present life divorced from a cosmic context. It is impatient with philosophical speculation, with Calvin's "contemplation", with metaphysics, with ontology, with ultimates. Neglecting these, it heightens the intensity of the here and now in its involvement in poignant personalness. Rejecting this, Calvin can only understand *here and now* in the light of *there and then,* the immediate in its cosmic context. "It is our established rule", he tells us, "that reflection precedes and experience follows" [2]. We may expect of him, then, practical realism and the command that we involve ourselves in his involvement in relativity; but we shall be somewhat surprised whenever we find

---

1) Charles Trinkhaus, "Renaissance Problems in Calvin's Theology", *Studies in the Renaissance* III, p. 62.
2) CG I, 174.

him absolutizing his involvedness in one partial segment of the *Heilsdrama.*

The Church Militant in the History of Theology

John Calvin was, par excellence, the Reformation's good soldier of Jesus Christ, unentangled in civilian pursuits [1] — just as Ignatius of Loyola was his opposite number in the legions of the Pope. Neither of them invented spiritual warfare, however, nor was it a discovery of the College de Montaigu in which they both studied within the same month. Though Calvin had found "to live is to be a warrior" (*vivere militare est*) in his studies of Stoic Roman legal theory by 1532, and Loyola had soldiered hard and literally, both depended for their views of spiritual struggle on a tradition already well-defined in the New Testament. From that point until its sixteenth century appropriation by Catholic Reformer and Protestant Reformer alike, the military metaphor played an astonishingly persistent role in the rationales for the life of the Christian man. Its importance can only be explained by its effectiveness in defining everyday ethics, in recognizing evil as a power which Everyman must combat, in doing justice to the forces within and around us which *we must deal with* in the shaping of our existence.

The authors of the traditional Pauline corpus refined and organized the metaphor drawn from Israel's bloody Holy wars until its apex in the formulation in Eph. 6. Thus, spiritual warfare became firmly established in the work and worship of the early church — partly because like most new religions of Rome, Christianity most readily infiltrated the most international arm of the empire, the army — and remained a persistent theme throughout the centuries before the Reformation. (This is clear from any reasonably thorough work on church history, e. g. Heussi's *Kompendium*, and such specialized studies as Adolf von Harnack, *Militia Christi*.)

The symbolic "beginning at the beginning" for the Christian combat takes place in the early Christian baptism with the ceremonial renunciation of the devil and the *pompa diaboli*. Similarly, the fasts of the early church were more than empty ascetic excess. The *milites Christi* were sentinels on station at their posts on Wednesday and

---

1) II Tim. 2:3 f.

Friday, each a *dies stationem* [2]. By the forth century the pattern linking progressive Christianity with the cities as opposed to the backward villages and hostile countryside had been established and fitted into the military metaphor. At first the village (*pagus*) gave its name to its not-yet-Christian villagers (*pagani,* pagans). Then by 365—70 the *paganus* was simply a spiritual civilian in contrast to the soldier of Christ. In a further development, the early Gothic Christians (Visigoths had settled on the lower Danube by the mid-fourth century) considered the priests primarily military officers. corresponding to the military constitution of the entire people. In Egypt, on the other hand, men like St. Anthony took over the popular conception of desert demons. The early hermits (desert monks) were not anchorites (escapees) in the literal sense. On the contrary, they lived at first in the vicinity of settlements which they protected from threatening demons. Later they went into the desert, where each lived in complete isolation, to do battle with the demons on their native terrain. St. Anthony himself was caught up in an inner struggle with the demons which appeared to him as wild animals, satyrs, centaurs and naked women.

Spiritual warfare raged on a much more visible and external — though to them no more serious — front where the *militia Christi* grappled with the formidable might of Rome herself. This campaign reached its decisive struggle in the persecution of Diocletian, which came near the end of his reign, and probably grew out of an increasing imperial concern over the large number of Christians in the army. Roman strategy for quelling Christianity had ranged from 1) a deliberate disdain designed to allow Christianity to run its course and exhaust its appeal, to 2) propaganda campaigns on both low level (calumny) and high (philosophical refutation), to 3) occasional outbreaks of violence (usually exaggerated by romantic Christian imagination). Diocletian, however, finally undertook a frontal attack, a vigorous campaign for the systematic elimination of Christianity. In 303 he destroyed the churches at Nicomedia, which had been his Imperial residence for almost twenty years, and followed this with a series of edicts calling for the destruction of all churches and the burning of Bibles, and the denial to all Christians, noble as well as slave, of the precious rights of the Roman citizen. The unbroken resistance of the Christians forced Galerius (also a

---

2) This again shows Stoic influence, III, x, 6, n. 9. Calvin still uses *statio,* sentry post, in III, ix, 4 and III, x, 6 in describing the spiritual warfare.

zealous foe of Christianity) to capitulate with an edict of toleration in 311, thus paving the way for the Constantinian era. (Among the reasons for the victory of Christianity, Heussi notes that the entire ancient world lived in horrified fear of the demons, which Christianity appeared to the popular mind to have the greatest power to combat [3].

As the power of Rome began to wane it became necessary to distinguish the Spirit of Christ from *Romanitas,* and the City of God from the City of man. Fortunately for Christianity, this was accomplished by probably its greatest mind, Augustine of Hippo. Thus, when in practice Gregory the great assumed the title and the authority of the *Pontifex Maximus,* resources for the survival of Western culture were at hand. Augustine in his early years as bishop of Hippo (396 or 397) wrote a simple little manual entitled *De Agone Christiano* (The Christian Combat) for the edification of his people, so we are not surprised that the theme of spiritual warfare recurs significantly in his magnum opus, *The City of God* (the 22 books of which were composed over the years 413—426 to refute the charge by pagans that the debilitating influence of Christianity was responsible for the conquest of Rome by Alarich in 410). The famous two Cities of this work are two ultimate *principles,* and history is understood as the struggle between them. (The two cities resemble Platonic *forms* or *ideas* which are then imperfectly realized and intermingled in the material realm. This evalution appears valid with reference to the heavenly city which often looks more like Plato's Republic than like the new Jerusalem which descends from heaven in Rev. 21. The concept of the *civitas terrena,* however, demonstrates the greatness of Augustine, whose thought in any area can never be described exhaustively in terms of one tradition, for it is of diabolical origin and no such things as an evil *idea* or form could exist in Platonism.) Augustine divides the history of the world into six epochs, the last of which is the one thousand year kingdom of Christ [4]. Thus, he overcame once for all the chiliasm which had reigned since the apostolic age. He simplified the Biblical apocalypticism into the idea that the first thousand years of the Christian era were to be a continual warfare of the kingdom of Christ on earth against demonic forces.

---

3) Karl Heussi, *Kompendium der Kirchengeschichte,* 10th edn. p. 95.
4) Rev. 20:2.

When the collapse of the empire, heralded by Alarich's conquest, carried classical culture to its doom, Europe was plunged into the Dark Ages. Consequently, even in the days of Carolingian Renaissance we find the popular Christian religion naive and realistic, hiding many pagan ideas under ostensibly Christian symbols, beginning with the devil, demons, angels, miracles and running down to blood revenge and divine judgments. One expression of this virile realism is the Old Saxon *Heliand* (probably before 850), an epic in which the story of Christ was Germanized. In this drama Christ has become a feudal German duke, and the disciples are bound to him by a Germanic fealty-oath.

Still more significant is the influence of St. Benedict upon the increasingly chaotic and problematic monastic life. He combined the ancient Christian tradition with the Roman military one. The monks, previously independent guerilla-like volunteers, were bound by a quasi-military oath or life-long vow to a *stabilitas loci* where they were under the discipline of St. Benedict's rule. The original locus of the Benedictine garrison was Monte Cassino, established in a strategic location, around 529. In spite of its fortress-like character it was destroyed by the Lombards in 589 for the first time. (The location and the formidable walls still formed a virtually impregnable keystone of the German defenses against the allies in World War II.) Its actual military value, however, is merely symbolic of its spiritual role, for after the death of its founder and more than a century before its refounding by the Langobards in 720, Gregory the great used its principles to forge a Christian culture and its spiritual soldiers as the first missionary shock-troops of the pope. Thus the *militia Christi* of St. Benedict became the dominant ideal in the west from the eighth through the twelfth century, and Benedict himself the patron saint of all Europe. We are not surprised, then, by the perduring validity of the picture drawn by Henry Adams in *Mont St. Michel and Chartres* contrasting to the thirteenth century Gothic cult of the wise and gentle Virgin the militant Norman culture of St. Michael. Ever since the fourth and fifth centuries the so-called lower cult (that of the saints) had especially honored the Apocalyptic Archangel, victorious in Dan. 10 and 12, Jude v. 9 and Rev. 12, and petitioned his help against the demons.

His Norman (and other) devotees now found far more concrete foes, for when Islam arose with *its duty* to do battle against unbelievers, Christians came to wrestle not simply with principalities and powers but (contradicting Eph. 6:12) with flesh and blood. The rationales for the crusades fit in with the whole medieval conception of honor and religious duty. The pilgrimage motif reached its fullest expression, and the knight's code of honor was extended to cover the honor of the church. But the papacy sponsored the idea of a *militia St. Petri* and the church consecrated military banners for its own service as early as the second half of the tenth century. Important orders of knights arose in connection with the crusades, some primarily as hospital orders, some which combined this function with armed service. The Knights Templar, for example, were the *milites templi* because they were originally based in the palace of Baduin II which was supposedly partially on the site of the temple at Jerusalem, and among their primary duties was the protection of the "Holy Sepulchre" and the pilgrims to it.

The convulsive disappointment of the crusades is symbolized by Adams as the transition in the popular mind of France from the cult of St. Michael to the adoration of the Virgin, and accompanies Scholasticism's preference (as shown in Act I) for the Neo-Platonic elements of Augustine's view of evil (i. e. as the absence of good) over his more Manichean devil. Even so, we find the first important publication of Erasmus his *Enchiridion militis Christiani* in 1503, and later in the century we discover the two giants [5] whose concept of the Christian's *spiritual* warfare exerted such vast influence. Their followers were to join the prohibited battle of flesh-and-blood in the succeeding centuries of religious wars, but the two primal strategists were devoted exclusively to the contemplation which sees "a great camp in all that region of Jerusalem, where the supreme Captain-general of the good is Christ our Lord; another camp in the region of Babylon, where the leader of the enemies is Lucifer" [6]. The author of these lines is the strategist of whose army Heussi says: "The *compañia de Jesus,* confirmed by Paul III in 1540, provided a revitalized Catholicism with its most battle-ready troops for the struggle with the Reformation" [7].

Ignatius Loyola was born in 1491 of the Basque nobility. He spent much of his youth as a professional soldier, and was severely

---

5) André Favre-Dorsaz, *Calvin et Loyola, Deux Réformes,* compares the two, "Reformation and Counter-Reformation incarnate", at many points (almost invariably and more or less subtly to the advantage of St. Ignatius).

6) Eph. 6:12. — Loyola, *The Spiritual Exercises,* p. 63.

7) Heussi, *op. cit.,* p. 340.

wounded in bold defence of Pamplona against the French in 1521. In 1522 after his recovery, he dedicated his weapons to Mary as her spiritual knight-errant [8] during a visit to the pilgrimage chapel Monserrat in Catalonia. As a thirty-three year old he began his formal education in Spain, during the course of which he composed his famous *Spiritual Exercises* and practiced them with companions before he ever began his studies at the Spanish universities of Alcala and Salamanca. Although the exercises — oriented as they were toward spiritual (Favre-Dorsaz emphasizes that his intention in them was "exclusively spiritual") warfare — were simply in the tradition made classic by St. Benedict, Loyola fell under the scrutiny of the Inquisition and wisely made his way to Paris. There he enter- ed the College de Montaigu and convened the first company of Jesus around the *Exercises* there on the Montmartre. Loyola entered the school in purposeful maturity in the same month of 1528 that the other genius of the strategy and organization of spiritual warfare departed from it at the age of nineteen. We will not speculate on the mutual influences of the Basque aristocrat and the Picard bour- geois in such a manner as, for example, Cecil Northcott (Did the future champions of Geneva and Rome meet in the lecture-room, or pass on the street? What a disputation they might have had!) [9]. Any influence of Loyola on Calvin was unconscious and undesired — in the approximately 1600 pages of the 1559 *Institutes* Calvin's only glance in that direction is "the Jesuits and like dregs" [10]. And the influence of Calvin's Geneva Academy on the Jesuit colleges is not more than, in Wendel's words, "very probable" [11]. Nevertheless, Calvin and Loyola — the two Reformers who, to use the words of Favre-Dorsaz, *embodied* the Reformation and the Counter Reforma- tion (or perhaps more properly with Ernst Staehelin, the Protestant Reformation and the Catholic Reformation) — made as much as possible of the metaphor of spiritual *warfare* and thus became the *operative* opposing forces in the "confessional struggle". Note that in 1534 on the Montmartre Loyola and Francis Xavier and their fellows vowed to be special servants (veritable commandos) of the pope, and that Pope Paul's Bull of recognition in 1540 was

8) See Unamuno, *The Tragic Sense of Life,* in which the parallel is drawn between Don Quixote and the Jesuits.

9) Northcott, *op. cit.,* p. 8.

10) III, iii, 2.

11) Wendel, *op. cit.,* p. 106.

named "REGIMINI MILITANTIS ecclesiae". It would be difficult to dispute Heussi's judgment that the success of the Jesuits has always been based on their strictly military constitution [12].

In spite of the military language used in his epistle dedicating the first edition of his *Institutes* to Francis I of France in August 1535, the Calvin "bullied and threatened" by Farel the next year *was* "only a poor, timid student", only a military theoretician without a single soldier to make up his first command. Soon, however, Calvin's preaching, teaching, and his writings both systematic and polemical, bristled with the same military language as Loyola's, so that H. D. Foster could call their legacies "examples of a faith carried to its logical limit with a marvellous loyalty and enthusiasm; each is the epitome of a church militant acting on the offensive rather than waiting to act on the defensive" [13]. They fight ostensibly under the *same* commander-in-chief and for the *same* ultimate goals, but with such different immediate loyalties that the whole of Europe was plunged into conflict between their armies. This is why we must now investigate precisely *how* and *why* Calvin *defined* the Christian life as a *warfare with the Spirit's sword.*

The nature of the warfare Calvin visualizes is determined by the character of the weapons, and Paul defines this as "spiritual": "The warfare accordingly is *spiritual.* Hence it follows by way of contraries, that it is not *according to the flesh.* In comparing the ministry of the Gospel to a *warfare,* he uses a most apt similitude. The life of a Christian, it is true, is a perpetual warfare, for whoever gives himself to the service of God will have no truce from Satan at any time" [14]. Let his statement, then, define our investigation, first of all, in the temporal dimension suggested in duration by "perpetual" and in inexorability by "at any time".

Calvin's Historical Framework [1]

The character of the Christian life, understood in terms of spiritual warfare, is determined by events outside of it. The struggle is, on the one hand, the result and continuation of the events described

---

12) Heussi, *op. cit.,* p. 341.

13) Foster, "Calvin's Programme for a Puritan State", p. 392.

14) *Comm.* II Cor. 10:4, II, 321 f.

1) At this point we must recall attention to the exhaustive treatment of this subject by Heinrich Berger, *Calvins Geschichtsauffassung.*

in Act I. On the other hand, the struggle moves toward its predetermined goal. This requires us to set the Christian's warfare in the historical frame described by Calvin.

The Christian faith asserts that the events of Christ's life, death, resurrection and exaltation are decisive for the course of history. There the current of corruption is halted and reversed, the face of man is turned toward God's *telos*. In an important sense the structure of the *Heilsgeschichte* should correspond to what we learn in an analysis of Shakespeare's serious plays. The climax of his dramatic logic comes not at the end, but in one of the middle acts. Many interesting and even unexpected events can and do occur after this climax, but the direction and character of the whole is set by the decisive event at the climax. So in the Christian Gospel, the life, death and resurrection of the incarnate Son of God decisively determine the whole of history. This chapter must try to measure the extent to which Calvin is successful in doing justice to this central truth.

The work of Christ operates to determine history first by altering the very character of the conditions under which that history unfolds. He has, subjectively, become our peace, for he has reconciled us to the Father, the Lord of that history [2]. Christ's work of reconciliation and peacemaking has, at the same time, been achieved by the objective overthrow of the powerful enemies whose tyranny casts a black shadow across the whole of history. Christ's death "destroys *sin*, by which the devil held us in captivity", so that it cannot now condemn us [3]; he has taken the sting from *death* itself, so that we need "no longer dread those things which our Prince has destroyed" [4]. In short, "Christ has once for all obtained the victory over the world" [5].

These triumphs of Christ have meant for him that he has ascended to the right hand of power to assume the decisive role of dominion over history. In the person of Christ, God himself triumphs, "inasmuch as he has conferred upon him all the glory of empire" [6]. Further, Calvin reminds us that the Christ who rules is man, our brother, in his flesh; yet he rules not in a "fleshly manner" but in a

---

2) *Comm.* Micah 5:5, III, 307.
3) II, xi, 15. e. a.
4) II, xvi, 11. e. a.
5) CE I, 297. e. a.
6) *Comm.* II Cor. 2:14, II, 158.

spiritual way, governing by the influence of his Spirit [7]. Calvin's Christ is no idle figure after his ascension: He ascended to the right hand of the Father, not to rest but to rule [8]. Since he is the "comrade and partner in the same nature with us" [9], his exaltation is by no means an honor conferred upon him alone; it has a vast effectiveness in man's history upon those who are united with their Head as his body. In the first place, it has an effectiveness which is surprising, because it goes directly counter to the concept of time implicit in the laws of causality. The visitation of God (Christ's coming) is looked upon by Calvin as the cause and origin of redemption for all God's people. Calvin thinks that the grace of Christ was *retroactively* effective to liberate believers before the event of his life in man's history, so that because of him they were not all their lifetime slaves of sin and death, for "the power and efficacy of that redemption, which was once [for all] exhibited in Christ, have been the same in all ages" [10].

The principal dimension of time effected by the Christ-event, however, stretches forward from Christ's ascension. Christ's historical work is like a mighty power station, transmitting spiritual energy to those united with him. Christ continues to triumph in the world through his body, joined to him by the Spirit which empowers the members [11]. These victories of Christ are continuous with those he gained "in his flesh", in fact they are largely the result of them [12].

At this point, we discover that Calvin is himself concerned about the actual effectiveness of Christ's victories, which he has described in such glowing terms. He is ultimately content with the fact that the victory of Christ is not, in his theology, effective for all men. If the Christian must still struggle with the same enemies which oppressed man before Christ came, however, how can we designate Christ's work decisive? The key to his solution of the problem is the statement we used at the end of the previous Act, that although the victory was complete in the Head, in the members it yet appears only in part [13]. Christ's victory progressively appears in the fellow-

---

7) *Comm.* II Cor. 5:16, II, 233.
8) *Comm.* Mark 16:19, III, 393.
9) II, xiii, 2.
10) *Comm.* Luke 1:68, I, 68.
11) See II, xvi, 16.
12) See *Comm.* Isa. 49:25, IV, 44.
13) I, xiv, 18.

ship of the body with its Head and in the communication of his life and strength to it. Being grafted into Christ we are delivered from the "miserable necessity" of sinning common to all sons of Adam, not that by and by we cease altogether to sin, but that at length we become victors in the fight [14]. Similarly, death was destroyed [15] in such a way as to be no longer deadly to believers, but not in such a way as to occasion them no uneasiness; or, in more pictorial language, "the sword of death which could penetrate into our very hearts has been blunted. It wounds nevertheless still, but without any danger; for we die, but by dying we enter into life" [16]. Finally, the same logic applies to Christ's victory over the prince of evil, who continues furiously to attack the believers: "He himself was so laid prostrate, that *no more account is to be made of him than as though he were not*" [17].

If this remarkable clause were taken literally, our study could, for all practical purpose, end at this point! Calvin has so subsumed the forces of sin, death and the old man — with which the Christian unquestionably still has to do — under the leadership of Satan that if we could literally "take no more account of him than if he were not", there would be no more need for talking about spiritual warfare and scarcely a need for a cosmic eschatology. What Calvin intends his assertion to say, of course, is that we need not — in fact, we can and must no longer — consider Satan as even potentially our master, no matter how vigorously he battles against the forces of God.

The victories of Christ's historical existence on earth are, then, like a mighty power station sending energy down through the succeeding eras of the Church. But how do the events at the *eschaton,* the goal toward which the spiritual warfare moves, affect the progress of that struggle? From our present position in history (and in this study) we can only here give an explication of hope and not of fulfillment. This is, however, quite appropriate to Calvin's pragmatism, for the refusal of such a thorough theologian as he to speculate when nothing practical and this-worldly is at stake is nowhere clearer than in eschatology [18]. As the relative thinness of our Act IV

---

14) *Comm.* Rom. 6:6, p. 225.

15) I Cor. 15:26.

16) *Comm.* I Cor. 15:26, II, 28 f.

17) *Comm.* Heb. 2:14, p. 72. e. a.

18) This is the context in which he wrote, I "refrain personally from superfluous investigation of useless matters," III, xxv, 11.

indicates, Calvin's operative and even his systematic eschatology consists of little more than the hope for and the contemplation of our future triumphs *here and now*. In terms of our present metaphor, the *eschaton* is not so much a power-station as a light-house which sends a brilliant beam to mark our goal and light our path to it. In his own pre-scientific terms, "the sun, before he is seen by us, chases away the darkness of the night by the pouring forth of his rays" [19].

Calvin, then, presents us a mixture whose flavor is a bittersweet combination of the hardships of this present warfare and the glories of the life to come. In the light of the coming triumph, we shall in general move from the sweet toward the bitter. Calvin can give full sway to the exalted Christ, give full credit — with respect to the elect — to Christ's glorious victory. He supplies all possible benefits to his people and fully protects them from evil. He now reigns *in full*, although "his manifestation is properly said to be delayed till the last day" [20]. Calvin's repeated call for meditation on the future life does not represent a world-fleeing asceticism engaged in fruitless dreams. He means instead that we should steadfastly fix our gaze upon the goal so that we may advance toward it along our *present* path with confident and well-directed strides. God calls us to the *hope* of eternal life, and it is the nature of a hope to be concealed; but we must keep it in sight in spite of all enemy attempts to allure us away from it [21]. Thus, in the darkest hour when the prisoners of Lyon face inevitable death, Calvin counsels: "Remember to lift up your eyes to that everlasting kingdom of Jesus Christ, and to think of whose cause it is in which you fight" [22].

During our earthly pilgrimage, then, the path is not smooth and free of obstacles, for the Christian is assigned a warfare until he reaches that *eschaton* toward which he moves [23]. The mortification of the flesh in this life must for Calvin precede the renovation of the world [24]. But while the day of triumph has not arrived and what we now see is not victory but a continuing need for struggle, Calvin insists that the assurance of faith is not diminished at all, but that

---

19) *Comm.* II Thes. 2:8, p. 335.
20) *Comm.* Luke 19:12, II, 441.
21) *Comm.* Luke 1:69, I, 68.
22) CE II, 394.
23) II, viii, 50.
24) *Comm.* John 12:31, II, 36.

we should wait patiently until Christ has finally disposed of his enemies and then accomplishes his kingdom in us in every respect [25].

When Calvin assures us that though the last judgment be delayed for a long time, yet it hangs over us every hour, he demonstrates that the fundamental tension of eschatology is from God's side [26]. Yet in a very remarkable statement of the problem Calvin points to a human hindrance within the forces of Protestantism, so that "our folly is made to supply much material" to Satan for delaying our arrival at the goal [27]. He chides Melanchthon for acceding to pressures in Germany and failing to cultivate solidarity with himself: "Surely it is indicative of a marvellous and monstrous insensibility, that we so readily set at nought that sacred unanimity, by which we ought to be bringing back into the world the angels of heaven" [28]. Calvin illuminates the eschatological tension — already now *and* not yet fully — and its relation to history when he visualizes Christ as finally destroying the Antichrist (the papacy) at the eschatological restoration, yet says that Paul intimates [29] that Christ will previously (in the success of the Reformation) put to flight the darkness of Antichrist's reign [30].

Though the *Heilsgeschichte* can be viewed from the standpoint of men, or institutions, or the doomed spiritual oppressors, it is more properly described in terms of Jesus Christ: "As he has already begun, so must he perfect his work, manifesting himself victorious in you against his enemies ... and our hearts are also strengthened to obtain the victory over Satan and all his supporters, while looking for the day when the glory of God shall be fully revealed" [31]. As we have seen, some of Calvin's descriptions of Christ's reign indicate progress within history toward the final victory. This aspect of the Gospel is clearest in the Christian's sanctification: for "As the kingdom of God is continually growing and advancing to the end of the world, we must pray every day that it *may come;* for to whatever extent iniquity abounds in the world, to such an extent *the kingdom of God* ... is not yet *come*" [32]. Calvin's conception of

---

25) *Comms.* I Cor. 15:57, II, 65 and I Cor. 15:25, II, 28.
26) *Comm.* Matt. 24:43, III, 164.
27) CE II, 362.
28) *Ibid.*
29) In II Thes. 2:8.
30) *Comm. loc. cit.,* p. 335.
31) CE II, 276.
32) *Comm.* Matt. 6:10, I, 320.

advancement in the Christian life is sometimes suspected of intro-
ducing a doctrine of the merit of good works into the Protestant
camp or of being a forerunner of the dogmas of *human progress*
which reached full flower in such utterances as Washington Glad-
den's that the kingdom of God might well come "right here in our
own Scioto valley". These charges may find an appropriate target
in the progressive Pilgrim of John Bunyan, heir not only of Calvin
but of the whole medieval pilgrimage tradition stretching back to
Augustine [33] — but Calvin's own idea is that *God's kingdom* advances victoriously in and through Christians in this life. Whatever
victories Calvin expected in this life and actually saw, he never
dreamed that he had reached or could ever achieve perfection. With
completely sincere fervor, he longed for the blessed future life where
this was to be received as the gift of God.

Finally, the eschatological perspective gives us an indispensable
warning in Jesus' disciples, who, "having been convinced that, as
soon as the reign of Christ should commence, they would be in
every respect happy, leave warfare out of account, and immediately
fly to a triumph" [34]. This desire to pass painlessly from the center
of the *Heilsgeschichte* to its end is a perfectly natural attitude — so
much so that Paul had to tie the hope engendered by I Thes. to the
ethical demands of II Thes. The Christian man must learn that
despite his contrary *natural* desires the past and future victories of
Christ are two edges of a frame. They do not simply coincide, but
they enclose a space — a space to be filled by the picture of what
Calvin calls the *militia Christiani,* the Christian's warfare with the
Spirit's sword.

The Necessity of the Spiritual Warfare

The necessity of which we speak — the necessity for this Act —
grows first of all out of the eschatological tension, but also out of the
presuppositions developed in our previous Acts. If we had used
different metaphors in describing the First and the Second Adam,
it would not be necessary now to speak of spiritual warfare. (The
exhaustive study by Wilhelm Kofhaus, *Vom Christlichen Leben
nach Johannes Calvin,* considers many metaphors Calvin uses to
describe the Christian life, including spiritual warfare.) The obverse

---

33) See III, vii, 3, n. 7.
34) *Comm.* Matt. 24:3, III, 117.

fact of composition, however, is that Calvin's insistence on the *militia Christiani* — not as one metaphorical possibility for describing the Christian life but as *the substantial fact* of that life — is the force which has driven us to discover Adam as the enslaved rebel and Christ as the Liberator. Calvin *feels* an overwhelming unavoidability which thrusts this warfare upon the Christian. On *systematic* grounds the Christian's warfare is the piece which fits into the historical framework of the *Heilsgeschichte*. Since we have continually to do with Satan, the Church shall be engaged in uninterrupted war *in this world* [1]. It becomes inevitable when a man ceases to be a slave of Satan and becomes an instrument of the Holy Spirit [2]. From another aspect, *justice* is not established in the world without a great struggle because of the devil's violent opposition [3]. Finally, in eschatological perspective, "Because God wills that Christ rule, we have many enemies, so that we must be soldiers and fighters" [4].

There are also powerful *empirical* grounds for this warfare. It is very simply a given situation into which the Christian is thrust. When a soldier, be he an officer or private, receives an order from the commander-in-chief he unquestioningly obeys. So Calvin carries on his struggles as a man who has received his orders from the heavenly King. God, the leader and supreme umpire of battle (*summus agonotheta*), has ordained that those who are one day to be crowned in heaven, must first engage in conflicts on earth [5]. Calvin's experience of the nature of the Christian life leads him on countless occasions to the conclusion that the present life is simply appointed as the field of conflict [6]. Calvin states that Christians always have been and always will be in the minority in this world, and therefore those who enlist in the cause of Christ must learn as one of their earliest lessons that they will have to fight for their faith [7]. The Christian warfare which is necessary for all, is doubly so for the ministers of the Church, "who go before the army and bear the standard" [8]. Shoulder-to-shoulder with the pastors, however, the

---

1) *Comm.* Isa. 27:1, II, 246 ff.
2) III, iii, 9.
3) *Comm.* Matt. 12:20, II, 62.
4) *Sermon* on Dan. 12:1, CR LXX, 115.
5) III, ix, 3, part. reten. Allen.
6) e. g. *Sermon* on Job 10:18—22, CR LXI, 508.
7) *Comm.* Luke 2:34, I, 147.
8) *Comm.* Phil. 2:25, p. 80.

leading political figures have a special responsibility to the Divine Captain [9]. (Calvin here sounds like the Luther of the open letter "To the German Nobility".) The most pragmatic reason of all for taking part in the Christian warfare is the blunt fact that the devil is actually assaulting us [10]. Since Satan wages *total* war on Christ, believers know that they worship God and profess faith in Christ on the condition that they are to have continual warfare with Satan, "for he does not spare the members who fight with the Head" [11].

Unquestionably Calvin, like all the Reformers, was faced with great difficulties because he remained faithful to the insights of the Reformation. We must now ask, however, whether much of the offensive character of life for him was not the product of his limited ability to see those who disagreed with him also under the sign of Christ's victory which reconciled men with God. (Perhaps we should speak of a mutual blindness, blind obedience to authority and blind independence, on the part of Loyola and Calvin, respectively.) Calvin uses Jesus' statement, "Blessed are they who suffer persecution", as the occasion for the questionable assertion that is "the ordinary lot of Christians to be hated by the majority of men" [12]. He unquestionably goes too far in this direction when he fails to recognize hyperbole and incorrectly claims that we should be earnest (sober and serious) because Luke 24:41 shows that joy was the cause of their unbelief when the disciples saw the Risen Lord [13].

The specific data of his experience is secondary, however, for here, as in every area of Calvin's theology, the ultimate answer, the underlying basis for what exists and occurs, is the purpose or decree of God. Sometimes Calvin is satisfied to leave us with the bare statement that God wills something to be so, but he often seeks to fathom the purpose of God. First of all, of course, Calvin's God wills to be glorified, but in addition, God has a purpose which concerns the Christian himself in his hard conflicts. The author and battle-umpire of our conflicts desires to test our faith, and exercise our patience [14]. But as the hardship of the struggle indicates, the purpose of God may be more earnest, namely, a chastisement for our

---

9) See *Ded. to Comm. on Gal.,* x.
10) *Comm.* Zech. 3:1 f. V, 82.
11) *Comm.* I Pet. 5:8, p. 150.
12) *Comm.* Matt. 5:10, I, 265.
13) *Comm. loc. cit.,* III, 372.
14) CG II, 275.

sins, particularly the sin of pride in exalting ourselves against him [15]. In one of his most effective scenes Calvin considers Paul's "thorn in the flesh": although Satan was a murderer from the beginning and the goad with which he prods Paul is dipped with poison, God in his kindness makes that poison medicinal to Paul so that Satan becomes a physician to him [16]. The picture which intrigues Calvin above all others, however, is that of Jacob wrestling with God. Here God, who elsewhere arms Satan to test man, himself fights against man and *also* strengthens him to resist or, as Calvin says, God fights against him with his left hand while he fights for him with his right [17]. This perfectly expresses the panergistic character of Calvin's God. Logically, this is a continuation of his conception of God's sovereignty over every aspect of man's slavery to the forces of evil. But both there and here one must ask if, after all, Calvin's God is not really responsible for the evil over which he reigns and judges in a way which compromises his goodness, and if, after all, Calvin's man is not a "tennis-ball" with which his God plays games. Neither the God who causes man to suffer so much in order to prove his character, nor the man who is thus tested, seems identifiable with the God and man revealed in Jesus Christ. The concept of God's testing his people through adversity is certainly in itself a legitimate idea, Biblically and theologically. We are here questioning, however, whether Calvin is wise to allow it, rather than the efficacious cross, to control his whole discussion of the problem of evil and the spiritual warfare it entails.

The role of Satan as the tempter is also a familiar one, connected with his role as *diabolos,* the accuser. Calvin thinks it is part of God's plan for strengthening the Christian that Satan fiercely attacks him, and that the afflictions which we endure are the Lord's rods with which he chastises us, or permits Satan to do so [18]. Nevertheless, the faithful member of Christ's body will come forth victorious because God's protection is a certainty on which Christians can rely. Calvin is so sure of this that he can even *turn around* the plea, "Lead us *not* into temptation" into a proof-text for his idea: "As God ... employs him (Satan) as the agent of his wrath ... He may also be said, in a way peculiar to himself, to *lead them into temp-*

---

15) *Comm.* Isa. 42:25, III, 314.
16) *Comm.* II Cor. 12:7, II, 376.
17) *Comms.* Gen. 32:24, II, 195 ff. and Hos. 12:3 ff., I, 422 f.
18) *Comm.* Isa. 10:26, I, 363.

tation" [19]. This very fact of God's hand in man's conflicts and distresses serves Calvin as a source of great comfort, for the final word is that "whatever poison Satan produces, God turns it into medicine for his elect" [20].

The Christian's confidence in God's protection and the benevolence of his ultimate purpose must not, however, lead him to doubt that further immediate struggles are necessary. When Jacob finished the fight he returned to his own land, but his wrestling with God had been for the purpose of preparing him not for rest but for the struggle there. "We, also, are to learn from him, that we must fight during the whole course of our life; lest any one, promising himself rest, should wilfully deceive himself" [21].

The Battlefronts of the Spiritual Warfare

Already in the biographical introduction we have presented almost all of the combatants who appear in the spiritual warfare. There, however, they were simply identified, whereas now we know the presuppositions which reveal their significance in combat. As we have followed the history of man's redemption we have met the all-operative God, the Satan who tyrannizes and the Divine Invader who as means of God's plan comes not to reinforce beleaguered allies but to liberate some captive victims. The victory of Christus Victor, then, makes possible and necessary the war between these freed-men and others still more or less under the Satanic spell. As we investigate now how effective the victory may be, we encounter a mighty new figure whose Sword will define the character of this Act and its outcome in the next, namely, the Spirit. (This aspect of Calvin's faith and life has received less attention than its centrality deserves, and is one of the areas still requiring sharper definition. The recent Harvard dissertation of B. C. Milner on the role of the Holy Spirit in Calvin's thought is an important step in this direction.)

The warfare carried on by the *militia Christi* is a multifront campaign, and all along the line of battle we hear Calvin's reminder that our warfare is not with flesh and blood, but with spiritual forces of

19) *Comm.* Matt. 6:13, I, 328.
20) *Comm.* Gen. 50:20, II, 488.
21) *Comm.* Gen. 32:24, II, 197.

wickedness at whose head we must always see Satan. There is, however, a basic distinction drawn by the first great Christian strategist,
the apostle Paul, between the battles to be fought against external
enemies and the one against those within the Christian man himself.
In Act I we learned that in a sense man is his own worst enemy; but
it is only after Christ's victory that we can see the struggle between
the old man of sin and the new man in Christ, between our flesh and
the spirit born of God, and thus appreciate the intensity and per-
vasiveness of the struggle within man. Paul's "fighting without and
fear within" makes clear that "even if there were not enemies to
make open war upon us, we find enough of aversion and indisposed-
ness in ourselves"[1]. The proof of the importance of his battle against
himself as flesh is that unless the Christian wins (that is, God gives
him) a significant measure of victory in this struggle against the
flesh he cannot hope to be effective in the struggle against other
foes. Therefore, we must consider first the battle front between the
flesh and the spirit.

"Flesh", for Calvin, is not simply a synonym for body, but com-
prehends the whole of the unregenerate or "old" man, that is the
whole man — body — and soul — insofar as he is in the state of
corruption and slavery. In fact, Calvin can go so far as to say of one
Pauline passage, "*Flesh* here, in my opinion, denotes — not the
body, but *that part of the soul* which has not yet been regenerated"[2]. There are many ways in which the flesh acts as a hindrance to
the Christian man, and not all of them appear as violent opposition.
In fact, one of the most discouraging characteristics of the flesh is
that its very weakness — here is a rare point of contact between the
Biblical view of man and classic dualism — makes it a treacherous
and unreliable soldier of the line. This is especially clear since the
Christian life must be lived in *faith,* for "believers have a perpetual
conflict with their own unbelief"[3]. The unwillingness of the flesh
to engage in the necessary struggles of the Christian life is most
annoying to Calvin. Even such a brave warrior as St. Peter is told
to expect to be led around against his will to show him, so Calvin
thinks, that we never serve God entirely without inner conflict, because our flesh flees the struggle[4]. But Calvin did not need to look

---

1) CE II, 189.
2) *Comm.* II Cor. 12:7, II, 373 f. e. a.
3) III, ii, 17.
4) CG II, 232.

beyond his own day to find evidence of the flesh's weakness. He was especially incensed by the conduct of the renowned play-boy prince Henry Navarre (later the notorious Henry IV) to whom he wrote that great regard for the body is great disregard for the virtues of the soul [5]. Unfortunately, this frailty of flesh is not confined to a few examples for no man can be found who is not still far removed from "evangelical perfection" and weakness so weighs down the majority that "with wavering and limping and even creeping along the ground, they move at a feeble rate" [6].

The weakness of the flesh leads Calvin to man's ultimate vulnerability, for he experienced that this life was lived in the midst of death. Not only were the members of the struggling infant Reformed Church never far from the possibility of violent death at the hands of their religious-political enemies, but also the weakness of the flesh made all men susceptible to innumerable forms of unexplained and therefore terrifying fatal disease. The artistic representations of death coming to claim people from all stations of life — the *Totentanz* paintings of Holbein, for example — suggest to us the intensity of the danger, and statistical reports of the effects of the plagues express its extent. Yet only through knowing a circle of acquaintances can we appreciate what that threat of death and disease meant to an individual. One would have to say that *most* of Calvin's family and friends — particularly the married women — died an early death as the result of disease. It can be no wonder that his view of the Christian's life in this world is always under the shadow of the struggle with the hidden enemy who has power to snatch away anyone, the moment God allows him the opportunity. Thus, Calvin is convinced that unusual diseases are, for the most part, inflicted on men through the agency of the devil, so far as God grants him permission to injure them [7]. It is well that Christ is king, therefore, "because if such excellence were not in him all of us would be oppressed with poverty and famine" [8]. Even allowing for the hard lot of Calvin and his comrades-in-arms, we can certainly not sympathize with his unrelieved somberness and the usual absence from his arsenal of spiritual warfare in this life of the joy which results from God's salvation in Christ! Calvin's battle-trumpet

5) CG II, 452.
6) III, vi, 5.
7) *Comm.* Luke 13:11, II, 154 f.
8) II, xv, 5. part. reten. Allen.

sounds a truer note, therefore, when he writes Denis Peolquin and Louis de Marsac as they approach martyrdom: "*As in the midst of this life we are in death,* you have now need to be well persuaded that *in the midst of death you are in life*" [9].

The flesh, however, is not just a weak and treacherous soldier of God. Far worse, it is his deadly enemy. The two ideas belong together, of course, because as Calvin says, we are not only cold and cowardly but so confounded that we desert Christ in the heat of battle, and thus our flesh is our greatest enemy [10]. For Calvin, not only do "fleshly lusts war against the soul", but in many passages he shows that the flesh is Satan's ally in actively opposing God. The very fact that we *stand* in grace [11] must be a dynamic rather than a static matter for Calvin, because it means "to stand firm against all the engines or devices of Satan and the flesh" [12].

Though systematically making "flesh" equivalent to the whole man, Calvin slips into asking what *part* of flesh is God's enemy. The most obvious candidates are the numerous *affections* which spring from our flesh and are so many enemies of God in us [13]. He can refer to sexual desires as Satan's darts against which we must be in constant conflict [14]. Such ideas could be expression either of Biblical insights or of the Classical-Catholic view of the flesh as the lower, material, non-spiritual-mental part of man's nature. The same might also be said of human pride. This fault is so radically involved in man's rebellion against God that Calvin connects it with the first sin, and is "so deeply rooted that even the most advanced are not thoroughly purged from it" [15]. Again, although his dealings with other men clearly show that he leaves rather too large a place for "holy anger", Calvin also occasionally recognizes that human anger can be a great hindrance to the advance of God's kingdom, not only in Farel but *even in himself*! [16] In tune with his anti-Classic doctrine of total depravity, Calvin blames not just the sensual and corporeal aspects of man, but also his thoughts, the studies and meditations

---

9) CE II, 403. e. a.
10) CG II, 291.
11) Rom. 5:2.
12) *Comm. loc. cit.*, p. 189.
13) *Comm.* John 12:27, II, 34.
14) *Comm.* I Cor. 7:9, I, 236.
15) II, i, 4 and *Comm.* II Cor. 1:9, II, 119 f.
16) CR XLVII, Epistle No. 3565.

of the flesh, for waging war against the will of God [17]. Even the very highest wisdom of man can be a very dangerous enemy of God's wisdom [18], for when Paul's preaching on Mar's hill was rejected, "the philosophers were captains and standard-bearers" in the assault. From these latter statements it is clear that Calvin — operatively as well as systematically — uses the term flesh to designate the whole old man and not merely the corrupt material or non-mental part of man.

The powerful and unending opposition of the flesh in this life is not a cause for despair, and this can chiefly be attributed to the fact that God gives his Holy Spirit to the members of Christ's body. Lutheran, or at least German, scholarship often criticizes Calvin for "spiritualizing" various aspects of theology, especially eschatology (as we shall see in Act IV) and the sacraments. Presumably this means that Christ's "spiritual" presence is less "real" than it must be, and that meditation on the future life is so abstract, irrelevant and other-worldly that indispensable supplies are suspended uselessly in a derelict balloon. For Calvin as for the Hebraic mind of the Bible, however, "spiritual" means "of *God* the Spirit", and designates *power* (from God's "other" world, to be sure, but) mighty and relevant to man in the highest degree. Calvin says Christ left us, "that his departure might be more useful to us than that presence . . . confined . . . within the humble dwelling of his body", and in the course of this same paragraph he (with Augustine) contrasts Christ's *spiritual* presence with his bodily absence [19]. The Christian, then, is understood as the man whose heart is armed with the heavenly power of God's Spirit against the fiery bombs and poison arrows of Satan, so that that man's own spirit is as quiet under his protection as "a mighty fortress" [20]. The principal activity of the Spirit in the Christian's life grows out of the Spirit's vital connection with the Word of God. Like Luther, Calvin insists that the *connection* of the Word and Spirit is a powerful force, while their separation is extremely dangerous, being the work of the spirit of Satan (specifically among the Anabaptists) [21].

---

17) *Comm.* Rom. 8:7, p. 287.
18) *Comm.* Matt. 16:22, II, 301.
19) II, xvi, 14, part. reten. Allen.
20) CG II, 48 and I, 385.
21) *Comm.* Isa. 59:21, IV, 271.

Calvin stresses that the warfare between the flesh and the Spirit occurs in man only after he is regenerated, because until the Spirit creates man's spirit anew, there is no real resistance to the flesh within him. Thus the warfare described in Romans 7 [22] can only take place after a man has received the gift of the Spirit from Christ who reconciles him to God! [23] Once a man is regenerated by the Spirit, then, the fight has just begun. Our righteousness is of such a fragile and fleeting character that it is perpetually corrupted, overpowered, and destroyed by subsequent sins [24]. Calvin is, therefore, sceptical of all religious revivals, sometimes even questioning the depth or the effect of the Reformation on the lives of the people in general! [25]

Interestingly, in the struggle between the flesh and the Spirit the character of the law of God as a weapon in the spiritual warfare is ambiguous. In Act I we saw that God's law, like his wrath, is an enemy which oppresses man, who is cursed because of his sin. In Act II we learned that God's enmity against man and God's condemnatory law have been overcome in Christ's victory over man's foes. Here we see that the law becomes a weapon of the Spirit in his warfare against the flesh: on the one hand, since the flesh is a lazy, dull and tardy servant of the man in God's service, the law serves as a whip urging it forward to its work [26]; on the other hand, "here is no greater variance in the world than of the Spirit and the flesh; the law is spiritual, man is carnal ... here is expressed an antithesis ... between the flesh and the Spirit" [27].

Two important considerations show that the struggle of the flesh and the Spirit within man is not merely a peripheral one but quite central and basic to the spiritual warfare. As we said earlier, victory in this struggle is a necessary precondition of the usefulness of a member of Christ's body in the rest of the warfare [28]. Far beyond this, Calvin can make the outcome of the warfare against the flesh decisive for the whole cosmos: "It is with us also that the renovation ought to begin; because we hold the first rank, and it is through our sin that 'the creatures groan, and are subject to vanity' as Paul

22) And more briefly in Gal. 5:16 ff., particularly v. 17.
23) See II, ii, 7 and IV, xv, 12.
24) II, xiv, 10.
25) *Comm.* Isa. 65:25, IV, 406.
26) II, vii, 12.
27) *Comm.* Rom. 7:14, p. 259 (author's transl.).
28) CG II, 276.

shows [29]. But when we shall be perfectly renewed, heaven and earth shall also be fully renewed, and shall regain their former state" [30]. This dramatizes the importance of man's inner struggle with the total spiritual warfare, however much we may deplore the shift of the point of control over creation's destiny from the Divine Invader to his militia. In point of fact, Calvin expected a Christian to win a measure of victory in his inward struggle sufficient to enable him to participate victoriously in the wider conflict. This victorious process is not a human possibility, but results — as is clear from the New Testament — from God's gift of the Holy Spirit [31]. The victory is not confined to the Apostoloic Age in direct proximity to Pentecost, but is a continuing fact down through the history of the Church. Calvin encourages Laurent de Normandie to believe that the victories of faith which he has won in the persecutions in France are examples which strengthen others to stand fast [32]. Finally, such victories belong not to a few, or even to a long list of saints of heroes of the faith, but Calvin holds it as a sure and steady truth that in the struggle of faith between the flesh and Spirit "the *invariable* issue of this contest is, that faith ultimately triumphs over these difficulties which besiege and seem to imperial it" [33].

When we follow Calvin's shift from the internal to the external battlefront we must immediately turn our gaze to the struggle for the faith within the Christian church, for it is there that God chooses to be worshipped and served, it is there that Satan attacks most boldly and insidiously, it is there that Calvin's own chief interest lies. One main battlefront claimed his attention, his strategic support, his command decisions, above all others — the one which, humanly speaking, *caused* the Reformation. It was the struggle against the Papacy, that Antichrist who usurped Christ's place as Head of the church [34].

---

29) Rom. 8:20.

30) *Comm.* Isa. 65:17, IV, 398 f.

31) *Comm.* John 16:20, II, 149.

32) CG I, 385.

33) III, ii, 18. e. a.

34) Calvin played an important role in the polemic struggle with Catholic thinkers which informs his entire discussion of the church in the *Institutes* of 1559. During his Strasbourg interim (1538—41) between his two tours of duty in Geneva Calvin was actually present at major colloquies. During most of his career, however, Calvin was forced to use long-range literary artillery.

Calvin's principal complaint is that once *God* has instituted means for making the Gospel known and effective in human society — the church, its ministry, the sacraments, the civil government — *Satan* has used the Papacy to corrupt "everything that God had appointed to be instrumental to our salvation"[35]. Thus, exactly as had Priestly religion to which God entrusted his Word before the coming of the Mediator, the church under the Papacy produced the chief enemies of Christ[36]. Since the corruptions of the church under the Papacy correspond to those under the Jewish hierocracy, Calvin sees himself and the other Reformers in the role of the prophets who under the Old Covenant rebuked the abuses[37]. Calvin proposes, therefore, to "look upon the poor Papists as lost sheep"[38], since they are but Satan's instruments. One suspects that it is a triumph of the forces of evil when in various practical situations Calvin deserted this sympathetic position and assaulted these human agents with that bitterness which can only deepen the wounds that separate. Although Satan has wreaked great havoc and confusion in the church through the Romanists, Calvin has confidence that God will protect Christ's body from ultimate destruction. In fact, some essential marks of the church still remain among the Papists, and "neither the craft of the devil nor the malice of men" can ever destroy their efficacy[39]. This fact by no means signifies, however, that a Christian who wishes to serve God purely may

Whatever Calvin's relation to Nicholas Cop's *Concio Academica* of Nov. 1533, his Prefatory Address to Francis I in August 1535 shows him thoroughly embroiled in the debate. The enumerations of Barth and Niesel, OS, III, 13—15 and of McNeill, PA 3, n. 8 obviate extensive citation here, but certain direct exchanges of fire deserve mention. Cardinal Sadoleto, who according to Bohatec had been one of those arousing King Francis against the evangelicals in 1534 f., wrote to the Genevans in Calvin's absence on March 18, 1539. He charged them to recant, asking how converts to the Reformation could possibly answer "before the dread tribunal of the sovereign Judge", to which Calvin effectively replied (see III, xii, 1, n. 2). Calvin's *Treatise on Relics* (1543) received reply from John Cochlaeus, *De sacriis religuiis Christi et sanctorum ejus* (1549), while, on the other hand, Calvin's *Treatise on Free Will against* [Albertus] *Pighius* (1543) and a second work against him, *Upon the Eternal Predestination of God* (1552) both answer Pighius' *De libero hominis arbitrio et divina gratia* in 1542, attacking *Luther's* doctrine of predestination.

35) IV, i, 1.
36) *Comm.* Acts 13:27, I, 526, 528.
37) See IV, i, 5 and IV, ii, 3.
38) CG II, 272.
39) IV, ii, 12.

legitimately remain under the yoke of the Papacy any more than he may remain in bondage to Satan, for "what are called temples among the Papists are only filthy brothels of Satan" [40]. The authoritarian jurisdiction of the Roman church over the faith and life of its adherents is, therefore, utterly intolerable to Calvin, "for if we allow Christ any kingdom among us, all this kind of domination must immediately fall to the ground" [41].

The usurpation of Christ's place of authority and importance in the church is the heart of Calvin's objection to Roman Catholicism. This is, in fact, the principal concrete form of what he treats as the unforgiveable sin — man's self-exaltation over against God. In a remarkable passage foreshadowing the spirit of Dostoevsky's Grand Inquisitor, Calvin says: "How foolishly the Papists boast that the church belongs to them, when they order Christ himself to be silent and cannot endure the sound of his voice, but proclaim aloud, with distended cheeks, their own edits, laws, decrees, and tyrannical regulations" [42]. Or, put in the metaphor of spiritual warfare: "They (the Popish clergy) affirm that the church cannot err, because it is governed by Christ; as if Christ, like some mercenary soldier, hired himself for wages to other captains, and if he had not, on the contrary, reserved the entire authority for himself" [43]. The most notorious instance of the Romanist imposture, is the institution of the Papacy itself. Calvin characteristically designates the Pope "Antichrist", a practice based on the conviction (common among the Reformers) that II Thes. 2:3 ff. gives a detailed description of the Papacy [44]. Calvin also employed other choice (often Biblical) epithets to describe the popes who had — as the very need for the Counter Reformation eloquently suggests — often been corrupt in that era. The popes are the false prophets who claim to come in God's name, a disguise for his agents Satan has used to deceive wretched men from the beginning [45]. Turning one of the Romanists' own favorite weapons against them Calvin says, "if they

---

40) *Comm.* Ps. 26:8, I, 447 (author's transl.).

41) IV, xi, 8.

42) *Comm.* Isa. 11:4, I, 382.

43) *Comm.* Matt. 28:20, III, 391.

44) Consult IV, ii, 12 n. 16, which gives an excellent survey of the usage of the term by Calvin and his predecessors. Calvin himself notes that Gregory the Great already spoke of the pride of his rival, John of Constantinople, as the precursor of Antichrist.

45) *Comm.* John 5:43, I, 220.

are determined to apply to Peter's successors every thing that was said to Peter, it will follow that they are all Satans, because the Lord also said to Peter, 'Get thee behind me, Satan, thou art an offence to me'" [46].

Calvin similarly attacks the Roman Catholic *clergy* for its opposition to the Gospel and its usurpation of Christ's authority in his church [47]. While Calvin hears Peter address, "You are a royal priesthood", to the whole church, Roman theologians apply the words to a "few shavelings" who are the most rapacious, ignorant and libidinous of men [48]. Calvin exhibits even less patience with the monastic institution and the pretensions of celibacy, "For if the lies of Satan wherewith he has blinded and bewitched the wretched world reign everywhere at present, they have their chief seat in those unhappy prisons (presumably cloisters) which he has reared up, that he may keep souls in a twofold captivity" [49]. Calvin considered marriage a holy institution of God and believed that it is Satan who has introduced the cult of celibacy to discredit marriage [50]. Further, coercive prohibition of marriage to priests is a terrible example of the impious tyranny by which the Papists destroy the God-given liberty of the Christian man [51].

This Christian freedom was expressly central to the Reformation from the moment of Martin Luther's *De libertate christiana* in 1520 [52]. Already in 1536, Calvin dedicated one-sixth of his first *Institutes* to his own "*De libertate christiana*". By 1559, essentially the same arguments crowned his treatment of justification by faith, defending Christian liberty against the Papists' claim to absolute authority in the church [53]. The usurpation of the prerogatives of God and of the government over Christian men is Calvin's target in every sector of ecclesiastical and political life, but it comes particularly to the fore along the sacramental front. (Much of Calvin's attack is directed at the theology developed by the Scholastics, esp.

---

46) IV, vii, 28.

47) *Comm.* John 7:48, I, 315.

48) IV, xix, 25.

49) CE II, 215.

50) See *Comm.* I Cor. 7:1 ff., I, 222 ff.

51) IV, xii, 23.

52) Melanchthon's treatment of Christian liberty in the *Loci Communes* (1521) seems especially to have influenced Calvin (See III, xix, notes 3, 5, 6, and 9).

53) See III, xix, esp. 1.

Lombard and Aquinas, and confirmed by the Council of Trent, e. g. session 7 in 1547.) First, Calvin levels his attack against the fabric and framework of the Roman Catholic sacramental system as a whole, saying that John 1:29, for example, "leaves no other refuge for sinner than to flee to Christ; by which he overturns all satisfactions, and purifications and redemptions, that are invented by men"[54]. Next Calvin systematically attacks each bastion in the fortress-like sacramental structure, from the Romanist conception of baptism to the rite of extreme unction!

Calvin's principal objection to the Roman Catholic conception of baptism is that it has critically weakened this sacrament by dividing up its significance among various other ceremonies[55]. The Romanists also recognized the terminology of spiritual warfare, claiming that in baptism we are regenerated to life, and that by confirmation we are armed for warfare. This means that the oil of confirmation replaces the water of baptism, because they taught that there is no promise in baptism to arm us for the spiritual warfare[56]. Although this is a manifest insult against baptism, Roman Catholic baptism is not invalid, "because although the devil has long reigned in the Papacy, yet he could not altogether extinguish God's grace"[57].

Far more serious in Calvin's eyes is the distortion of the Lord's Supper in the Roman Mass[58]. That it was, to him and his fellow officers in the regiments of the Reformed, the central abuse of the sacramental system is clear from the fact that they, in contradistinction to Luther and his followers, basically re-formed the celebration of the Lord's Supper[59]. The subtlety of the devil, says Calvin, has so bewitched the world that the "monster of transubstantiation" will no longer allow the light of true interpretation to fall upon the words "this is my body"[60]. This "monster of transubstantiation" drags many tails behind it, for it requires a host of other ceremonies to complete its effect — and Calvin attacks them all. He freely admits that God, in his mercy, instituted "certain exercises of

54) *Comm.* loc. cit., I, 65.
55) IV, xv, 19.
56) See IV, xix, 5, 8, 12 f.
57) *Comm.* Ezek. 16:20, II, 120.
58) See Calvin's attack on the Mass as a sacrifice in IV, xviii, as defended by Eck and De Castro: see notes 2, 4, 6, 7, 9.
59) *Comm.* Hos. 4:15, I, 173.
60) *Comm.* Matt. 26:26, III, 207.

piety" but adds that Satan later corrupted these into the impious and idolatrous worship seen in the Roman Church [61]. Interestingly, Calvin's tactics in dealing with the rituals and so-called sacraments of the Roman Church depended largely on the individual case. He could counsel acquiesence or ruthless rejection, depending on the seriousness of the excess, and the prevailing trend of practice [62].

Calvin likewise looked upon the attempts of the Roman Church to preserve the apostolic activities of miracle-working and exorcism as presumptuous games played directly into the hands of Satan [63]. Perfect examples are the counterfeit (Allen, "fake", Battles, in LCC) exorcists, the "Pope's clerks and door-keepers, for not only do the demons refuse to obey them but actually exercise dominion over them" [64].

Calvin concerns himself most deeply, however, with the theological implications of the sacramental structure, which systematically and operatively requires penance, indulgences and satisfactions. They are part of the elaborate legalistic scheme of salvation by works substituted for true repentance, which is an act of faith, a gift of God, in which the Christian maintains himself in the attitude of turning toward God [65].

There are also innumerable isolated theological battle-areas, because of the large numbers of the Romanist philosophers and theologians, "scribes, who in the present day sell their labors to the Pope to make war with Christ" [66]. The veneration of Mary had not in Calvin's day achieved the dogmatic significance it has since gained, but he had words of warning against Mariolatry, for in honoring her the Papists "stripped Christ of his spoils" [67]. The principal example of their activity in Calvin's time was the Council of Trent, where Antichrist, the sworn and professed enemy of

---

61) IV, xiv, 19.

62) CG II, 10 and CE II, 215.

63) *Comm.* John 3:2, I, 106 f.

64) IV, xix, 24. — The official Roman Catholic position still insists on the power of the church to dispel demonic influence not only generally, in baptism and the sacraments, but specifically in actual cases of possession. The development of modern psychological sciences and such charges of negligence as those by Calvin have led to careful control and extreme caution in exercise of the power claimed by the church.

65) See III, iv, 21; III, vi, 4; III, v, 6 and 10; and *Comm.* John 12:42, II, 47.

66) *Comm.* John 8:10, I, 322.

67) *Comm.* John 1:51, I, 85.

Christ, presided over the slaves of Satan [68]. De Quervain may well be right in making the work of the Council of Trent one of the two great concrete enemies which Calvin kept constanly before him [69].

Finally, Calvin had to content not only with a church which distorted and tried to overwhelm the truth of God by theological subtleties and the weight of ecclesiastical authority and long custom, but also employed force and political power. Calvin was deeply distressed, of course, by the general persecution of Protestants as a group in France, and the martyrdom of individuals [70]. Yet in the face of all the forces of the Papists, which enabled them to maintain the battle along so many fronts, Calvin expressed unfailing confidence in the victory of the Reformation [71].

From this struggle based on fundamental disagreement we pass not to Calvin's repeated warm disagreements with his allies, but to two quite ambivalent fronts, one intellectual, one ecclesiastic. Renaissance humanism itself represented a type of Reform movement within Christendom, an attempt to correct the barbarism, parochialism and temporal limitations of the supposedly One, Holy, Catholic, Eternal Church. In contrast to the nineteenth century image of the Renaissance as pagan and secular, modern scholarship is increasingly uncovering its Christian and religious aspects, certainly in the northern Renaissance where the broad circle symbolized by the name of Erasmus revived knowledge of the Church Fathers and *Christian* antiquity and also recaptured skill in the Biblical languages and laid the groundwork for modern scientific exegesis. More surprisingly, perhaps, is the tendency of greater scholarly familiarity to force recognition of the Christian elements of the two centuries (fourteenth and fifteenth) of the Italian Renaissance. (One gains the

---

68) *Ded. to Comm. on Catholic Epistles,* p. xv. This letter was addressed to Edward VI, boy-king of England on Jan. 24, 1551. The Council of Trent convened in 1545 and ran intermittently until 1563, the year before Calvin's death. Calvin devoted a tract to it, *Acts of the Council of Trent with the Antidote* (1547), and his subsequent writings are filled with allusions to its pronouncements, specially with reference to justification by faith and the relation of faith and works, in addition to the items discussed directly in our text (the sacraments and the primacy of the Roman See). McNeill notes thirteen points of contact with the Acts of Trent in the 1559 *Institutes,* esp. III, xi, "justification by faith" and IV, xiv—xviii, on the sacraments.

69) See de Quervain, *op. cit.,* p. 14, and Ded. to *Comm. on Acts,* I, xxiii.

70) See CG II, 366 and CE II, 38.

71) *Comm.* Isa. 54:17, IV, 153.

impression when reading Delio Canitmori's Italian Heretics of the Sixteenth Century that these men were primarily Anti-Medieval rather than Anti-Christian.) The term itself, "rinascita", was already used by a committed Renaissance man, Giorgio Vasari, to designate the current rebirth (the word "renaissance" stems from the Vulgate equivalents for Paul's description of "the man in Christ": *renasci, renovari, reformari; regeneratio, renovatio, nova vita*) of Italian painting since Cimabue and Giotto. Of fourteenth century humanists, Petrarca was a cleric and even Boccacio his admirer was aware of no contradiction of the church when planting the Renaissance in Florence. The beginnings of historical criticism with Laurentius Valla in the fifteenth century were ultimately beneficial, at least to the Reformed churches, while the leading minds of Florence, Marsilius Ficino (*Restitutio Christianismi*) and Pico della Mirandola sought to effect a renewal of the church. (Van Gelden, *Two Reformations of the Sixteenth Century,* finds the distinction between these thinkers and the medieval church in that while it concentrated on salvation they were interested in a doctrine of life. From this point of view, Luther would, as in many important areas, remain a child of the Middle Ages, while both Calvin and Loyola would stand shoulder-to-shoulder with the Renaissance.)

The tendency was tremendously broad and since it represents perhaps a mood rather than an organized movement it sometimes seems to be simply a matter of definition (on this problem, see Erwin Panofsky, *Renaissance and Renascences*). For some like Jacob Burckhardt, *The Civilization of the Renaissance in Italy,* "Renaissance" means the flowering of individual personality and a return to pagan antiquity. For others such as Michelangelo specialist Henry Thode and K. Burdach, the latter element is non-essential and "Renaissance" really refers to the rebirth of fourteenth century man. It is no surprise, then, that in the spiritual warfare of Calvin the Renaissance has the most variable allegiance, sometimes neutral, sometimes opposing, sometimes allied.

The effect of men like Marsilius Ficino and Pico was greater in the north than in Italy itself so that all of the Reformers except Luther[72], whose philosophical heritage — outside of the Augustin-

---

72) Wilhelm Pauck, "Historiography of the German Reformation during the past twenty Years", *Church History* IX (1940), pp. 305—40, points out that the Lutheran *Loci Communes* in which Philip Melanchthon first formulated Lutheran piety into a theological system is a Humanist form.

ianism which led him back to his Pauline Bible — extended Nominalist critiques of medieval Romanism into many areas from which Ockham deliberately shrunk back. Calvin's legal training in Bourges and Orleans brought him in touch with ancient Stoic and contemporary Italian philosophy, in addition to those contacts with humanism common to Swiss and French Reformers familiar with Paris and the Rhineland. This aspect of Calvin's mind, which calls for still further study, has been most fully explored by J. Bohatec[73]. While Augustin Renaudet (*Préréforme et Humanisme à Paris pendant les premières guerres d'Italie,* 1916) claims that Faber Stapulensis (Lefevre d'Etaples) exerted the greatest influence on Calvin of any French Christian Humanist, Bohatec demonstrates a fairly extensive though strictly limited influence by Erasmus, whom Budé vainly sought as head of the Royal Readers, forerunner of the College de France. But Budé himself, according to Bohatec, was most important, for he symbolizes the ambiguity of the Renaissance in Calvin's spiritual warfare. On the one hand, Bohatec claims that Budé was involved with Cardinal Sadoleto in arousing Francis I against the evangelicals in 1534 f.,[74] and that he is a more important opponent for Calvin than any mentioned by Barth and Niesel[75]. On the other hand, Q. Breen claims that Bude's *Annotationes in Pandectas* was the model for Calvin's *Commentary on Seneca's De Clementia* of 1532[76].

It is this writing alone which presents us with Calvin the humanist not yet Reformer, and therefore gives us an invaluable tool evaluating the humanism *which went into* the Christian-humanist synthesis of which R. Seeberg says: "Calvin really arrived at that union to which Melanchthon aspired but never attained except in a rather external manner"[77]. H. Berger finds Calvin, whom he believes raised the problem of power and the tyrant because of Francis I[78], ultimately a far truer — because more noble and uncompromising

---

73) Esp. *Calvin und das Recht,* 1934, 'Calvin et l'humanisme,' 1938—9. "Budé und Calvin," *Studien zur Gedankenwelt des französischen Frühhumanismus,* 1950.

74) J. Bohatec, *Budé und Calvin,* pp. 128 ff.

75) OS, III, 13—15.

76) Q. Breen, *John Calvin, a Study in French Humanism,* p. 96.

77) R. Seeberg, *Lehrbuch der Dogmengeschichte,* 2nd edn., 1920, 2, p. 558.

78) H. Berger, *op. cit.,* pp. 22 f.

— Stoic than Macchiavelli [79]. The method of Calvin illustrates the quality of his writing, for, as Wendel points out, although Budé blazed the trail with his use of philology, grammar, logic, rhetoric and literary comparison in his *Annotationes* and Valla and Erasmus both employed the humanist method in exposition of the New Testament, "it was Calvin who first made it the very basis of his exegesis, and in so doing founded the modern exegetical science" [80].

Why then did Calvin desert the ranks of Humanism, and to what extent was his defection an effective rejection? Wendel points out that "with a touch of arrogance, he presented his work to the humanists as thought he had been their equal. They judged him presumptuous, self-important . . . the reaction almost everywhere was one of cold disapproval . . . His literary self-esteem . . . had suffered its first — and last — humiliation" [81]. Breen and Cadier imply that Calvin went over to the Reformation partly because it was on the rise and the Renaissance was on the wane when Calvin was seeking the audience he had not found with his commentary on Seneca [82], although Seeberg thinks that Calvin's humanistic competence was the cause of his eventual success with the intellectual elite [83]. The Protestant mind would insist that Calvin's famous and largely secret "sudden conversion", which in all circumstantial probability occurred before his surrender of his ecclesiastical benefices in Noyon in May, 1534, swept all other considerations aside. Nevertheless, the humanistic method continued to in*form* all his intellectual work, so that from this point of view Wendel can say: "Just as Luther never managed completely to efface the intellectual imprint of Ockham, so Calvin remained always more or less the humanist he had been in 1532" [84]. Neuenhaus correctly traces a development in which Calvin, while absorbing all the elements of humanist culture, endeavored to use them in the service of his faith, and avoided the dangers which might have arisen from them. The Hellenic spirit faded little by little before the Christian spirit; nevertheless, Calvin

---

79) *Ibid.,* p. 29. *Il principe* was in press at the same time as Calvin's work but was not translated into Latin until 1553.

80) Wendel, *op. cit.,* p. 31.

81) *Ibid.,* pp. 36 f. with n. 66.

82) Q. Breen, *John Calvin: A Study in French Humanism,* p. 93 and Jean Cadier, *Calvin,* p. 31 (German edn.).

83) Same reference as in note 18 above.

84) Wendel, *op. cit.,* p. 33.

preserved to the end the reputation of an excellent humanist" [85].
Yet form and content, though distinguishable, have an *unio perso-nalis* of their own which forces us to investigate the thesis of Roy
Battenhouse that "Calvin's rejection of humanism for theology, and
of reason for revelation, seems to have been a rejection more often
of conclusions than of basic definitions and assumptions" [86]. Charles
Trinkhaus suggests that one of these fundamental carryovers occurs
from Renaissance optimism about rational man in general to Calvin's ultimate optimism about the renascent man in Christ. Others
have found a strong Platonic strain [87], but as Wendel says, "the limits of the Platonic influence are well drawn by Bohatec, *Budé und
Calvin,* p. 417" [88]. Actually, the quantity of Platonic material is misleading, and one would suspect that the Platonic dynamic in Calvin
was almost invariably pre-digested by his revered Augustine, and
the primary direct influence of antiquity on Calvin is indubitably
Stoic. With reference to the Renaissance, Trinkhaus has probably
led us in the most fruitful direction when he delineates "Renaissance problems" Calvin was still solving in the *Institutes* of 1559
(i. e. near the *end* of the Biblicizing-de-Hellenizing process described
by Neuenhaus above): "(a) the epistemological question of the
relation of subjective perception to objective truth, (b) the related
question of man and the universe — microcosmos and cosmos —
(c) the question of the fortuitous or providential character of events,
and (d) the question of man's free will" [89]. In any case, the Renaissance remains the most ambiguous battle-front of the spiritual
warfare. Its line of battle ran through the heart of Calvin himself
and of individuals in every camp of the sixteenth century, continually creating friends and neutrals and foes in the spiritual
struggle. For example, the effect of the Renaissance on Calvin may
be symbolized when we applaud the humanistic exegesis Calvin used
to sharpen the Spirit's sword for his dramatic conflicts but question
the Stoicism of the Deity who wields it and "indifferently" destroys
many men.

85) J. Neuenhaus, "Calvin als Humanist", *Calvinstudien* (1909), p. 2.

86) Roy W. Battenhouse, "The Doctrine of Man in Calvin and in Renaissance Platonism", *Journal of the History of Ideals* IX (1948), pp. 469 f.

87) J. Boisset, *Sagesse et Sainteté dans la penseé de Jean Calvin,* pp. 225 ff.
and Battenhouse, *op. cit.*

88) Wendel, *op. cit.,* p. 33, n. 52.

89) Trinkhaus, *op. cit.,* p. 79.

Unfortunately, his relations within the Protestant camp did not set Calvin completely free for his great struggle on the *ecclesiastical* front with the Romanist foe. He, like Luther and Zwingli, had to learn early that there were those among the loose confederacy of rebels against Rome who must be opposed. The Reformers found them especially among the Anabaptists, those Enthusiastic advocates of the freedom of the spirit granted the Christian man. The Protestant polemics against "the Anabaptists" was overdrawn — partly because Romanists charged all of the rebels with the same Enthusiastic excesses — and the polemic post held by Calvin against the left wing of the Reformation has largely been by-passed by modern scholarship [90].

There were four principal, separate but related, areas of dispute whenever the Reformers debated with the Anabaptists. The first of these was, of course, baptism, for the Anabaptists claimed that the baptism of infants (therefore divorced from faith) administered by the impure Roman Church was invalid and, claiming the precedent of Acts 19:5, they advocated a re-baptism. Calvin, who largely reproduced the Augustinian answers to Donatism [91], denied the lack of ground for the institution of infant baptism [91a], denied that the primary significance of baptism is as a sign before men of one's religion [92], and insisted that God's promise even in an infant baptism by an unbelieving priest is legitimately answered by faith occurring years later [93]. The second area concerns the relation of the Spirit to the Word. This was perhaps nearer to the heart of the Reformation because there, in contrast to the first area, the Reformers held a position against the Papists as well as the Anabaptists. The Enthusiasts considered the Bible the "dead and killing letter" which Paul rejected in adherence to the Spirit. Calvin replied that the Spirit *binds* himself to the Scripture lest "under his sign the spirit

90) See, for example, LCC XXV, *Spiritual and Anabaptist Writers*, ed. G. H. Williams and A. M. Mergal, and the literature cited by Prof. Williams in "Studies in the Radical Reformation: a Bibliographical Survey of Research since 1939", *Church History* XXVII (1958), pp. 46—69, esp. R. Bainton, "The Left Wing of the Reformation", *The Journal of Religion* XXI (1941), 2, 124—134 and F. Littel, "The Anabaptists and Christian Tradition", *The Journal of Religious Thought* IV (1947), 2, 168—171.

91) IV, xv, 16, n. 26.

91a) IV, xvi, 1 ff., and esp. n. 1, 2 and 4.

92) IV, xv, 1, here especially also against the Zwinglians, see n. 3.

93) IV, xv, 17.

of Satan should creep in" [94]. The third battle area grew out of the Anabaptist tendency toward a doctrine of Christian perfection, an inclination derived from the idea of contact with the Spirit "immediately" (i. e. unmediated through the Word). The Enthusiasts held that a Christian returns to innocence and need no longer restrain the flesh but has simply to follow the leadings of the Spirit. Calvin considered this dangerous precisely because it ignores the fact of the conflict between the flesh and Spirit *in* the Christian [95]. The fourth area of controversy, the relation of the Christian to the world, grows out of the Anabaptist desire for perfection and separation from everything which does not partake of it. Some fanatics, says Calvin, think it is a degradation for us to be occupied with secular cares, such as those relations to laws and courts, which are "unnecessary" for the Christian [96].

Calvin summarizes his attitude toward the Anabaptists when he asserts that Satan is the source of their delusions [97]. We may still recognize — all current corrections of the Reformers notwithstanding — that the oversimplified view of the Gospel and its relation to the world held by at least some left wing Protestants represented a real menace to the Reformation. Yet we who are the ecclesiastical and theological heirs of Calvin can probably be thankful that he was not faced with precisely the same problem as that which confronted Martin Luther (just as Lutherans may be glad that Servetus did not camp at Wittenberg). Without high expectations, we can only wonder if Calvin would have uttered something closer to the heart of the Gospel than Luther's thunderous exhortation to the princes to wipe out the pestilent fellows involved in the Peasants' Revolt.

Athough Calvin could join hands with the Lutherans as fellow Protestants fighting along the battle-fronts against the Papists and the Anabaptists, he was painfully aware that the peace within this alliance was far from idyllic. The choleric temper of Luther, which we have just seen directed against the Enthusiasts, was certainly one cause. Understandably — after all of the originality and courage

---

94) I, ix, 2.

95) III, iii, 14, see n. 30.

96) IV, xx, 2, see n. 7. IV, xx, 11 and 12 are directed against Anabaptist pacifism, cf. n. 30.

97) *Comm.* Acts 7:31, I, 278.

with which he had stood against the wrath of Rome — he wished to be heard as God's definitive prophet for the sixteenth century. Understandably, Zwingli and his followers refused to allow the almost equally early and courageous contributions of the Zürich Reformer to be forgotten in a flood of reverence for the Saxon. A generation later, Calvin found himself caught up in the tension between Lutheran and Reformed. Luther's followers had already begun to elevate his words to virtual canonicity and the Reformed leaders were equally unable to get beyond the terminology of disagreement. There were certainly also important differences in their views of the Gospel, for the Reformed thinkers had found other grounds, in addition to those used by Luther, for attacking the corruption of the Roman Church (cf. Alexander Schweizer's famous aphorism: Lutheranism attacked the Jewishness of Rome, while the Reformed attacked its paganism) and these became in part controlling in Reformed theology. Thus, theological and personal incompatibilities were intertwined to create a battle-front between Calvin and his Lutheran contemporaries [98].

One vital theological issue (together with his third use of the Law) between Calvin and the Lutherans was the latters' insistence on their understanding of the sacraments. Calvin had at first advocated a generally more Lutheran conception, but after being "shot at" by the Bernese and some Zwinglians as well as by the Lutherans, he developed his own interpretation. This represented a third viable alternative, which, in place of Zwingli's, actually gained more general acceptance on the Reformed side of the front [99]. Calvin's doctrine of the sacraments represents a more radical reformation of the Roman teaching and practice than does Luther's. Perhaps the most clear-cut example of this is the Lutheran continuation of emergency baptism, which was eradicated among the Reformed [100]. In other particulars Calvin would not have considered the Lutheran understanding of baptism dangerous were it not for the intimate connection between baptism and the Lord's Supper. But because of this link, Calvin wrote to the Flemish and French communities in Frankfurt that when they presented their children to be baptized by the Lutheran pastors who had been set over them, the parents must express their own opinion of the meaning of the Lord's Sup-

---

98) See CG II, 155 and 256.
99) See e. g. CE II, 155.
100) IV, xv, 20, esp. n. 39. See also CG II, 263 and CE II, 38.

per [101]. Calvin's chief objection to the Lutheran conception of the Supper was expressed in the struggle over the Lutheran doctrine of the ubiquity of Christ's glorified body [102]. From Calvin's point of view this appears to require a too "fleshly" (in this case that would mean "material") connection between *res* and *signum,* whereas Calvin advocates a "spiritual" relationship. The Lutheran adherence to consubstantiation ("with", "in", and "under" are the *termini technici* of consubstantiation) [103] and ubiquity is so unavoidable that Calvin feels constrained to ask rhetorically about the Lutheran Mass: "For what else is the adorable sacrament of Luther than an idol set up in the temple of God" [104].

Calvin's disagreements with Lutheran allies did not mark the end of his skirmish area, for his struggles extended inside the borders of the Reformed camp and even into the heart of Geneva. One of Calvin's most frustrating and discouraging struggles was against the weakness and indifference of his own friends and allies. This gives rise to the oft-repeated truism, which he applied to the whole history of God's people, that the worst enemies of God are the members of the church [105]. The most painful fact of all is that the very men entrusted with the wielding of the Spirit's sword, the ministry of the Word of God, can bring the greatest disgrace upon the Gospel [106]. Therefore, Farel must be censured for his excessive ardor and the tedium and prolixity of his invariably extemporaneous discourses [107]; Beza for his lack of wisdom [108]; Bucer for his lenience and overeagerness to compromise [109]; Knox for his rigorism [110]; the chaplain of the Duchess of Ferrara for the not unusual tendency to

---

101) CG II, 409 and 414.
102) See again IV, xvii, 16—31 and especially notes 54, 73, 3 and 67.
103) See IV, xvii, 20 and n. 66.
104) CE II, 220.
105) *Comm.* Matt. 13:24, II, 119; *Comm.* Isa. 11:13, I, 392; etc.
106) See esp. *Comm.* II Cor. 6:3, II, 248.
107) CE II, 322.
108) CG II, 397.
109) CE II, 219.
110) CG II, 350, a letter from April 23, 1561. Knox was squaring an old grievance with Mary Stuart, the queen responsible for his years as a galley-slave aboard a French vessel, when he wrote "The First Blast of the Trumpet against the Monstrous Regiment of Women" — during the reign in England of Catholic queen Bloody Mary Tudor, but its publication in 1558 coincided with the rise of Elizabeth to power. Thus Knox embarrassed Calvin, costing Calvinism any chance for success under Elizabeth who, although imprisoning

flatter those in high places [111]; and, above all, Melanchthon must be chided for his lack of courage, particularly in the face of the loud Lutheran accusers of the Reformed [112]. In fact, the only leader who escapes unscathed by Calvin's scrupulous attempts to correct those faults which hinder God's Reformation — is Calvin himself. In place of what frequently became, with Calvin, personal belligerence we must suggest that the advance of God's armies against the forces of evil could better be served by an unswerving love for even bitter human enemies and weak allies, based upon unwavering confidence in the power of God's accomplished victory in Christ to overcome evil and to redeem men. Though he might become displeased with individual ministers and earthly leaders of the church, Calvin gives *worthy* counsel when he advises us to honor their honorable rank even when we consider Judas himself [113].

Calvin also skirmishes with those he designates heretics. In addition to the historical heterodox, whose teachings lived on or were revived, he had to do with a few contemporary domestic heretics and others who, although Calvin duelled with them in Geneva, were actually a breed of itinerants there for refuge along with the large numbers from every land in western Europe where Papists persecuted adherents of the Reformation. The points at issues between Calvin and his opponents varied, but there were several recurrent areas of conflict. Calvin was attacked first, and probably most often, in relation to his doctrine of God. The first assault, coming from Peter Caroli, was based on Calvin's refusal to acknowledge the Trinitarian symbols of the ancient Church as binding. This attack was followed by others on his doctrine of predestination, or God's eternal decrees. These assaults became so persistent as to assume the character of a permanent perimeter of defence and attack around Calvinism. (During Calvin's life, perhaps the most serious internal attacks came in consecutive opposition by Jerome Bolsec and Jean Trolliet in the 1550's). A related aspect of Calvin's doctrine was under fire when Sebastian Castellio berated the severity of the cold and apparently despotic decrees of Calvin's Deity. None of these, however, were so troublesome to

---

Mary Stuart in 1568 and having her executed in 1587, also persecuted the English Calvinists, setting up a High Commission for the purpose in 1583.

111) See CE I, 275.
112) CE II, 257 ff.
113) *Comm.* John 6:70, I, 280.

Calvin as the fertile-minded and erratic Spaniard, Michael Servetus, physician and sometime theologian [114]. It appears that the feud between the two went back to the early 1530's in Paris. Servetus, who was condemned in absentia after escaping Vienne, made the fatal mistake of stopping in Geneva on his way to supposed asylum in Naples. We must not underestimate the theological aspect of the warfare between the men. Calvin had had to deal with a crude "attack on the person of Christ" in the affair of Gruet, one of whose more restrained statements was that Jesus Christ was a wicked person who deserved to be crucified [115]. But in Servetus, Calvin had to do with Christological and Trinitarian heresies of a somewhat more refined thinker. Servetus had real theological affinities with his Anabaptist contemporaries (Calvin tended to "smear" them by association with him), but a list of his often mutually contradictory views would read like a catalogue of traditional heresy. It is inconceivable that Calvin would agree with such a man theologically; but while one must grant Calvin's claim to orthodoxy we cannot applaud the use to which he and his fellow Genevans (including his opponents) put their theological victory. (It is perhaps "ironic justice", a "divine judgment" — which must, however, be corrected — that Calvin has popularly been charged with a doctrine he opposed. It was Servetus who taught the damnation of unbaptized children, which Calvin rejected) [116]. Like Luther, Calvin insisted that personal attacks, such as those of Servetus, meant nothing to him so long as the faith were not assaulted. In several cases, however, Calvin made himself as the minister of the Word assigned by God to a specific battle-post, the theological issue [117].

In addition to the domestic theological struggle, Calvin was engaged in a running battle over the morals of Geneva with a tendency sometimes crystallized into a party known as the Libertines [118]. This group was made up largely of the "old settlers" of Geneva who wished to be free of the strict control of the Romanist

---

114) See R. H. Bainton, *Hunted Heretic*, 1953 and Wendel, *op. cit.*, 93—99.

115) CE II, 276.

116) See IV, xvi, 26, n. 46, sec. 29, n. 52, sec. 31, n. 56 and sec. 31 point 3 on Servetus, and IV, xv, 20, n. 39 on Calvin.

117) See e. g. CE I, 176 and CG II, 266 as well as Wendel, *op. cit.*, 95 f. on the Servetus problem.

118) As Wendel reminds us (*op. cit.*, p. 87, n. 53): "We must remember not to confuse the party of the "libertines", of which Perrin, Vandel and Favre

Church, and also of any other strong restraint [119]. A constant conflict raged between Calvin's desire to control every tendency to evil and the Libertines' desire to enjoy the pleasures of life with aristocratic freedom [120]. Under the leadership of Amy Perrin, one of Calvin's earlier supporters, the Libertines were able to wage an at least partially successful campaign against Calvin's moral strictures (and sometimes even invaded his ecclesiastical realm of authority) until the middle of the 1550's. By then the votes of new citizens who had come to Geneva as refugees under Calvin's aegis were sufficiently numerous permanently to overthrow the pre-Calvin Genevans and their supporters (although, as Wendel points out, Calvin never succeeded in withdrawing the church from the control of the magistracy) [121]. This battle was as fierce as any Calvin had to wage, both in prolonged intensity and bitterness [122]. We can appreciate that in the whole moral area Calvin was to be commended in his desire to assist weak brethren apparently losing the battle between the old man and the new. We can admire his feat of making from such a pleasure-loving center one of the most tenacious social structures in Christendom. Yet was he not guilty of one of his own favorite charges against the Roman clergy, that of binding the consciences of believers, not with false hopes and doubts, but with legalistic strictures often presumptuous and unnecessary?

These struggles have drawn us into a discussion of the political aspect of Calvin's spiritual warfare. His legal training and aptitude fitted him for the political conflicts into which he was thrown in his effort to reform the church [123]. This is fortunate since the ever-present problems which arise from the plain fact that the church *is*

---

were leaders, with the sect of "spiritual libertines" against which Calvin launched his treatise *Against the Fantastic Sect of the Libertines* (1545) ... These spiritual libertines were mystics, more or less connected with the Reformation ... See W. Niesel, "Calvin und die Libertiner", *Zeitschrift für Kirchengeschichte,* 1929, p. 58—74.

119) See CG I, 38.

120) Calvin maintained the strict limitations on dancing instituted long before his day. Abstaining from alcohol, on the other hand, was hardly an issue. See Peter Brunner, *Die Alkoholfrage bei Calvin.* In fact, a considerable portion of Calvin's annual salary was paid in wine.

121) Wendel, *op. cit.,* p. 53.

122) See *Preface* to the *Comm. on the Pss.,* I, xlv.

123) See J. Bohatec, *Calvin und das Recht,* 1934, and *Calvins Lehre von Staat und Kirche,* 1937, an admirable decade in which to contribute objective scholarly knowledge to *Untersuchungen zur deutschen Rechtsgeschichte!*

now *in* the world, created *political* fronts along which Calvin actually had to do battle. These principally take us to France, to the political arena of Geneva, and to that of Bern, that mightiest of Swiss cantons whose authority (often unfriendly to Calvin) extended over many of the French-speaking communities served by Calvinist pastors.

After his conversion to Protestantism, Calvin soon made himself unwelcome in the strongly Romanist centers of learning in France and felt obliged to leave at the age of 27 to return only on one brief trip [124], so far as we know, during his remaining 28 years. His dedication of the earliest *Institutes* to the king, Francis I, reflects the hope of creating sympathetic understanding, but although the temper of the situation in France shifted at various periods, the overwhelming tendency was in a direction unfavorable to the Reformed. This tendency reached its climax in the Huguenot war of 1562—3 and in the massacre of St. Bartholomew's night in 1572 when 50,000 Protestants, including most of the leaders, were exterminated. It is small wonder that Calvin saw these persecutions of his friends and followers in France as a black and white morality play, a clear-cut struggle between Satan and God.

The situation within the ranks of the Swiss Reformation was markedly better — certainly there was no such physical violence among brothers. Nevertheless, Calvin exerted little influence in Bern and especially the civil authorities there had little inclination to support his policies, sometimes opposing his influence even in Geneva itself. He in turn trusted them so little that he could write to Viret in Lausanne: "As you know, the Bernese are people from whom one must hide the truth" [125].

In Geneva itself, Calvin was obliged to grapple along three principal fronts. He found it necessary to fight for the freedom of the pastors to administer the affairs, particularly the discipline, of the church itself; to fight immorality and he organized resistance of the Libertines; to fight religious heretics with political means when the occasion demanded. The three fronts cross and merge repeatedly, partly because the opposition between Calvin and his foes was so clear-cut and diametrical that the opponents remained the same regardless of the front involved [126]. The political aspects of the

---

124) See Wendel, *op. cit.,* p. 48.
125) CG I, 287.
126) See, for example, CE II, 120, 428, and 406 f.

Servetus affair demonstrate the way in which Calvin used political measures to further matters having to do essentially with church discipline. When Calvin learned that his old enemy was in Geneva, he considered it his duty to have him arrested. Servetus' intransigence sealed his unhappy fate. Once set in motion, the Geneva officialdom rolled on speedily to crush the heretic. (The other Swiss churches supported Geneva's action. In the city itself, Calvin's old enemy, Amy Perrin, now hopelessly outnumbered, pleaded in vain for Servetus' release.) Despite repeatedly charging Servetus to retract and live, and despite his final, sincerely humane attempt to secure a less inhumane method of execution, Calvin was basically satisfied with the judgment.

As the relation between his understanding of predestination and providence would imply, Calvin believed that the state exists for the basic purpose of preserving the ordered structure of human society, and thus to further the salvation of the elect. This goes so far as to include the repression of enemies by force, when and if the occasion requires. In the exercise of his principles of government, Calvin believed his own function should be limited to the exposition and proclamation of the Word, and the administration of the sacraments and of church discipline. He consistently attempted to free himself from political involvement and rejoiced whenever he felt that he was being allowed to retreat from political affairs.

Surveying now the network of battle-fronts along which Calvin carried on his spiritual warfare, we find familiar friends and foes. Calvin presumes to identify the elect, the liberated army of liberation, with himself and his associates in the Reformation of Christ's body on earth. He states systematically that he still exists as the old man, God's enemy, but operatively he identifies this old man, the flesh, with the diseased body which "imprisons" his militant spirit, his burning heart. Empirically, the line he drew was hard and fast, a line setting the "real" Calvin — the man who understands God's will — together with his followers, over against his own flesh allied with those men who refused to obey the will of God. Practically, Calvin's confidence in his own understanding of the Gospel was a powerful force for the success of the Reformed Church. As Calvin evaluated his military intelligence, however, his confidence also critically limited the possibility of God's working through other members of Christ's body, and even checked the possibility of God's correcting Calvin's own theological and ecclesiastical program. Does this not reflect a lack of confidence on Calvin's part in God's freedom to work victoriously upon any man through the power of his decisive self-revelation in Jesus Christ without requiring his Christian soldiers to destroy (by logic if possible or by force if necessary) those who refused to cease opposing the advancement of the Calvinistic Reformation?

The Weapons of Our Warfare

. . . are spiritual. This recalls us to the exposition with which the Act began, and reminds us that "the warfare corresponds with the kind of weapons" [1]. Therefore, Paul "glories in being furnished with spiritual weapons" [2]. Calvin hopes by these statements to insure that he and we will be equipped with the weapons which alone are legitimate and useful in the war we have to fight, and that we may lay aside all others, for they could only hinder the proper prosecution of the spiritual struggle.

To set these limitations is not to say that the *spiritual* conflict does not have to do with the whole man, for Christians ought to esteem all their members to be weapons of the spiritual warfare [3]. It is, in fact, necessary to put on the *whole* armor of God. This already puts a real qualification upon the Christian's "whole armor", for it is the armor of *God*. God's role in our warfare is dramatized in Calvin's statement to the courageous imprisoned women of Paris: "The One who leads us into the battle, also again and again arms us with the necessary weapons and teaches us to use them. We simply need to take them and to allow ourselves to be led" [4]. But when we take up these weapons, victory is sure. In fact, "we know for certain, that while we wage war under the banners of our Christ, and fight with the weapons of his warfare, we shall be unconquerable" [5]. Here Calvin sounds the true call of triumph on the victory trumpet of Christ. There is not a false or presumptuous note in his statement! [6] Many of the practical situations of Calvin's

---

1) *Comm.* II Cor. 10:4, II, 321.
2) See CG II, 114.
3) *Comm.* Rom. 6:13, p. 231. See also *Comm.* Eph. 6:11, p. 334.
4) CG II, 193.
5) CE I, 287.
6) See I, vii, 4 passim and esp. *Comm.* Eph. 1:13, p. 208.

life work teach us, however, that no Christian, no matter how earnest, intelligent, or even "spiritual" he may be, invariably wars under Christ's banners and fights with his weapons. When he fails to do that, he is not unconquerable; and should he win a victory, it will not be the victory of Christ. It becomes increasingly clear that in the spiritual warfare, the Christian does not fight alone: since it is God's warfare not only do we fight for God with weapons he provides, but God himself is also actively engaged in the struggle. Since God the Holy Spirit is especially engaged in the process of sanctification, he is directly concerned in the warfare against the flesh. But beyond that, the Spirit brings to the Christian soldier the benefits of the Word of God, that sword of the Spirit which is one of the most powerful of his weapons and also the source of many others. The rich panoply in this armory of the Christian warfare becomes available to the Christian only through the internal testimony of the Holy Spirit that God's Word is true in itself and also true for him. Since the Spirit speaks not of himself but leads us to Christ, Calvin assets that the Holy Spirit is the bond (*vinculum* can even mean fetters or chains) by which Christ efficaciously unites us to himself [7]. This means that Christ in no sense deserts his own in their day of battle; in fact, he who has won the decisive victory does not cease to carry on his triumph here in his body which, in Karl Barth's terminology, is his "earthly-historical form of existence". The Christ who is exalted to the right hand of the Father is so closely united with his members that Calvin can say, "He reigns rather for us than for himself, and that both internally and externally" [8]. From this "it follows that it is impossible for the devil, with all the assistance of the world, ever to destroy the church, which is founded on the throne of Christ" [9].

Just as the Spirit speaks not of himself but of Christ, so behind Calvin's Christ stands the all-mighty, all-knowing, *all-determining* God, who — in spite of Calvin's orthodox assertions in his statement of the Trinity — acts like the First Person understood as the Old Testament God of glory. This God "furthers and promotes the kingdom of his Son", so that "a few men unarmed, furnished with no garrisons, do show forth more power in their voice alone, than

7) III, i, 1.
8) II, xv, 4.
9) II, xv, 3.

all the world by raging against them" [10]. The role Calvin's God most often plays in the actual spiritual warfare he assigns his children is that of Protector. Therefore, even though the church shall never enjoy complete peace, yet God, bearing with the weakness of his people, defends them "so that at least the kingdom of Satan might not grow out of the ruins of the church" [11].

In addition to his own intervention, God sends his elect angels to the defence of his elect men. Calvin assures us that the angels of God, armed with invincible power, constantly watch over us, and array themselves on every side to aid and deliver us from all evil, and adds that they are prepared for fighting, because they cannot succor the elect without also opposing their enemies [12]. One of the principal weapons of the Christian's warfare is to maintain confidence in this powerful assistance. Thus, Calvin thinks that Paul in Romans 8:33 desires to arm the sons of God from head to toe with the *confidence* of God [13]. If we wish to dwell in safety, therefore, Calvin advises us that we must remain in the church, for the Lord protects it [14]. A related armament is reliance on God's promises, for depending on them, Calvin's garrison expects deliverance from the "wretched bondage and wicked yoke" of Antichrist; they boldly defy Satan and all the ungodly, when they endeavor to drive Christ from his throne; they pray confidently for the Spirit of wisdom, who exposes the tricks and impositions of Satan [15].

Similarly, Christians rest on God's providence, since this doctrine teaches that the devil and his whole army are powerless to do anything against God's people without the permission and even the command of God. It is most comforting to be certain that although God arms them for the testing of his people, he also fixes the limit of their fury [16]. God's predestination of the elect to eternal life applies still more directly to the struggle which they experience now. The Christian's struggle — no matter how difficult and precarious his position may become — cannot mean that this salvation could be overthrown, for that depends solely on God's eternal election [17].

---

10) *Comm.* Acts 4:4, I, 167.
11) *Comm.* Isa. 49:19, IV, 35.
12) *Comms.* Ps. 34:7, I, 563 and Ps. 35:46, I, 578.
13) *Comm. loc. cit.,* p. 323.
14) *Comm.* Isa. 26:1, II, 210.
15) *Comm.* Isa. 14:3, I, 437.
16) I, xvii, 11.
17) *Comm.* II Thes. 2:13, p. 342.

Sometimes, Calvin's overwhelming confidence in the rightness of his cause could be dangerous, as we can see when he dares to say: "Though our weakness prompts our enemies to growing insolence, yet the Lord is near and will defend us as with an ample shield, for they who fight against us wage war with the living God [18]. This is perilous overconfidence — not overconfidence in God, for Calvin is right — that is impossible. Calvin, however, identifies his present empirical *will*ing self too unqualifiedly with God. The Christian as a member of Christ's body *is* united with God; but Calvin, who knew the Old Testament so well, failed to realize that at this point he committed the sin of Israel, the sin of believing: "God will not allow us to fall, for that would be his own defeat". Calvin, who detests the pretences and presumptions of perfection in the Anabaptists, fails to detect its flagrant presence in his own existential ethic. He identifies his imperfections, which he recognizes in moments of quiet reflection, almost exclusively with the prison of his body. Thus, he effectively denies that the flesh can at any time win the upper hand in him in such a way as to control his decisions and action. He so emphasizes his *confidence* (in God) that he excludes the possibility that human confidence (even in God) could become presumption, which is an ally of Satan.

Calvin's weapon of confidence in God took a theologically more concrete form in his confidence in Christ as the Head of his body, the *ecclesia militans*. Since the faith which overcomes the world is a real apprehension of Christ, Calvin holds that only he who rests solely on Christ's power can conquer Satan and the world, and not succumb to his own flesh [19]. Thus if we are to win, firmness *in Jesus Christ* must support us under the pressures of battle. This union with Christ as members of his body provides an additional weapon — solidarity with other members of Christ. Therefore, Calvin admonishes the persecuted French Protestants: "Think of the fact that in distant lands your brothers, who with you are members of one body, have to withstand the same struggle as yourselves" [20]. In Jesus' prayer in John 17, "He began with his Apostles, that their salvation, which we know to be certain, might make us more certain of our own salvation; and, therefore, whenever Satan attacks us, let us learn to meet him with this shield, that it is not to no

---

18) *Comm.* Isa. 37:23, III, 128.
19) *Comm.* I John 5:5, p. 255.
20) CG II, 291.

purpose that the Son of God united us with the Apostles, so that the salvation of all was bound up, as it were, in the same bundle" [21].

An especially important weapon is the solidarity with the ministers of the Word, who serve as officers in Christ's army. Faithful pastors protect the church from the snares of Satan, and therefore the church should pray to be surrounded by such sentinels [22]. Their importance lies, of course, in their special relationship to the Spirit's sword, that distinguishing mark of the church — the Word. Calvin repeatedly asserts that the decisive characteristics of the church are the pure preaching and interpretation of the Word, and the proper administration of the sacraments. Close behind these, but markedly less definitive in character, is the maintenance of order in the church through church discipline [23]. It is small wonder that when he comes to speak of the spiritual warfare, Calvin thinks of these as powerful weapons.

We may understand Calvin's conception of the Word from its threefold character as God's eternal Word (incarnate in Jesus Christ), the Scripture, and the Church's proclamation. In the warfare of the *militia Christi* Calvin thinks primarily of the Word as the *third* form in dependence on the *second's* witness to *Jesus Christ.* This weapon is forged and sharpened by the minister of the Word as exegetes. It is the duty of interpreters of Scripture to supply weapons to fight against Antichrist [24]. The best quality of steel is provided for the Spirit's sword by the property of the Word as truth. We already know from Act I that Satan always considers truth a primary target. This truth of God is a powerful and active thing which, therefore, ought to have such a firm hold on us that all the schemes and attacks of Satan shall not draw us from our course [25]. Truth for Calvin comes to man through the conjunction between the Word and authentic faith, the two armaments of

---

21) *Comm.* John 17:20, II, 181 f. — Such statements are not intended to diminish the Christocentric character of our assurance and joy. I shall never forget the look of rapture on the face of a theological student of the Eastern Orthodox Church as he tried to explain to us sober Westerners the joy of the fact that "I am one with John Chrysostom." We should always remember that we *are* one with the Apostles, Chrysostom, Augustine, Aquinas, Luther, Calvin and Schleiermacher — but one only *in Christ.*

22) *Comm.* Isa. 62:6, IV, 328. See also *Comm.* Acts 4, I, 164.

23) See IV, i, 9, n. 18.

24) *Ded.* to the *Comm. on Cath. Epistles,* xx, and *Comm.* Matt. 4:6, I, 218.

25) *Comm.* Eph. 4:15, p. 286.

"highest rank": "for the Word of God is not received by faith, if it floats on the surface of the brain; but when it has taken deep root in the heart, so as to become an impregnable fortress to sustain and repel all the assaults of temptation" [26]. A related weapon is *Christian doctrine,* which is truth on an adjacent level, for it grows out of Biblical truths and (as in the case of his *Institutes)* conversely should serve as an introduction to the Bible. Thus, it is Christ's royal banner which assembles believers under his dominion [27]. Calvin slightly changes the metaphor when he refers in his letter to Richard Le-Fevre, a prisoner approaching martyrdom, to a confession of faith as a shield held up against the enemy [28]. He also always joins the sacraments to the Word of God, and it is to be expected that he would give them prominence in the conduct of spiritual warfare. It is with a measure of surprise, then, that we read in his letter to Bullinger: "I am not pleased that in your second chapter you declare that the word sacrament is a military expression" [29]. Calvin agreed in the same letter that there is a "certain connection corresponding to the military oath of the soldier", and himself many times used the metaphor, but he was concerned that it be understood in the light of the fact that God always remains the principal party *spiritually* present and active. Bullinger's conception tended to fit in with the Zwinglian idea making *sacramentum "nothing else than* an initiatory ceremony of pledging" by the soldier of Christ [30]. Baptism becomes a weapon when Calvin says that in it we are armed for spiritual warfare (rather than in confirmation, as the Roman Catholics insisted) [31], and, in a statement reminiscent of Luther's use of the words *baptizatus sum*: "Therefore, as often as we fall away, we ought to recall the memory of our baptism and fortify [or arm] our mind with it" [32]. The usefulness of the Lord's Supper in the spiritual warfare grows out of its very character as a meal: just an ordinary meal provides strength for the body, so the Lord's Supper "arms us for our spiritual struggle" [33]. Calvin refers to "the celebration of the Supper" when he says: "Since the Lord is pleased to

---

26) III, ii, 46.
27) *Comm.* Isa. 11:4, I, 381 f.
28) CE II, 276.
29) CG I, 265.
30) See IV, xii, 13 and n. 21, and IV, xv, 1, n. 3.
31) IV, xix, 8.
32) IV, xv, 3.
33) CG II, 465.

exercise and drill us in his warfare, let us fight on with deliberate and constant valor, *only let it be with those weapons with which he furnishes us*" [34].

Following — not alongside — the preaching of the Word and the administration of the sacraments comes church discipline, which Calvin thinks of as the sinews of the body of Christ (although some Calvinistic churches make discipline the third mark of the church, Calvin does not add it to pure preaching of the Word and the right administration of the sacraments as essential to the true church [35]). Calvin looked upon this discipline, including its severest form, excommunication from the visible church, as legitimate [36]. The kingdom of Christ represents to Calvin a sort of island in the sea that is the kingdom of Satan, the world. Excommunication means that the offender is, to use our figure, banished from the island and cast adrift on the sea, for being cast out of the church can only mean to Calvin being placed under (actually, returned to) the dominion of Satan. Calvin, like Paul, expresses every hope that the offender will repent and, after only a temporary banishment, return [37].

In addition to the weapons appropriate to Christ's church as a corporate whole, there are arms suited to the *individual* Christian. First, we must know the source of these weapons, the armory from which he draws them. In one passage, Calvin makes the source of our weapons to consist in the forgiveness of sins [38]; but ordinarily he turns to Holy Scripture as the source of the Christian's armaments, because "out of it come faith, hope, love, wisdom, patience and all the virtues with which we are to withstand the attacks of the enemy until we win the victory" [39]. Calvin's inventory lists the weapons which come out of the Bible — as from a kind of spiritual armaments factory — in an order useful for our consideration.

Faith, from God's side his gift to the elect, from man's side requires a veritable battle to acquire and maintain, for the forces of evil and of unbelief are always attempting to persuade us that because of our sins God is our irreconcilable enemy [40]. But faith

---

34) CE I, 283. e. a.
35) See IV, i, 9, and n. 18.
36) See *Comm.* John 16:11, II, 141.
37) *Comm.* I Tim. 1:20, p. 48 and   *Comm.* I Cor. 5:5, I, 184.
38) *Comm.* John 21:31, II, 271.
39) *Sermon* on I Sam. 19:17—21, CR LVIII, 329.
40) II, ii, 20.

answers that he is merciful even when he afflicts, because chastisement proceeds rather from love than from wrath[41]. This genuine evangelical note, which makes despair of God's mercy a weapon for Satan's army, is unfortunately outweighed in the totality of Calvin's life and thought. Had he met a man whom he felt sure was one of the *reprobi,* Calvin would no doubt cheerfully have told him that God was his irreconcilable enemy. Even with respect to the elect, Calvin was an advocate of the use of despair in leading men to Christ (as in the argument of III, xii). So great is the power of God's grace which bestows faith, however, that when the Christian struggling with his own weakness, presses toward faith in his moments of anxiety, is already in large part victorious[42]. The fact that faith is based upon the Word of God is another indication of its complete reliability[43]. Perhaps the most poignant use of the shield of faith by those around Calvin was by the imprisoned Protestant women in Paris, to whom he wrote that their faith — no less than of male counterparts — was the victory overcoming the world, and that through it God was defeating his foes, for there was no more effective preaching[44].

Hope is the second member of the famous Pauline trio of theological virtues, which, in the metaphor of spiritual warfare, become mighty weapons in the Christian arsenal. "So long as we are in this world, our warfare is sustained by hope"[45]. Even faith itself must be supported by hope, when scoffers stir up doubts as to Christ's return to bring justice to the earth, and the flesh and the world whisper the same things in our ears[46]. Probably Calvin's most characteristic expression of the Christian hope is his conception of meditation on the final resurrection and the future life[47]. The second dimension of the *duplex cognitio,* the knowledge of ourselves, has as its primary end that man should "arouse himself to meditation upon divine worship and the future life"[48]. Though the sabbath is a symbol of *rest* it is a *symbol* of rest and not the substance, and "because there is still a continual warfare with the flesh", the sabbath is to provide

---

41) III, ii, 21.
42) III, ii, 17.
43) See *Comm.* Eph. 6:16, p. 339.
44) CG II, 193.
45) *Comm.* Eph. 1:14, p. 209.
46) III, ii, 42.
47) III, xxv, 1 and passim.
48) II, i, 3.

material for this warfare, being filled with unceasing meditation on the symbol, upon the spiritual rest [49]. We must remember the nature of hope, if we do not wish to find it depressing still to face severe warfare, as though we derive no benefit from Christ's victory. We would certainly and rapidly succumb to the temptations which beset us on every side if we did not become accustomed to continual meditation on the blessed resurrection [50].

The alliance of faith and hope, however, is an incomplete part of the triple entente Calvin considers sufficient to equip the Christian for spiritual warfare: "He (Paul) does not, however, enumerate *all the parts of the armor (panoplian),* but simply makes mention of two, the breastplate and helmet. In the meantime, he omits nothing of what belongs to spiritual armor, for the man that is provided with faith, love and hope, will be found in no department unarmed" [51]. Paul's conclusion concerning his famous trio is that "the greatest of these is love". One sometimes wonders if Calvin agrees with the Apostle. He says that the teaching of the Scholastics that love (*charitas*) is prior to faith is mere madness, since it is faith alone which produces charity [52]. Calvin makes this subordination still more explicit when he says that as Christian liberty "must be subordinated to *charitas,* so love in turn ought to abide under purity of faith" [53]. Wilhelm Kolfhaus says, "The church of Calvin is a *community of love,* not ... primarily a *battle-community*", and Kolfhaus is an honorable Calvin scholar; but he hastens to add that the two are not mutually exclusive [54]. Calvin himself says that Satan brings forward many causes of offence to the good pastor, so that only if the love of Christ shall reign in his heart does he overcome every obstacle [55].

Yet out of the more than a thousand passages from Calvin's writings which stand behind this chapter, we have found only these very few which connect love with the Christian warfare. If spiritual warfare is, as Calvin insists, a legitimate metaphor describing the Christian life, must we not assume that there is not only a dangerous

---

49) II, viii, 30 and 31.
50) III, xxv, 1.
51) *Comm.* I Thes. 5:8, p. 289.
52) III, ii, 41, part. reten. Allen. See also n. 61 on II, viii, 54.
53) III, xix, 13, part. reten. Allen.
54) W. Kolfhaus, *op. cit.,* p. 350 (e. a.).
55) *Comm.* John 21:15, II, 288.

breech in the defence-attack perimeter of Calvin's conception of spiritual warfare but a serious flaw in his view of the Christian life. The New Testament validates Kolfhaus' assumption that the church of Jesus Christ is primarily a community of love; but this should have immense implications for the spiritual warfare which is the Christian's assigned duty. The breastplate of love in I Thes. 5:8 should be given a central place in a discussion of the Christian armor. "We wrestle *not* with flesh and blood *but* against the spiritual hosts of wickedness in the heavenly places", and this classic definition should operatively shape the local commander's conception of battle and his specific orders. Just as we know no true fatherhood except that of the Father of God the Son, just as we know no true justice except his justification, just as we know no true love except his — each time because both our human counterparts and our human ability to understand the original relationships are corrupt — so we learn little about the spiritual warfare from human conflicts, for IT IS NOT *A* WARFARE OF *DESTRUCTION* BUT THE WARFARE OF *SALVATION*. The goal of his human soldiers in this conflict must correspond to God's own goal of destroying enmity and reconciling men to himself. The victory which our strategy must serve is the freeing of man's understanding from its slavery to the forces of evil, freeing man to the knowledge of God's victory *for* him in Christ. The principal weapon in this warfare must be love with its winning wisdom. All of this we find only on the periphery of Calvin's conception. What a different face Calvinism might have worn — not less successful but perhaps more effectively Christian — if Christian love had shaped Calvin's entire strategy, while in turn losing shapeless sentimentality by being forged into the chief weapon of his arsenal.

The title of the chapter on prayer in the 1559 *Institutes* asserts that it is the "chief activity of faith". We are not surprised then when it is also designated Christ's chief armor, of which his enemies attempted to strip him [56], and, correspondingly, the first part of our armament [57]. At the source of weapons Calvin says that prayer digs out these treasures, which the Gospel discovers to our faith [58]. Calvin welds prayer as "chief activity" into the spiritual warfare

---

56) *Comm.* Matt. 27:47, III, 320.
57) See Kolfhaus, *op. cit.,* p. 470.
58) III, xx, 2.

by connecting Eph. 6:18 with the inventory of armor in verses 10-17. When the Christian has donned his armor he is merely *ready* for battle; he must "fight by prayer" [59]. Finally, prayer sustains the Christian in the heat of battle so that he does not faint [60].

Where does the *miles Christi* use this weapon, however; what should we pray for? "Thy kingdom come", the heart of the Lord's prayer, teaches us that God's Word resembles a royal scepter ... and that we are commanded to pray that he will subdue the hearts and minds of all men to a voluntary obedience to it [61]. Similarly, the petition, "Lead us not into temptation, but deliver us from evil", teaches us to pray for arms, and defensive protection to enable us to win the victory [62]. Finally, in a note of true Christian understanding, Calvin says that we must pray for our enemies, above all for the tyrants into whose power it may please God to place us [63]. Does the Divine commander-in-chief answer our prayers. however, filling our requisition for the material needed for victory? Often, yes, but if the result be not what we expected, let us blame our own sins and ingratitude; for the Lord was ready to bestow those blessings abundantly upon us [64].

Another powerful armament of the Christian is his good conscience, for only here does its operation justify Calvin's claim for its importance. Calvin used to say that conscience is a "brass wall" against all reproaches, calumnies, accusations and slanders [65]. Like the Word and faith, conscience as a weapon is bound to the Holy Spirit. Therefore the Spirit furnishes the consciences of the pious with strong and effective weapons against the ferociousness of those who, under a false pretext, boast that they are the church [66]. Though in practice his "I know that my conscience is surer than yours" [67] is quite typical, in statements of principle Calvin asserts that not even

---

59) *Comm. loc. cit.*, p. 340. See Knox's battle prayer after the sermon in Spiott and Leishman, *Book of Common Order,* pp. 96 f. with its petition for strength "to persevere in this spiritual battle against sin."

60) *Comm.* Rom. 12:12, p. 467.

61) III, xx, 42.

62) III, xx, 46.

63) CR LIX, 145.

64) *Comm.* Isa. 49:17, IV, 33.

65) *Comms.* John 10:33, I, 418 and Isa. 36:10, III, 86.

66) *Comm.* Gen. 21:12 f., I, 547.

67) CE I, 173.

the conscience is completely free from the possibility of error [68]. Usually the conscience, though it can be bound from without, appears almost exempt from total depravity, but one passage finds "enemies who rise up *in our conscience* against his kingdom" [69]. Like all other weapons in the Christ's spiritual arsenal, conscience is useless without the specific empowering of the Spirit. (It is interesting that Calvin with his great humanistic respect for the power of man's mind in matters irrelevant to salvation has so little to say for the role of even the *regenerate* reason in theology, where our knowledge is totally dependent on the Bible authenticated in our hearts (or consciences) by the Spirit, I, vii, 4-5. The way to the kingdom of God is open only to him whose "*mind* has been *made new by the illumination of the Holy Spirit*" [70] but the way to theology has apparently not. Although in practice Calvin the theologian always utilized the tools of reason the only *direct* reference to the phrase "renewal of your mind" in the *Institutes* [71] uses it to prove that the mind is involved in total depravity, and in his commentary on Rom. 12:1-2 he uses the phrase as an occasion to separate himself from the Sorbonists who put the mind as Queen.

A weapon designed to complement assurance and compensate for uncritical confidence is patience. Calvin believes that the design of the parable of the wheat and tares is to teach God's children that they must be "armed with patience, and in the midst of offences which are fitted to disturb them, may preserve unbroken steadfastness of faith" [72]. "Keeping in mind the conscience's infirmity" and "patience", the certainly bound to faith leads us to flee in humility to God, that strengthened by his promises we may boldly oppose Satan and sin [73]. These reservations about human frailty and pride, however, do not dull or muzzle the final weapon of the Christian, his assurance of victory. Calvin boldly asserts: "He is no believer, I say, who does not rely on the assurance of his salvation, and confidently triumph over the devil and death" [74]. The foundations of the assurance of victory are said to be God's spiritual assistance

---

68) *Comm.* I Cor. 10:12, I, 330.
69) II, viii, 58. e. a.
70) II, ii, 20.
71) II, i, 8.
72) *Comm.* Matt. 13:24, II, 119.
73) *Sermon* on Job 40:20—41:25, CR LXIII, 476.
74) III, ii, 16, part. reten. Allen.

and God's decrees [75]. Though this promise of victory is sure, it is a *promise* of victory, and "The security which we have in God, does not serve our carelessness . . . but strengthens us so that we shall not be fatigued in the battle" [76].

This survey of the Christian's legitimate weapons has revealed the power of Calvin's metaphor and the multitude of his incisive insights. Only at a few critical points — particularly with reference to the role of love and to Calvin's unshakable confidence that *his* enemies are the enemies of *God* who must be destroyed — have we found it necessary to suggest a Christocentric critique of his impressive array of weapons.

There are, however, other weapons upon which the Christian's hand may fall which do not serve the purpose for which he is commissioned as a warrior of God. The criterion for the legitimacy of the weapons to be used is that God must offer them for our warfare. The first class of arms excluded by this criterion may be designated by terms familiar in this age of rapid technical advance in military science: there are weapons once valid in the Christian warfare which are now outmoded or obsolete. Of the ministerial gifts listed in Eph. 4:11, Calvin says the first three "were not instituted in the Church as permanent ones", but that God now and again revives them as the need of the times demands [77]. In the ecclesiastical orders of the Roman Church he finds some offices wrongly perpetuated, to which "outmoded" weapons of the spiritual warfare appertain. Exemplary in this category are the counterfeit exorcists who, unlike Jesus and, to a lesser extent, his immediate followers, "cannot persuade the demons that they are endowed with such power" [78]. Thus, what had been a weapon in the arsenal of Christ and his army became by obsolescence effectively a weapon of Satan within the church [79]. Similarly, a miracle, looked upon as a weapon, has a rather neutral character. Miracles and magic in general, however, fall systematically under his assertion that God has revealed all that is necessary to be known by means of the arts and sciences. If any man

75) *Comm.* Ps. 19:13, I, 332.

76) *Sermon* on Dt. 8:39, CR LIV, 611.

77) IV, iii, 4.

78) III, xix, 24.

79) Eduard Thurneysen, a contemporary Reformed professor of pastoral theology, would reintroduce the possible relevance of exorcism in the cure of souls (see "Seelsorge als Exorzismus", *Die Lehre von der Seelsorge*).

shall wish to be wise in any other manner, he adds, he must have Satan for his teacher [80]. In practice, however, Calvin's attitudes toward necromancy, astrology, lunacy and dreams, indicate that while in individual cases he showed sober common sense, he was not as progressive as Melanchthon in using the tools of C. P. Snow's second (or scientific) culture to distinguish between the weapons of superstition and those of truth [81].

Calvin knows of a second class of weapons even more dangerous than the once valid now outmoded ones. Just as there are weapons which by their God-given character insure victory as soon as they are in hand, there are weapons which by their demonic character cannot be used to the ends and goals of the Christian's warfare but insure the defeat of his purpose as soon as he begins to use them. Such weapons falsify the infamous maxim popularly attributed to the Jesuit army, "The end justifies the means", because such weapons are incapable of leading to the desired end. "Overcome evil with good" is a far better criterion of quality control for spiritual weapons: "He who shall go about to overcome evil with evil, may perhaps outdo his enemy in maliciousness, but to his own destruction; *for, in so doing, he fights for the devil*" [82].

Specifically, lying is an example of a technique of war which cannot serve Jesus Christ who is the Truth. Calvin says of those Protestants who still go to mass for the sake of their own safety and advantage, that God is not so weak that he needs our lies [83]. In general, man has neither the right nor the power to find *within himself* weapons to defeat the forces of evil. Calvin is, therefore, sceptical about the "carnal judgement" which leads self-righteous man to "declare war against vice" [84]. The doctrine of free will can be a camouflage for this tendency, and even Church Fathers err, seeming sometimes "to provide (man) with armor naturally his own" [85]. Finally, in principle, Calvin clearly opposes the right of any man, Christian or not, to use actual destructive violence. In a

80) *Comm.* Isa. 19:3, II, 52.

81) Wendel, *op. cit.,* p. 36, makes the contrast in the areas of natural science and mathematics, adding that Choisy's defence of Calvin here, "Calvin et la science", *Recueil de la Faculté de Théologie Protestante,* University of Geneva, 1931, tends to *dis*prove its thesis.

82) *Comm.* Rom. 12:21, p. 477. e. a. author's transl.

83) CG I, 371.

84) II, i, 3.

85) II, ii, 9.

letter to the persecuted Protestants of France, as late as 1559, Calvin admonishes them to limit themselves to the weapons given by God, for "we are not permitted to want to win this struggle by force", even though the enemies rage against innocent people [86]. In practice Calvin, like anyone "in the flesh", finds this idea difficult to retain as a criterion for all his actions. Therefore we must investigate with some care the legitimacy of using political power as a weapon in the spiritual warfare.

In addition to IV, xx [87], Calvin gives a useful discussion of the relationship between the kingdom of Christ and the world in commenting on John 18. Like all the Reformers, he is centrally interested in Jesus' statement, "my kingdom is not of this world", for no matter how strongly we are attacked our salvation remains secure because it is founded on this kingdom of Christ, which is not subject to the caprice of men. The kingdom does dwell *in* the world in the hearts of those renewed by the Holy Spirit [88]; but as Jesus commands Peter to sheath his sword, "We must also beware of repelling our enemies by force or violence, even when they unjustly provoke us, except so far as the institutions and law of the community admit" [89]. This does not mean that the pure worship of God ought never to be defended by arms [90]. These passages reflect Calvin's view that God's providential ordering of the state serves his eternal election. The Christian government (the Reformers usually thought of local city government) must painstakingly provide for the Church and protect it from external physical danger and rid it of annoying heretics and other troublemakers [91]. The state may not, however, extend the dominion of Christ and the church by external means, because that by its nature is an internal, a spiritual affair. Calvin tries to steer a course between extremes of complete separation of church and state, advocated by the Anabaptists, and of close identification of the two, represented by certain Roman Catholic and Lutheran leaders [92]. Although Calvin admits that the edicts and statutes of

---

86) CG II, 405.

87) See LCC n. 1.

88) *Comm.* John 18:36, II, 210.

89) *Comm.* John 18:11, II, 195 f.

90) *Comm.* John 18:36, II, 210 f.

91) Doumergue emphasizes Calvin's view of the state as a *"remède divin"* (*op. cit.,* V, 399).

92) IV, xx, 1. Martin Bucer seems to have exerted a formative influence on Calvin's political ethic during the latter's Strasbourg interim (1538—41). This

princes are good helps for advancing and upholding the state of Christianity, yet he is confident that God is pleased to declare his sovereign power by the *spiritual sword of his Word,* when it is made known by the pastors [93]. The repression of heresy by the power of the state is most revealing: "In vain will the magistrate employ the sword [94], which undoubtedly he must employ, to restrain wicked teachers and false prophets; in vain, I say, will he attempt all these things, unless this sword of the Word go before" [95].

Calvin was certainly convinced that whenever he was directly concerned — for example in his treatment of Servetus — the sword of the Word had gone before. With that condition fulfilled, the magistrate had undoubtedly to employ the secular sword. We must ask, however, the source of the imperative quality of this "undoubtedly". Calvin's "the magistrate must employ the *sword*" does, after all, fall under his own condemnation of the Papists who, when their attempts to use the Word fail, take up other weapons [96]. As Calvin should have realized when his treatment of Bolsec drove de Falais from Calvin's camp, such destructive force used by the soldiers of Christ is a weapon of Satan which invariably defeats the cause of the church. Calvin also asserted the Reformers' common opinion that the church owes political loyalty to the existing authority (a legitimate inference from Rom. 13), even when, as in Calvin's own day, kings are not the "foster fathers" but the executioners of the church [97]. This *political* loyalty, however, by no means implies that the king is, or can become "the chief head of the church under

comes as no surprise if E. A. Dowey is correct in asserting that Bucer's *De Regno Christi* is the strongest of the Reformation attempts to restructure politics on the Biblical model ("Bucer Studies since 1918", *Church History* XXVI [1957], p. 82).

93) Charles Mercier, "L'esprit de Calvin et la démocratie", *Revue d'histoire ecclesiastisque* XXX (1934), points out the limited but real democratic tendency in Calvin. J. T. McNeill, while concurring, asserts that Calvin characteristically "associates theocratic with democratic concepts and blends the patterns of government for church and state" ("The Democratic Element in Calvin's Thought", *Church History* XVIII [1949], p. 165).

94) See Rom. 13:4, which gave rise to the familiar two-sword theory of church and state.

95) *Comm.* Isa. 11:4, I, 381.

96) It might be granted that certain extreme and stubborn heretics must be excommunicated (temporarily, it is to be hoped) from the Church and even restrained from actively disturbing it, but this has nothing to do with destroying these men politically.

97) *Comm.* Isa. 49:23, IV, 41.

Christ" as Calvin makes clear against that claim by Henry VIII of England [98].

One important related question remains: the relation of actual overt warfare and the spiritual warfare which, for Calvin, was far more real [99]. Calvin treats briefly the commandment, "thou shalt not kill", and does not directly connect it with war in the *Institutes* [100], although in commenting on the Deuteronomic version he grounds it interestingly: "You battle against men (says God), when you strive to injure each other, for I have stamped my image upon you" [101]. Still he can speak of possible justification for a specific war by the special providential direction of the Spirit [102]. While Calvin did not instigate the one war in which he played an advisory role, and denounced the active role played by the pastors of Lyon, he felt justified in supporting the Huguenots in what began as resistance to murderous persecution, and was willing actively to enlist assistance for his already partly successful friends [103]. Perhaps most revealing is Calvin's attitude toward the end of the war: on the one hand he deeply regretted that de Conde had made a separate peace for his own advantage and forced the other Huguenots to give up the fight when they were in a very good military position; but, on the other hand, Calvin says: "My advice will always be not to take up arms and rather see everything lost than to have to experience such evil confusions" [104].

Theoretically and systematically, then, Calvin deplores the destructive character of war and counsels avoiding it at *almost* any cost. He finds war legitimate only in extreme cases where a defensive war must be fought for the direct protection of the proclamation of the Gospel and the church, and to prevent the establishment of a *spiritual* tyranny. When he connects mortal combat with the spiritual warfare, providence, and predestination, however, he leaves an open door for Cromwell and the militaristic Dutch Calvinists. Calvin himself would probably have condemned their specific actions, but he prepared the way for them, first, by

---

98) *Comm.* Amos 7:10, 349.

99) See F. C. Palm, *Calvinism and the Religious Wars,* 1932, and R. M. Kingdon, *Geneva and the Coming of the Wars of Religion in France, 1555—63.*

100) II, viii.

101) *Sermon* on Dt. 5:17, CR LIV, 325.

102) *Comms.* Gen. 14:13, I, 384 and Isa. 5:26, I, 194.

103) CG II, 405 f.

104) CG II, 436.

his insistence on the assurance of the salvation of the elect and, second, by his idea that the victory of Christ failed to extend over the world outside the church so that "the world" remained under the sovereignty of Satan. It was a relatively short and direct road from assurance to arrogance and a conviction that the servants of Satan who oppressed the church must be destroyed. We are not surprised by the significant fact that Kolfhaus, loyal Calvinist *and* German, can say in a book about Calvin, "How much more in the spirit of the Reformation rings the word of Bismarck: 'I am God's soldier, and where he sends me I must go, and I believe that he sends me and alters my life as he needs it'" [105].

These are the powerful weapons of the Christian's warfare; but they would be of little use in the hands of those who have no idea of how to use them, of or the objectives toward which their warfare aims. We must therefore concentrate on strategy to utilize men and material in the spiritual struggle.

Strategy and Conduct of the Spiritual Warfare

The complexity and hardness of the spiritual warfare suggest that in general here we begin with a statement of the strategic action of the *sancta militia* in each area under discussion and then proceed to spotlight Satan's opposing action in the shadow of the first. In welding an effective fighting force one must attend to its organization, first to the corps of officers. Calvin believes that only the offices of pastor and teacher remain as legitimate ranks within the *militia Christ,* but he refers to these warriors in a wealth of military terminology: the French words which appear in his sermons as designations for Christ, the pastors, or the faithful, include *lieutenant, chef, capitaine, port-en-seigne, officier, prince, gendarme, vassal, archier* and *haquebutier* [1].

The honor which a Christian will eventually receive when the church shares in Christ's triumphs comes "according to the station assigned him in the army" [2] in highest measure to the apostles and ministers of the Word, just as the lieutenants (in ancient Rome's armies) accompanied on horseback the chariot of the commander-

105) W. Kolfhaus, *op. cit.,* p. 243.
1) Erwin Mühlhaupt, *Die Predigt Calvins,* p. 40.
2) *Comm.* II Cor. 2:14, II, 157 f.

in-chief, sharing his honor. In this life, however, the soldiers of Christ have little time for concern about the distribution of medals, for the main accent is on the larger share of the burden and heat of battle which falls upon the officers of Christ's militia. Calvin says that although all Christians are soldiers, the pastors and ministers of the Word are the standard-bearers who must go ahead of the others and, equipped with exceptional courage and bravery, normally bear the brunt of Satan's assault [3].

The problem of authority is analogous for the minister of the Spirit's sword and the military officer. Paul struggled to assert his true apostleship for the purpose of edifying or constructing the church, building up Christ's army, while attempts to tear down his authority were plots of Satan to undermine the church [4]. God commands that the minister *of the Word* be honored "as an angel of God" but the devil instigates contempt of them, and ministers of Satan hope by producing this dislike they may displace them, thus rupturing the chain of command [5]. Calvin considers the unity of the officers corps the keystone in the structure of the *militia Christi*. With Cyprian he says: "I long that all our fellow soldiers be gathered within Christ's camp", even those who have deserted or otherwise broken military discipline [6]. Consequently Satan's strategy aims at dislodging the keystone of unity among the officers and thus destroying the morale and discipline of the army of God. Therefore, Calvin finds it necessary to write Pellikan assuring him that the reported malevolence of Farel toward him is non-existent, and admonishing him to exert every effort to eradicate the idea before Satan can exploit it in the church [7]. Calvin was conscious that in unusual times such as his own — in which, for example, laymen turned to the freedom of the Protestant churches faster than the priests (i. e. "enemy officers") were converted or ministers could be trained — certain irregularities in the ministry could be overlooked without harm [8]. (On May 24, 1561 Calvin writes to Bullinger that he is besieged with requests for newly-trained ministers and regrets that he is entirely "sold out".) Every craftsman in the

---

3) *Comm.* Philemon 2, p. 348.
4) See esp. *Comm.* II Cor. 10:8, II, 329.
5) *Comm.* Gal. 4:14, p. 128.
6) IV, xii, 8.
7) CE II, 355.
8) CG II, 272.

workshops of Geneva who had the least literary and theological training had been drafted and sent to the front [9]. But this provided no excuse for evangelical ministers handing over a weapon to Satan by their covetous desire to replace another pastor at a more "desirable" post of duty [10]. In spite of such dangers, he believed that God has made the rank of *minister verbi divini* so important to the church that as long as even weak pastors present the chief points of the Christian religion and administer the sacraments, the church ought to adhere to them [11].

Ministers do not stand alone as officers in God's army, however, for teachers to train and drill the common soldiers and future officers for the rigors of the spiritual warfare are indispensable. When negotiating with King Sigismund August of Poland for the entry of his domain into the Reformed camp he counsels (in 1554) against arbitrarily replacing Catholic priests. Instead, evangelical teachers should be brought in provisionally until the church of Poland be reformed [12]. One would think that at least the task of teacher might be a quiet one; indeed Calvin himself had at first hoped so. He had to learn the inexorable fact, however, that those who could not themselves do battle were not fit to train others for the perilous and strenuous assignment. Therefore, all who are sent to teach the Word are sent to carry on a contest: it is not enough to teach faithfully what God commands, unless we also contend [13].

The teacher is so important to the success of the *sancta militia* because the warfare is so hard that only the well-trained soldier can withstand the heat of battle. The ministers of Satan are highly skilled in deception, and actually seek out the careless to trap [14]. Therefore, God "never brings his people into the field of battle till they have been fully trained" [15]. To a layman imprisoned and later martyred for his faith, Calvin writes that he is an exception to his rule [16]. In general, the church must systematically undertake the task of training and drilling foot-soldiers and officers. In more ordered times the church gives intensive preparation for the spiritual struggle

9) CG II, 356.
10) CE I, 116.
11) See CE II, 121 ff.
12) CG II, 52.
13) *Comm.* Micah 3:8, III, 234.
14) *Comm.* Eph. 4:14, p. 286.
15) *Comm.* John 18:9, II, 194.
16) CE I, 366.

to the recruits it trains for the ministry of the Word. Calvin claims that in the ancient church, the bishops labored hard to teach the younger men, who had enlisted in the sacred army [17]. Training began when youths, with the consent of their parents, "enlisted in the spiritual army", and it continued through a long period of increasing exercise of their skills and strength. "Just as army recruits are instructed through sham battles for real and serious warfare, so the clergy were prepared by certain prescribed training exercises before they were actually promoted to officers" [18]. Calvin makes familiarity with Scripture and in particular with the discourse of Jesus essential in the training of an officer of Christ's army. As long as these words are imprinted on our minds, we may march on the field of battle as soon as necessary, confident of victory [19]. To insure that his trainees might not retreat the moment they enter actual combat, Calvin the drill-sergeant insists: "Let us, therefore, accustom ourselves to use this armor in such a manner that it may never drop out of our hands" [20], but he saves his toughest terminology for the less diligent recruits [21].

Whenever a Christian has a rest leave, he must not understand it as a sign that the spiritual warfare is ended. Rather, it is a time given him to prepare for the battles ahead, since Jesus immediately adds the assumption of the yoke to his invitation to rest: "And hence we obtain a definition of that rest of which he had spoken. It is not at all intended to exempt the disciples of Christ from the warfare of the flesh, that they may enjoy themselves at their ease, but to train them under the burden of discipline, and keep them under the yoke" [22]. This is no idle rumor, for the recruits and those granted "leave from front-line duty" for recuperation and further training are all called soon enough into battle. Then the careful drilling, the preparation of legitimate weapons, and the lessons in strategy serve the *sacra militia* well. Now all of the admonitions to use only the correct weapons must be scrupulously observed even

---

17) IV, iii, 2.

18) IV, iv, 9, part. reten. Allen.

19) R. M. Kingdon, *Geneva and the Coming of the Religious Wars in France, 1555—63*, unpublished diss., speaks of the militant missionaries, French (and other) nationals trained in exile in Geneva and then returned to extend the battle-line in their native land.

20) *Comm.* John 16:1, II, 133.

21) *Comm.* Matt. 4:4, I, 214.

22) *Comm.* Matt. 10:29, II, 44.

in the heat of battle, for our battle is not justified simply by the fact that we have a good cause: "In order to protect ourselves in a proper and permissible manner, we must lay aside all hate and irascibility, vindictiveness and unbridled passion" [23].

In view of our intelligence about the nature of the enemy and the struggle we must formulate an overall strategy, being "well aware how necessary it is to reconnoiter an enemy to know by what method to counteract his strategems". This strategy is grounded on three premises: first, if we centered our attention on inflicting vengeance on Satan's human agents we would be following a method by which we would ourselves be vanquished by the devil; second, if we avoid all conflict with men except as *they* actively oppose Jesus Christ, we *do* resist the wiles of the devil and *are* using the Lord's armor; third, laying aside malicious prejudice and refusing to repay evil with evil, we must "be guided solely by zeal for the service of God, moderated by his Spirit according to the rule of his Word" [24]. Here Calvin has unquestionably given us sound advice, but not a simple formula for automatic victory. Each command decision requires the grace of God and the full use of every bit of ability and training at the disposal of the soldier or officer of Christ to determine precisely when men are actively opposing Christ, when human zeal is being moderated by the Spirit and when the Christian follows the rule of the Word. But we are to pray, as Calvin prayed for Farel — who was "neither so raw nor inexperienced in this warfare as to be alarmed even by great danger" — to be filled with the "Spirit of wisdom, of prudence, of moderation, of zeal, of fortitude, to be armed at all points for an undertaking so difficult and arduous" [25]. Two terms remarkably placed side by side in this last directive give us a practical motto to describe the conduct of the Christian's campaign. We are to fight under the watchword of "zealous moderation", for "our Lord has furnished us with spiritual prudence, which, as it neither slackens nor weakens our zeal, so, on the other hand, it stills and regulates it by a wise moderation" [26]. The Christian soldier must consequently be alert *at all times* to the danger posed by strong and resourceful enemies [27], for Satan

---

23) See Kolfhaus, *op. cit.,* pp. 458 f.
24) CE I, 60 f.
25) CE I, 325.
26) CE I, 288.
27) *Comm.* John 10:10, I, 401.

can transform himself into an angel of light [28], or even assume the disguise of God himself [29]. On such occasions, Satan directs his ministers to agree with the servants of God, if this opens the door to turning them aside from their mission [30]. Such insidious and dangerous infiltration tactics force the army of Christ to develop a criterion for "testing the spirits" [31]. Although the Biblical author defines the criterion as the confession that Jesus Christ has come in the flesh, Calvin prefers to stress the Spirit's sword, the relation between God's Spirit and the Bible [32].

For Calvin, Reuben's adultery shows Satan's sabotage penetrating into the holy house, casting doubt upon God's election [33]. This is merely a clear specimen of Satan's most common and insidious stratagem for weakening the church by destroying confidence in God and the fulfillment of his promises. The most devastating example of this tactic occurs when Judas, one of Jesus' personal choices, falls away. That one so chosen could fail "was a powerful instrument of Satan" for shaking the disciples' faith [34]. Similarly, Calvin believes that Satan uses the Romanist practice of suspending the soul between hope and fear to undermine faith even where he cannot utterly destroy it [35].

However, Calvin knows the defence which must always be victorious against this tactic: "Whenever Satan would drive us to despair, we ought to hold out this shield, that God is unwilling that we should be overwhelmed with everlasting destruction, because he has appointed his Son to be the salvation of the world" [36]. Furthermore, combatting such stratagems of Satan demands of the Christian soldier a spotless military conduct. Presenting oneself blameless is a tactic of defence which was as a foundation a powerful struggle of personal discipline and restraint. Since victory in the internal struggle is indispensable to the conduct of the external one, Calvin displays great interest in a strategy for winning this inner

---

28) II Cor. 11:14.

29) *Comm.* Isa. 36:10, III, 86.

30) *Comm.* Amos 7:10—13, II, 347.

31) I John 4:1.

32) I, ix, 2.

33) *Comm.* Gen. 35:27, II, 246.

34) *Comm.* John 6:70, I, 280.

35) III, ii, 24.

36) *Comm.* John 3:17, I, 126. In spite of his physical pain and weakness

conflict, and he finds this strategy in *mortificatio* [37]. Calvin is so impressed with this strategy that he can say: "... the life of a Christian man is a continual effort and exercise in the mortification of the flesh, till it is utterly slain and God's Spirit reigns in us" [38]. This strategy is perpetually valid, for "we are baptized into the mortification of the flesh, which begins with our baptism, and which we pursue day by day and which will be accomplished when we shall pass from this life to the Lord" [39].

Other weapons combine with this strategic action and are, at the same time, "interchangeable parts" in the machinery of the *militia Christi*. For example, *repentance,* which "consists in the mortification of our flesh and of the old man" [40]. When the Christian "takes up his own cross", Calvin sees the Lord subduing "the wanton impulse of our flesh" [41]. Note, however, Calvin's distinction between the bitter cross assigned the *reprobi* and the Christian's cross made sweet by being borne by Christ [42]. Likewise Calvin understands *self-denial* in terms of mortification of the flesh, since self-confidence wars with God [43]. Yet again, *mortificatio* is replaced by the *destruction of the old man* as well as the denial of ourselves [44].

In spite of the great weight he places on these forms of strict military discipline, Calvin is not advocating an exercise of human ascetic virtuosity. Not unlike the Luther who explored every avenue offered by the elaborate spiritual road system of Roman piety and learning before breaking with it, Calvin had lived a veritable monastic existence as a teen-ager in the College de Montiagu, and made more progress at disciplining his mind, developing a tendency toward migraine, and ruining his stomach than at saving his soul [45]. The tendencies toward a *spiritual* asceticism which appear on the horizon are contrary to Calvin's expressed

---

Calvin seems never to have been seriously threatened by that all-engulfing foe portrayed by Dürer, Melancholia, which besieged Luther.

37) Calvin draws here upon Melanchthon — see III, iii, 3, n. 9 — while rejecting Loyola on exterior and interior penance — see III, iii, 2, n. 8.
38) III, iii, 20, part. reten. Allen.
39) IV, xv, 11.
40) III, iii, 5.
41) III, viii, 5.
42) *Comm.* Luke 12:51, I, 469.
43) *Comm.* Luke 18:9, II, 202.
44) *Comm.* Matt. 6:10, I, 320.
45) J. Cadier, *op. cit.,* p. 18 f.

belief that *mortificatio* is ultimately a work of God not of man, a benefit of the work of Christ. (That famous half-truth called the Weber thesis makes a (this) worldly asceticism definitive for the Calvinist "Protestant ethic". See R. W. Greenlaw ed. *Protestantism and Capitalism: The Weber Thesis and its Critics*.) This is clear from Calvin's full definition of repentance as a "*True conversion of our life to God, a turning that arises from a pure and earnest fear of him, and consists in the* mortification *of our flesh and of the old man, and in the* vivificatio *of the Spirit*"[46]. Defining *vivificatio* Calvin can say: "In one word I interpret repentance as regeneration, the sole end of which is to restore in us the *imago dei*"[47]. But *vivificatio* is a pure act of God to which no works of man contribute, so Calvin does not make it an element of strategy for the Christian army. (This fits, however, into the general pattern in which *vivificatio* is a relatively pale tactical counterpart of *mortificatio,* which Calvin vigorously prosecutes.)[48]

Mortificatio carnis, therefore, remains legitimate for the whole spiritual conflict so long as the flesh refers to the whole man subject to sin, while the new man or spirit in man refers to the whole man in Christ through his Spirit, that is, subject to *vivificatio.* How, then, do we account for the violent fury with which Calvin attacks the flesh as a *lower part* to which man's spirit (almost his soul) as the *immortal higher part* corresponds. It would seem more consistent with the Biblical conception, which Calvin's systematic statement appears to understand, simply to say that mortification ought to consist of the starvation of the entire old man through deliberate neglect, while the whole new man should be strengthened by nourishment and training.

We find violent fury astonishingly absent when we turn from this inner warfare to Calvin's systematic statements concerning the Christian's strategy for treating human enemies. In its place we find a true considerateness born of Christian love. Here, perhaps more than at any point in the conduct of the Christian life as a part of the spiritual warfare, Calvin displays a thorough understanding of the implications of the Gospel for the character of the struggle. He looks upon our human enemies sympathetically as

---

46) III, iii, 5. See again III, iii, 3, n. 9 for Melanchthon's prior use of this terminology.

47) III, iii, 9.

48) See K. Barth, *op. cit.,* IV, 2, 651.

victims of their spiritual masters and as potential brothers in Christ to be won over rather than destroyed. His view *is* controlled by "We wrestle not against flesh and blood"; "Our natural disposition would lead us to direct all our exertions against the men themselves; but this foolish desire will be restrained by the consideration that the men who annoy us are nothing more than darts thrown by the hand of Satan" [49].

More positively, of the seven thousand hidden faithful Israelites Calvin says: "If God's grace is able to do so much in the worst of times, we may not immediately look on all those whose piety is not yet visible as slaves of the devil!" [50] Granted that all who serve Christ are warriors, their style of living as warriors consists not in inflicting evils, but rather in patience [51]. Satan's strategy at this point is to lead us beyond Christian discipline to Pharisaical rigor and cruel domineering which will cause a Christian delinquent to despair and to be lost to Christ's cause [52].

From Calvin's own practice we have to learn that carrying out such excellent strategy is as difficult as it is important. To his statement, "The church militant, which is under the standard of Christ, has no permission to execute vengeance", Calvin found it necessary to add, "*Except* against those who obstinately refuse to be reclaimed", and "*until* it appear beyond all doubt that they are irrevocable and hopelessly depraved" [53]. We scarcely need add that Calvin felt fully justified to judge such cases. Although he actually made far less frequent of this "except" and "until" than many readings of church history suggest, the relatively few uses he made of it cast serious doubts on all exceptions to his salutary systematic statements.

Finally, we must discuss the strategic use of certain specific weapons: prayer and worship, the Spirit's sword, theological symbols and truth in general. As a general base for all other forms of fighting, prayer, the chief exercise of the Christian life, pervades every area of the battlefield whether the war be "cold" or "hot". While at the Worms Disputation in 1540, Calvin wrote to the pastors at Neuchatel that he and his comrades-in-arms were sitting inactively in the

---

49) *Comm.* Eph. 6:12, p. 335.
50) *Comm.* Rom. 11:4, p. 413 (author's transl.).
51) *Comm.* II Tim. 2:3, p. 210.
52) *Comm.* II Cor. 2:7 ff., II, 151.
53) *Comm.* Ps. 18:47, I, 305. e. a.

camp because the enemy would not come out to fight. Nevertheless the hidden battle was to be carried on in prayer, so that those at home could assist in it too[54]. Further, we must guard against Satan's attempts to dull the cutting edge of the sacraments[55], and to corrupt every aspect of Christian worship, for example, in almost all ages "endeavoring to make the bodies of God's saints idols to foolish men"[56].

Several strategic considerations attend the use of the sword of the Spirit, God's Word, in the conduct of the Christian warfare: "The ministers of the Word are called by God that they may save men from the power of death and bring them to life, and to make slaves of the devil into children of God"[57]. The enemy cannot allow this offensive to be carried out unchallenged[58]. But while the devil labors with all his might to undermine the authority of Scripture and to bury its truth under false interpretations, to "disparage" the Gospel[59], to spread a cloud of error to obstruct the progress of sound doctrine[60], to corrupt doctrine by tainting its purity with his leaven[61], to darken the pure doctrine of Christ by his false-hoods[62], to inspire Christians with offence at the degradation of the cross[63], it is for the officers and men of Christ's troop to follow Paul who "builds up the authority of the Gospel"[64]. Calvin can also make strategic use of theological formulations in the spiritual struggle. He writes to Martin Schalling that he would willingly subscribe to the Lutheran Augsburg Confession, not because it was in his mind the finest statement of the Christian faith, but because it might prove a means of strengthening the unity of the Evangelical camp to present a united front against the foe[65]. At the same time, Calvin uses theological formulations to hold other soldiers of Christ to their commitments to his conception of the struggle and its con-

---

54) CG I, 114 f.
55) e. g. baptism IV, xix, 8.
56) *Comm.* Jude 9, p. 439.
57) CG I, 271.
58) *Comm.* Gal. 4:22, p. 135.
59) *Comm.* Eph. 1:8, p. 203.
60) *Intro.* to *Comm. on Harmony of Gospels,* I, 4.
61) *Comm.* Gal. 5:9, p. 154.
62) *Comm.* Eph. 4:14, p. 285.
63) *Comm.* John 1:46, I, 76 f.
64) *Comm.* Eph. 1:8, p. 203.
65) CG II, 169.

duct [66]. Thus, the soldiers of Christ must continually be alert for the ever-shifting attacks of Satan's army upon every form of Christian *truth,* whether attempts to destroy or weaken justification by faith [67], or assaults on the purity of marriage and the legitimacy of sexual relations within its bounds by profane jests on the one hand and by asceticism on the other [68]. The attack on the certainty of the resurrection and hope of ultimate victory and eternal life emphasizes how indispensable is morale in warfare. "Satan has not a more deadly dart for wounding the souls of men than when he endeavors to dislodge hope from our minds", Calvin says, "by turning the promises of God into ridicule" [69]. Similarly, the Christian must be prepared to face the onslaughts of Satan by which he tries to wound them by slander and to render them totally ineffective by terror [70].

Finally, the responsibility and freedom accorded the officers in Christ's army, as well as the interdependence of its various units, is underlined by Paul's statement that he "robbed" other churches to the advantage of the one in Corinth. This is not to be understood in terms of the "robbery" which some have claimed General George Patton perpetrated on the vital roads and supplies needed by the allied armies in World War II to the advantage and glory of his army and the detriment of the others. Instead, Calvin points out that what Paul took — although it was in a sense his "by right of spiritual warfare" as spoils of his missionary victories — was actually donated voluntarily and gratuitously by one division of Christ's army for the relief and assistance of another [71]. This quite practical problem brings us to the border of the strategic relationship between the *ecclesia militans* and the supporting political governments. Just as the Jews accused Jesus of plotting revolt against Caesar, so, in Calvin's view, "Satan labors to expose the Gospel to hatred or suspicion on this plea, as if Christ, by erecting his kingdom, were overturning all the governments of the world, and destroying the authority of kings and magistrates" [72]. This statement explains why Calvin, like the other Reformers, employed

---

66) CE II, 320.
67) III, xvii, 1.
68) *Comm.* I Cor. 7:1 ff., I, 224 ff.
69) *Comm.* Ps. 22:7, I, 367.
70) *Comm.* Micah 7:8, III, 373.
71) *Comm.* II Cor. 11:8, II, 347.
72) *Comm.* Matt. 27:11, III, 276.

the strategy of rejecting the Anabaptists as fellow-soldiers in the ranks of the Reformation, and also why he put so much weight on the politically conservative interpretation of Rom. 13:1-6. Calvin's characteristic strategems therefore included 1) assurances to kings and governors in areas where the Reformation was gaining a foothold that it meant order, not chaos; and 2) his admonition to churches even under unfriendly governments to support the government as long as it did not require a denial of their faith. In an extreme case, however, he counselled the ministers at Montbeliard to flee rather than capitulate: "Your lot, however hard, will be more blessed than if you had maintained a name and a place where the Son of God was exiled. Yet we shall soon see him so reigning in heaven, as to make his power appear also on earth. Meanwhile, it becomes us to be ready for the warfare, since it is not yet the hour of triumph" [73].

From the organization and training of the common soldiers and the "corps of officers", and the strategic use of the weapons God provides, we turn to the primary qualities required of the soldier of Jesus Christ in this life: perseverance and endurance. Since the very character of the warfare itself, and the tenacity and power of the enemy makes necessary this command to persevere, Calvin generalizes Jesus' story of the displaced demon who returned: "Let us not then suppose that the devil has been vanquished by a single combat, because he has once gone out of us. On the contrary, let us remember that as his lodgment within us was of old standing, ever since we were born, he has knowledge and experience of all the approaches by which he may reach us ... We must, therefore, endeavor that Christ, holding his reign within us, may block up all the entrances of his adversary" [74]. Then as Christ "governs those whom he has elected, all the engines which Satan can employ will not prevent them from persevering to the end with unshaken firmness" [75]. Calvin attempts to impress the importance of perseverance on his fellow-soldiers with every means at his disposal. Jesus foretold his coming in glory so that his disciples "might keep their minds in warfare till Christ's second coming" [76], and Paul persevered, not

73) CE II, 195.

74) *Comm.* Matt. 12:45, II, 86.

75) *Comm.* John 13:18, II, 63.

76) *Comm.* Matt. 25:31, III, 175.

only as a "veteran soldier" but even as a "raw recruit" [77]. Calvin exhorts the troops to *Meditatio futurae vitae* so as to be weary of and despise this life in comparison with the next. Yet this life is a post (*statio*) at which the Lord has placed us, and which we are to *hold* till he recalls us [78]. Kolfhaus conjoins this classic term of the spiritual warfare with *vocatio* to describe the locus for the Christian life [79]. Resigning an officer's commission, on the other hand, is tantamount to desertion and is completely excluded as a possibility open to the Christian soldier [80]. The austere Reformer is almost as hard on those who look forward to retirement in this life [81]. When we hear the flat statement that there are no *emeriti* — discharged veterans — in this life [82], we must remember the picture of Calvin who died not simply "with his boots on" but with his sword in hand. Then we appreciate his argument that death itself is the only release from active service, and that it is in fact intended for that purpose: "There is therefore no reason for us to ask a discharge from the Lord, whatever service we may have performed; for Christ will have no discharged soldiers, but those who have conquered death itself" [83].

Thus, Calvin formulated for the army of Christ a strategy covering the entire period of earthly service, from the first days of training through the heat of battle to the end. It is a strategy geared to warfare which demands the entire strength of Christ's body and all its members, a warfare so difficult that they must not be surprised if the cannot triumph after every skirmish, "since Christ himself did not always succeed" [84]. Nevertheless, Calvin believes that God will keep his imperfect soldiers faithful to the end, for "the truth of God ought to have such a firm hold of us, that all the contrivances and attacks of Satan shall not draw us from our course;

---

77) *Comm.* II Cor. 11:31, II, 363.

78) III, ix, 4.

79) W. Kolfhaus, *op. cit.,* p. 235.

80) CE II, 45. In a letter to Francis Daniel in 1534, that familiar military type, the malingerer, is condemned along with the scribe in Matt. 8:19, who seems to want to fight in the shade at ease, untroubled by sweat or dust, and beyond the reach of the weapons of war.

81) *Comm.* Heb. 10:32, p. 252.

82) *Intro.* to *Comm.* on *Acts,* I, xx.

83) *Comm.* Heb. 12:4, p. 315.

84) *Comm.* John 5:18, I, 197.

and yet, as we have not hitherto attained full and complete strength, we must make progress until death" [85].

The Goals of the Spiritual Warfare

The warfare imposed on the Christian by his Divine Commander is no purposeless exercise. Each topic discussed in this chapter both presupposes and requires certain goals and purpose of the spiritual warfare. The evangelicals imprisoned in Paris hear in 1559: "You know the things for which you fight; that God may be glorified, the truth of his Gospel confirmed, and the kingdom of our Lord Jesus Christ be praised as it deserves" [1]. Here again, the *gloria dei* occupies Calvin's first theological concern. Kolfhaus [2] in company with Doumergue [3] considers the *gloria dei* both motive and goal of Christian morality. Since in everything we must endure on this earth the glorification of the name of God is the ultimate goal [4], Calvin is so convinced that this *gloria* is as important to God as it is to him that he can ask those in danger of weakening in the face of the enemy, "Do you *think* that God does not value his glory much higher than your life?" [5] This does not denote quite the sharp alternative between the glory of God and man's preservation from extinction it might seem to imply, for Calvin refers to "mere" earthly life and certainly not the soul's eternal blessedness, which is inextricably bound up with the glory of God as a goal of the spiritual warfare: in the battle which our highest king leads, "His glory *and* our salvation are at stake" [6].

Our own salvation might be suspect as an unworthy goal of the spiritual warfare. Subordinated to the *gloria dei,* however, it takes on a somewhat different appearance. Calvin exhorts us to "to fight under the banner of our Lord Jesus Christ for our own salvation, since we are sure of the victory" [7], but not as a solipsistic matter. While he tells the congregation at Orbe that they are fighting an

---

85) *Comm.* Eph. 4:15, p. 286.
1) CG II, 256.
2) *Ibid.,* pp. 510—25.
3) E. Doumergue, *op. cit.,* IV, 283.
4) *Sermon* on Ps. 115, CR LX, 455.
5) *Sermon* on Dan. 11:23 f., CR LXX, 64.
6) CE II, 109. e. a.
7) CG II, 358.

engagement intimately connected with their own salvation, he also counsels an active sympathy for the unbelievers bewitched by Satan, a sympathy which does for them good they do not know or desire [8]. One attitude and tactic is so fundamental to God's glory and our salvation that it becomes a goal of the Christian life, namely, obedience, which in the terminology of spiritual warfare, is a *captivité voluntaire* [9]. Just like the soldier who carries out the orders of his commander, the Christian who lives in constant obedience to God achieves an important goal by that very fact. Even when the fruits of our labors are scanty, and even though there be no ears to hear our proclamation of the truth, we must not throw away our weapons, "for it is enough for us that we labor faithfully for the glory of God" [10].

Obedience extends far beyond all limits human weakness would place upon it, for the Divine Commander "who spared not his own Son" may also require of his soldiers that they follow him in "obedience unto death". Thus, when Paul speaks of the marks of suffering which he bears about in his body as a result of his obedience, Calvin insists that these *stigmata* are the marks which Christ our leader confers upon his most distinguished soldiers, just as in "earthly warfare" a general decorates a soldier for bravery [11]. Moreover, Calvin can look upon a human death — if not as meritorious — at least as the accomplishment of the process of mortification, the death of the old man. Calvin rejoices in the hour "when, the old man slain and utterly destroyed in us, the divine goodness will receive us into blessed peace with the New Adam" [12].

We should not be misled at this point into thinking that Calvin had an individualistic conception of the goals of the Christian life. A principal objective of the Christian warfare as he understood it was to win men and nations to Christ and to the Reformation understanding of the Gospel. The empirical evidence that more people have been influenced by his work than by any other leader of the Reformation except Luther emphasizes this. Although during his life he represented only one branch of the Swiss and south German Reformation, the form of polity and faith of the Reformed

---

8) CG II, 7.

9) See II, ii, 7, n. 37 and CL, CR, XXIX, 254, as well as Kolfhaus, *op. cit.,* p. 266.

10) *Comm.* Isa. 6:10, I, 215.

11) *Comms.* Phil. 1:28, p. 48 and Gal. 6:17, p. 187.

12) III, xiv, 12.

Church to which he gave decisive expression became definitive, in varying degrees, not only for parts of Swiss and German, Gallic, Scottish and Lowlands Protestantism, but also had its effect in England, the Western Hemisphere and the Eastern border of European Protestantism, while Lutheranism was limited to Germanic and related Scandinavian cultures.

Calvin's powerful conviction inspires an almost poetic flight when he proclaims that the minister of the Word is called by God to save men from the power of death and bring them to life, and to make servants of the devil into children of God [13]. As a result of Calvin's vigor in pursuing this conviction, by the middle of 1551 with refugees daily streaming into Geneva, permission was granted them to assemble for public worship in their own languages. English was preached at the Auditoire, Italian at the college, Spanish at St. Gervais, and Flemish in St. Germain. And then, as the situation permitted, the tide turned and some of the refugees — now leaders trained by Calvin as at a spiritual military academy — returned to spread Calvin's conception of the Gospel.

By no means all of Calvin's attempts to capture men and lands for Christ were successful. Yet even when the chances of success were slim, as in Poland, where the flickering flame of the Reformation was quickly snuffed out by the Counter Reformation, Calvin was as good as his word: "It is our duty, indeed, to labor diligently, and to strive by every possible method, that the whole world may be brought, if possible, into the unity of the faith" [14]. The grand scope of such a statement might lead one to expect that Calvin had a genuine world mission in view, which would have made him unique among the Reformers [15], but we find no developed program or even a solid theological basis for extension of the visible triumphs of Christ over the "heathen" realms. In this sense, the Roman Church had a truer claim in the sixteenth century to the term "Catholic" because some efforts had been made in the world mission. The terms "Protestant" and "Reformation" symbolized real limitations. The

13) CG I, 271.

14) *Comm.* John 10:8, I, 400.

15) Calvin's association with the mission to Brazil in 1556 should be noted as an exception indicating his disposition. See K. Fröhlich, *Reichgottesidee,* p. 7 and R. Rouse and S. Neill, *A History of the Ecumenical Movement 1517 to 1948;* also K. Barth, *op. cit.,* IV, 3, pp. 18—40, in which Calvin's discovery of the prophetic office of Christ is seen as a root of the modern Christian world mission.

sole central Protestant goal in the Christian warfare, was to reform the existent European church of Christ by restoring the purity of the *faith* and the *order* of the Church. Calvin's program for the Reformation of Polish Christianity makes the ultimate goals the glory of God and the kingdom of Christ, while the proximate ones are the purity of holiness and the good of humanity [16]. We miss once again among Calvin's goals the love which is the content of both Jesus' great commandments. It was unquestionably sound Biblical insight which led the Reformers to stress *faith* over against the concept of love which reigned in the Roman Church at the time (exaggerated though Nygren's critique in *Agape and Eros* may be). But when Calvin can go so far as to make the statement, in discussing Christian liberty, "as our liberty should be subject to *charitas,* so *charitas* itself ought to be subservient to the purity of faith" [17]. One must ask — in Calvin's terminology — whether Satan has not used the over-ripeness of Scholastic *charitas* to spoil Calvin's taste for *agape.*

Finally, Calvin makes the maintenance and restoration of the *order* of the Church a basic goal of the Christian conflict. When the protector of the church at Montbeliard was militarily defeated, Calvin asserts that "Satan has, by the aid of his ministers, overturned among you also the order of the church as established by God" [18]. But for Calvin the order of the church is understood in terms of the faith to which love must be subordinated. Calvinism is always right to set aside a love which is abstracted from faith and also devoid of true joy, but it must always guard against replacing it with a "faith" which is abstracted from love. If the goal Calvin set for his struggle for the purity of the faith had been a church centered on the love which is greater than faith, the love of God *in Christ,* the mark left by the warfare of Calvin and his followers would have been of a decisively more evangelical nature.

Since he does not fully employ the mandate of God's *love* for the world in his theology, Calvin's view of the objectives in the spiritual warfare must necessarily lack a dimension which must not be lacking in a complete statement of the implications of Christ's victory. Calvin and the other Evangelicals of his day did have one definite attitude toward the heathen, one they shared with their Papist con-

---

16) CG II, 48.
17) III, xix, 13.
18) CE II, 194.

temporaries. It was a defensive attitude based on the threat of the Mohammedan armies to the Christian West. Calvin as historian considered Mohammed the leader of a heretical sect of Christianity, similar to Antichrist the pope, and these sects (Islam and Roman Catholicism) "are streams of revolt" which divert water from the main course of Christianity [19]. Faced with "the Turk at the gates of Vienna", Calvin counsels his followers not to fear that God has lost his power because the Turk has conquered such a great multitude of (mainly Oriental and African) Christians. Instead, with the confidence of an Old Testament prophet, Calvin assures us that it is precisely the wrath of God evoked by the licentiousness, wickedness and superstitions of those in Greece and Asia which have accounted for the Turk's success [20]. Significantly, Calvin not only does not counsel political action (Europe was exhausted with crusading), but does not attempt to formulate any strategy for, even declare as a goal, the spiritual conquest — or more properly re-conquest — of millions of people who, according to his own view of history, were led by a heretic to rebel against the Gospel and apostasize from the church of Christ.

The Certainty of Victory

Calvin's goals for the Christian's warfare are no shimmering set of wispy ideals but — as is clear from the historical framework in which the Christian's struggle is set — are the goals of God's own irresistible, victorious plan of salvation. Therefore, "when you have Satan to combat, and fight under Christ's banner", as Calvin puts it, "he who girds on your armor and has drawn you into the battle, will give you the victory" [1]. To the prisoners for their Evangelical faith Calvin expresses this assurance with beautiful tenderness. He does not attempt to hide the fact that the "slaves of Satan tread us under feet", but in the very teeth of it adds that we look "for that happy issue which is promised to us" [2].

The Christian's certainty of victory is wholly dependent on the guarantee of God, to be sure, primarily Calvin's God of changeless glory. Calvin can put this in terms of *God's power,* which is "a sure

---

19) *Comm.* II Thes. 2:3, p. 327.
20) *Comm.* Isa. 36:20, III, 99.
1) CE I, 261.
2) CE II, 395.

and invincible munition", for there is "no danger which may not be successfully met by the power of God" [3]. Secondly, we are able to rely on *God's immutability,* his very reliability: the fact that God cannot lie is a defence against which no contrivance of Satan can prevail [4]. Thirdly, Calvin gains assurance of victory from *God's protection,* because "under the banner of Christ we battle only as victors, so that we triumph in trusting in this protection" [5].

Fourth, our certainty of victory depends on *God's promise.* Since "it is impossible that God shall not govern successfully", it is enough for Calvin that "he never commands us to advance without at the same time adding a promise to encourage us" [6].

There is always the danger that confidence will cross the border into overconfidence, that assurance will pass over into arrogance, of which Cromwell's Puritans are proof enough. Calvin himself approaches the border even systematically. Commenting on the "unconditional covenant" of Gen. 12:3: "We may therefore infer this general doctrine, that God so embraces us with his favor, that he will bless our friends, and take vengeance upon our enemies", but he sounds a warning in inferring the opposite: "nor ought it less to alarm us, that he declares war against us, if we hurt any one belonging to him" [7].

His concept of incorporation draws decisive certainty of victory from the statement that "the gates of hell shall not prevail against the church" all who are "*united to Christ,* and acknowledge him to be Christ and Mediator, will remain to the end safe from all danger; for what is said to the body of the church belongs to each of its members, since they are one in Christ" [8]. This goes beyond abstract assurances by Calvin's God of glory. Although the emphasis on God the omnipotent sovereign is by far the most common, and probably controlling, the Christological emphasis is also significant. Yet assurance in Christ need not wait, for "we shall be named victors not only in heaven, but Christ forms our earthly life like his heavenly life" [9].

---

3) CE I, 172 and *Comm.* Eph. 6:13, p. 337.
4) *Comm.* John 3:33, I, 138.
5) CL, CR XL No. 931 and *Comm.* Hos. 12:4, I, 423.
6) *Comm.* John 11:10, I, 429.
7) *Comm.* Gen. 12:3, I, 378.
8) *Comm.* Matt. 16:18, II, 292.
9) *Comm.* Rom. 6:10, p. 228 (author's transl.).

Calvin's Christ who assuredly triumphs, however, also wears a face resembling that in Michelangelo's Last Judgment, the face of so many Roman (and Protestant) "Christs". This is the face of the vengeful counterpart needed if our enemies are identical with the enemies of God. "We will pray Christ", Calvin can say, "that he may not only be our advocate with the Father, but that he may manifest himself as the just avenger of his [Reformed is clearly meant] church" [10].

As a good Trinitarian theologian, Calvin also connects the Holy Spirit with the warrior's certainty for the Spirit powerfully regenerates the Christian and is thus the guarantor of victory: "We know that believers are regenerated by the Spirit of Christ, that they may finish, with unshaken fortitude, the course of their warfare" [11]. Here certainty depends on the Regenerator rather than on the regenerate man's possession of regeneration. Even Calvin's monumental confidence in his own conscience is dependent on his calling by the Spirit: "If I am a servant of Christ", he writes the pastors of Neuchatel, "the witness of my conscience alone will always be worth more than the applause of the entire world"[12].

Finally, what effect has the Christian soldier's certainty that he is fighting in a cause that will be, and in a real sense already is, victorious. The whole metaphor of spiritual warfare depends on Calvin's confidence in the triumph of God's purpose: "He will protect and fortify the work he has begun not only in spite of Satan, but also in spite of the opposing malevolence of men. Thus we will in the meantime patiently submit to the period of testing which we need" [13]. Calvin's Christian soldier bears — along with several dissimilarities — one important resemblance to the soldier in our age of world-wide warfare. The modern warrior, officer or man, realizes that the war in which he takes part is so complex and of such a vast scope that whatever he may do will not be sufficient to bring victory to his cause. He also knows, however, that he has been given a specific assignment for which he is responsible, and that he must maintain constant vigilance to protect himself and the members of his own "combat team" from possible disaster. Finally, a good soldier fights in the confidence that victory will be achieved by a power

---

10) CG I, 329.

11) *Comm.* Isa. 66:7, IV, 422.

12) CG I, 328.

13) *Ibid.*

far beyond his own and that he will participate in it. Calvin's soldier of God, after realizing the necessity of fighting the good fight of faith, after receiving his training in the nature and use of the Spirit's sword, bends every effort in the *sancta militia,* but always in the hope of God's sure triumph in which he shares as a member of the body of the victorious Christ. This hope is the reason that the *true* word, "the Christian soldier must battle as long as he has breath", must not and cannot be the *last* word. The *ecclesia militans* must become the *ecclesia triumphans* and the God of battle must reign triumphant over all his foes.

ACT IV: TOWARD COSMIC VICTORY

Ecclesia militans becoming *ecclesia triumphans*

"I *have fought* the good fight . . ." (II Tim. 4:7).

Calvin's whole teaching, still more than Luther's, is worked out eschatologically — according to Heinrich Quistorp's important study of Calvin's eschatology. Just as Luther's name is synonymous with "faith", so Quistorp ventures to identify Calvin as the theologian of "hope"[1]. Similarly, Kolfhaus can say: "Without the eschatological perspective, we cannot at all understand Calvin's outlook on the whole of the Christian life"[2]. One can see why Martin Schulze thought that the *meditatio futurae vitae* was foundational in Calvin's thought (e. g. in defining human nature in the state of *justitia originalis* Calvin can say, "man *was made for* meditation on the heavenly life")[3], determining his entire conception of Christianity to such a great extent that his whole theology really becomes eschatology[4].

For ourselves, however, we must turn again to the analysis of the plays of William Shakespeare for analogy, and designate Calvin's eschatology in its futuristic component as an *anticlimax*. For dramatic criticism, "anticlimax" does not so much refer to a disappointing decline in importance as to the predetermined character of the end. Thus, although the murder of Desdemona and the suicide of Othello are much more violent and perhaps exciting, they represent the *anticlimax* of the dramatic logic which climaxes at the apparently more innocent moment in which Othello becomes convinced she is unfaithful. For Christian theology the *eschaton* — *telos* and *finis* of human history — is in a certain sense the anti-

---

1) Quistorp, *Calvin's Eschatologie,* p. 4.
2) Kolfhaus, *op. cit.,* p. 542.
3) I, xv, 6. e. a.
4) M. Schulze, *Meditatio futurae vitae.*

climax reflecting the past climactic event of God's reconciliation in Christ. For Calvin, the eschaton is doubly anticlimactic because God's decree is dramatically prior to the whole *Heilsgeschichte*. The brevity of our Act IV is symptomatic of this anticlimactic character of Calvin's eschatology.

Quistorp also knows that Calvin's eschatology has its limitations. He notes that the Reformers had no driving interest in last things and that they were suspicious of eschatology as such because their opponents used it in dangerously premature ways: the Roman Catholics tending to find *eschatology realized* in the church and the Enthusiasts making the end so *imminent* as to obviate all this-worldly ethics. The Reformers highest service in this area was to pass on simple and orthodox teaching in an era of exaggerated extremes. Calvin's saving grace in eschatology (even more than Luther's) was that he confronted all his dogmatic formulations with vast expanses of Scripture and thus was forced to face the implications of eschatology for his total theology. But the very fact that the major gap in Calvin's Biblical commentaries is his failure to deal with the Apocalypse (like Luther whose "spirit would not enter into the book", Calvin is said to have admitted that he did not understand it) indicates that his eschatology per se had to be an anticlimax [5].

Therefore, Quistorp is ultimately correct in accusing Calvin as well as Luther of "de-eschatologizing" the Gospel. In the first place this de-eschatologizing means that Calvin did not think that the authoritative figures of the New Testament — above all, Jesus and Paul — expected the second coming of Jesus to occur before the Protestant Reformation. He believes that Jesus in Matt. 24:3 ff. did not consider the destruction of the Temple eschatological, and chided the disciples for doing so [6]. Particularly embarrassing to Calvin are passages like I Cor. 15:52 and II Thes. 2:3 which "associate" Paul and his contemporaries with those who "*would at that time* [the *parousia*] be alive" [7]. Calvin de-eschatologizes in a second dimension when he dispenses (in general) with the cosmic breadth of Christian eschatology [8]. This tendency is clearest in Calvin's reduction of the effective scope of eschatology to a considera-

---

5) See Quistorp, *op. cit.*, pp. 1 ff.
6) *Comm. loc. cit.*, III, 117.
7) *Comm.* I Cor. 15:52, II, 60.
8) Quistorp, *op. cit.*, p. 3.

tion of the Christian's future life. Calvin says systematically that the end of the spiritual warfare does not simply coincide with the end of *our* lives but awaits *Christ's* victorious return to raise us from the dead. When he interprets the eschatology of Paul's Thessalonian letters, however, he emphasizes not the Lord's return but the hope for the resurrection of Christians [9].

The importance of these limitations emerges when we present our discussion of Calvin's eschatology in terms of *Heilsgeschichte* and discuss the *eschaton* and the church triumphant. This definition of eschatology immediately leads us to ask about the relation between the already accomplished victory of Christ and the awaited final triumph. We can best deal with this question in terms of Christ's exercise of kingship, of which Calvin says: "The noblest triumph which God ever gained was when Christ, after subduing sin, conquering death, and putting Satan to flight, rose majestically to heaven, that he might exercise glorious reign over the church ... No ascension of God more triumphant or more memorable will ever occur than that which took place when Christ was carried up to the right hand of the Father, that he might rule over all authorities and powers, and might become the everlasting protector of his people" [10]. The contrast between victory and triumph here dramatizes the shift from *ecclesia militans* which *wins* victories to the *ecclesia triumphans* which only *celebrates* them. In the light of this, Calvin's view of the *Heilsgeschichte* more closely resembles Karl Barth's conception that the decisive victory has been won objectively in the Christ-event and that its significance will be revealed fully to men at the eschaton rather than Reinhold Niebuhr's conception that we now have (subjective) clues to God's plan as the result of the Christ-event but the judgment takes place objectively for all things at the end of history [11].

Calvin, however, is not satisfied with this definition, but also says: "By 'the kingdom of Christ', I mean not only that which is begun here, but that which shall be completed at the last day, which on that account is called 'the day of renovation and restoration' (Acts 3:21)" [12]. He sees Christ's kingly power demonstrated in his

---

9) See *ibid.*, p. 22 and also *Comm.* II Thes. 2:1, p. 322.

10) *Comm.* Eph. 4:8 (Ps. 68:18), p. 272.

11) See Calvin's Christ *now* reigns in *full*, although "his manifestation is properly said to be delayed till the last day." *Comm.* Luke 19:12, II, 441.

12) *Comm.* Isa. 35:1, III, 62.

dominion over his enemies, and in this context he explains the relation of the accomplished reconciliation to ultimate redemption: "Indeed (Satan) is once overcome of Christ, but yet not so but he may continually renew war. (Paul) promises, therefore, the *last* putting of him to flight" [13]. This perspective of Calvin makes the scene of triumph the realization of the goal of the preceding warfare: "Thus, Paul teaches that when Christ shall ascend his judgment-seat to judge the world, then shall be fully accomplished that which began at the commencement of the Gospel, and which we still see done from day to day" [14].

In full, then, Calvin sees the victory of Christ in his earthly life, death, resurrection and ascension as decisive but still in need of completion. Calvin, who looks to the return of Christ for the final unalterable victory over his enemies and ours, thinks that the *parousia* represents an extension of Christ's kingship, and understands the appearance of the Son of Man — likened to a lightning flash in Matt. 24:26 — as the "further spread of the kingdom of Christ, which suddenly and unexpectedly enters and whose way will be like that of the lightning flash" [15].

Many of the enemies will have been conquered effectively before the coming of the last day — sin and its entourage on the cross and our flesh at the death of our body — but in addition to Satan, two of his allies remain: *Antichrist* to plague men in this life, and *death* to threaten them beyond. Therefore, Calvin is careful to make it clear that Antichrist will be destroyed wholly and in every respect when that final day of the restoration of all things shall arrive [16]. The destruction of death is best expressed, of course, in terms of I Cor. 15:26, Paul's proclamation that death (the last enemy) will be destroyed. In view of this, Paul taunts death with the loss, even now, of its barb or, as Calvin puts it, with the blunting of the *fatal* edge of *its* sword. In another metaphor, "The substance of death in us will one day be drained off" [17]. And the devil himself, even though he does not voluntarily bow, must be subjected, because the completion of Christ's kingdom means that his kingship is com-

---

13) *Comm.* Rom. 16:20, p. 551.

14) *Comm.* Isa. 45:23, III, 428.

15) *Comm.* Matt. 24:26, III, 142 (author's transl.).

16) *Comm.* II Thes. 2:7 f., pp. 335 f.

17) See *Comm.* I Cor. 15:26, II, 29, I Cor. 15:57, II, 65 f.

pletely demolished [18]. Further, the Pauline conclusion that God shall be all in all does not mean that Satan shall be reconciled, but precisely the opposite — that he who is incorrigibly evil must be destroyed and, in this destruction, God's glory displayed [19].

This negative aspect does not, of course, fully describe the final realization of Christ's kingdom. The destruction of death fulfills our rebirth "of incorruptible seed" [20]. Calvin paints the eschatological realization of life's victory over death in dramatic military hues: "Just as a commander assembles his army to battle at the call of the trumpets, so Christ will call together all the dead with a penetrating voice understandable throughout the whole world" [21]. The comfort which Calvin offered to those approaching martyrdom for their faith was, of course, this dramatic portrayal of God's ultimate victory for them and their participation in the everlasting kingdom of Christ [22].

Calvin connects these two apparently contradictory elements — negative and positive, destruction and eternal blessedness — by making the completion of Christ's kingship at the *parousia* and the resurrection of the dead synonymous [23]. Thus, Calvin thinks the New Testament uses Psalms 12:10 and 110:1 to describe the eschatological war between death and life: "Now, death will not be destroyed till the last day. The kingdom is, then, given to Christ till the end of the world, and his kingdom cannot exist without his life" [24]. Calvin had no sympathy with a Millenarian attempt, represented in his day by Enthusiasts or Anabaptists, to interpret Rev. 20:4 as identical with the content of the blessed hope. With Augustine he thought that this thousand years refers to "the various agitations which awaited the Church in its militant state upon earth". He feared that chiliasm represents human ignorance and perversity led by Satanic influence "to overturn all the grace of God and power of Christ". He opposed this by insisting that there will

18) *Comm.* Phil. 2:10, p. 63.

19) *Comm.* I Cor. 15:28, II, 33.

20) *Comm.* I Cor. 15:26, II, 28 f.

21) *Comm.* I Cor. 15:52, II, 59 (author's transl.).

22) CE II, 394.

23) Quistorp, *op. cit.,* p. 108, thinks because of this that a representation of the eschatology of Calvin in the more exact sense could also be headed: the future of Jesus Christ.

24) *Comm.* John 20:9, II, 253.

be *no end* of the happiness of the elect, or the punishment of the reprobate [25].

The claim that the dead are raised includes the problem of the relation between "the immortality of the soul" and "the resurrection of the body". We have previously shown that the immortality of the soul as the answer to the problem of death plays a vital role in Calvin's thought. Beyond this, as Quistorp points out, the Reformers' complete rejection of purgatory gave a greatly heightened significance to the hour of death as the eternally decisive moment [26]. The fact that Calvin's *Psychopannuchia* is the only significant writing of either his or Luther's which has an eschatological topic as its main theme underlines the place of this problem at the heart of his eschatology. As the name of this writing — *Wakefulness* (through the whole night, *pannuchizein*) *of the Soul* — indicates, Calvin engaged in a controversy (against spiritual Libertines and Anabaptists) about the sleep of the soul [27]. In this writing, interestingly, the body is not so much devaluated as the soul is exalted, although many sentences (for example, "The difference between the heavenly soul and the earthly body is as great as the distance between the heaven and earth", *Psychopan.* 55; 197) make it clear that Calvin cannot hold the two of equal worth. The issue for Calvin is that the soul (or spirit) is an independent substance, different from the mortal body, created by God as immortal [28]. To make this point, Calvin can, in the extreme case, go so far as directly to emend Paul [29] by referring to the soul or spirit as the temple of the Holy Spirit [30].

Although Calvin thus robs the body of an important New Testament attribute and bestows it on the soul, he is by no means unaware that the resurrection of the body is essential to the Christian conception of the future life: "I readily acknowledge that the philosophers, who were ignorant of the *resurrection* of the body, have many discussions about the immortal essence of the soul; but they talk so foolishly about the state of the future life that their opinions have no weight ... But since the Scriptures inform us that the

---

25) III, xxv, 5. See note 9.
26) Quistorp, *op. cit.,* p. 2.
27) See *Intro.* to *Comm.* on I Cor. 15.
28) *Op. cit.,* 23; 177 and 32; 184.
29) I Cor. 6.
30) III, xxv, 6.

spiritual life depends on the hope of the resurrection, and that they should, when separated from the bodies, look forward to it, ... Whoever destroys the *resurrection* deprives souls also of their immortality" [31]. Since the immortal wakeful soul goes directly to Christ upon the death of the body, the day of resurrection sees the raising of the body but not the soul. Calvin is here concerned that there shall be continuity between the body which walked this earth and that in heaven, lest the union in Christ's body — the *conformitas* between Head and body — be destroyed [32].

The question of life after death is probably the master key to a theologian's eschatology. It reveals first whether his view of man is primarily Hebraic or Idealistic, and then reveals the consequences of this first discovery for ethics. Calvin seems to affirm both Hebraic and Idealistic views, resurrection of the body and immortality of the soul [33]. Quistorp refers to this double affirmation as a contradiction between Calvin's "Biblical realism" and his tendency toward "spiritualism". We have just seen a sample of the former in Calvin's concern for human continuity between life and life after death, which can only be assured by the resurrection of the body. The realism of the Bible could conceive of no form of human existence which could be dis-embodied [34]. For late Old Testament apocalypticism, the Pharisees, and their Christian allies in this area of theology, God's *justice* requires life beyond this life where justice is meted out for deeds, both good and ill, "done in the body". Man's embodiment individuates him and makes him responsible. Therefore, life beyond death is only significant on the basis of the resurrection of the body, and Calvin affirms this "Biblical realism". His systematic affirmation is immediately suspect because he also affirms Plato's "immortality of the soul". Actually, at this juncture Calvin accepts Plato's Idealistic or "spiritualized" dualism for the sake of its possibility (unique among classic philosophies) for a conception of life after death, and against the more materialistic dualism of Aristotle which, like the wisdom literature of the Old Testament

---

31) *Comm.* Matt. 22:23, III, 48.

32) At this point Calvin follows Augustine in differentiating between the *substantia* and the *qualitas* of the body. While the substance remains the same in the resurrection, the quality is changed. See III, xxv, 5, 7, 18 and *Comm.* I Cor. 15:53, II, 61.

33) III, xxv, 6.

34) Note Paul's horror of such nakedness of the conscious "we", II Cor. 5:3.

(especially Ecclesiastes) excludes life after death[35]. Calvin's position, however, is also distinct from Plato. He is willing to use Plato's word "immortal" — as is Paul on rare occasions such as in I Cor. 15:53 f.[36] — but immortality belongs properly, *de natura,* to God alone[37]. For Plato, then, man's soul is divine and therefore innately immortal, but Calvin attacks this opinion as one of the points at issue in his *Treatise on Free Will against Pighius*: "... we do not agree that the soul is immortal of itself"[38]. As Wendel correctly paraphrases Calvin: "Not only is the soul created but its immortality is a gift of God which he could withdraw from the soul if he wished"[39].

Classical Idealism is not the real enemy Quistorp fears, however, when he speaks of Calvin's "spiritualizing". When Calvin uses the word "spiritual" it conjures up for Quistorp idealization, abstraction, the imaginary, the nebulous world of mysticism which crystallized in the German soul in Meister Eckhardt, 1260—1329, with his personal mixture of diverse elements drawn from such sources as St. Thomas, Neo-Platonism, St. Bernard, Averroes, Avicenna, and Maimonides. "Spiritualized" for the German mind refers to the influence of Eckhardt on Luther (who knew his ideas only through such works as Tauler's *Theologia Deutsch*), on Jacob Böhme (1575—1624), and on the German Idealism of the nineteenth century, especially Kant, Hegel and, through them and Schelling, Paul Tillich[40]. But Calvin is no mystic, German or otherwise, and Quistorp's two-dimensional representation of the mind of the enormously complex Swiss Reformer is a false alternative. For Calvin, "spiritual" is not the antithesis but the essence of Biblical realism. For the Old Testament — where Lutheranism has always charged that Calvin lives — "Spirit is power is God" in contrast to "flesh is weakness is man". For Calvin, therefore, the *spiritual* presence of Christ in the Lord's Supper is more effective, more real than the presence in the Zwinglian memory *or* the presence in the

---

35) See I, v, 5 and esp. n. 16.
36) See also II Tim. 1:10.
37) I Tim. 1:17 and 6:16.
38) Quoted in Wendel, *op. cit.,* p. 175, see n. 77.
39) *Ibid.*
40) See Heussi, *op. cit.,* p. 248 f., and behind him the texts and studies written and edited by K. Werner, W. Preger, F. Pfeiffer, A. Spamer, K. Grunewald, R. Otto, H. Denifle, M. Grabmann, O. Karrer and H. Ebeling and cited on p. 246.

Lutheran "Real" ubiquity. For Calvin, the Spirit never works *immediately* (this mystic and Enthusiastic term is one of the words Calvin most derides). His longest book (IV of the 1559 Institutes) is dedicated to the *external media* by which God (the Spirit) invites us into the society of Christ and holds us therein. Calvin can outdo the Bible in "Biblical realism" precisely in this "spiritualism": for him the weight of the Spirit's action in the conversion of Paul falls not upon the experience on the road to Damascus, which the sermons attributed to Paul in the book of Acts stress and which was unmediated by the church, but on the reception of Saul by the church and the interpretation of his experience by Ananias [41].

Therefore Calvin's *meditatio futurae vitae* cannot be written off as empty mystic contemplation but is an element of tough-minded practical calculation for the present life. Really, only in the remotest eschatological future after Christ has peeled off the armor, the person of the Mediator, and we are left alone with God (if not absorbed in him) could Calvin conceivably be charged with Quistorp's kind of "spiritualizing", so different from his own.

Following the resurrection of the dead, Calvin expects the great judgment of Christ. That judgment precedes grace in Calvin's theology is directly stated with reference to the eschatological events: "The grace of God is never manifested for the salvation of the godly, till his judgment first appears for the destruction of the world; and for two reasons; because God then separates his own people from the reprobate, and because his wrath is kindled anew by the ingratitude of the world" [42]. Calvin looks to this judgment as the complete extension of Christ's authority over the whole world, as the ultimate justice toward which we must now look when injustice appears to prevail, as the decisive moment which, though possibly long delayed, hangs over us every hour [43]. And Calvin looks upon this judgment as a sort of personal triumph, for he prefers to understand "we shall judge angels" [44] to mean that we shall judge the devils [45]. Unfortunately, Calvin's conception is not free from "un-

---

41) Acts 9:17 f.

42) *Comm.* Matt. 3:10, I, 192. Note also the title of Book III, Chapter xii, "Consideration of the Divine tribunal is necessary to a serious conviction of gratuitous justification".

43) *Comm.* Isa. 45:23, III, 428

44) I Cor. 6:3.

45) *Comm. loc. cit.*, I, 201.

evangelical" vindictiveness when he writes Beza (at at time when the French royal court was unfavorable) that we shall sit at the feet of the triumphant Christ and be able from this height "to scorn all his enemies and ours!" [46]

The negative aspect of the final defeat and judgment of the enemies in the spiritual warfare — as important as it is to Calvin's eschatology and as deep an impression as it leaves upon us — is only the preparatory stage for the restoration of God's creation in and by Christ. When Calvin sees all creatures in the height and in the depth as heralds calling men to the judgment, he envisions the whole creation pressed into the service of its Lord who is being revealed [47]. Interestingly, however, he provides the restoration of all things (after the judgment) with a double foundation. In the first place, he says that Christ will appear openly to establish perfect order in heaven and earth, not as a simple ratification of the creation's present form of existence, but because through Christ the whole cosmos is promised an imperishable life [48]. The whole creation must be reformed and transfigured, passing through a sort of condemnation to death into a new life [49]. In the second place, Calvin makes the redemption of the whole creation dependent upon that of man. This is already clear when he writes: "Lastly, the renovation of *the world* must be preceded by (our) mortification" [50]. This point becomes unmistakable in the extensive statement which climaxes in the words, "But when we shall be perfectly renewed, heaven and earth shall also be fully renewed, and shall regain their former state" [51]. In this idea we encounter two serious limitations of Calvin's eschatology: First, we meet once again with creation's anthropocentricity which in general limits the freedom of God to act directly upon it and in particular has cancelled its original goodness; second, we see clear evidence of Calvin's tendency to relegate the cosmic dimension of eschatology to an importance secondary to the perfection of the elect.

After the judgment, which has resolved the last remaining human tensions, we come to the peculiar, difficult and dangerous doctrine

---

46) CG II, 381.
47) *Comm.* Matt. 24:30, III, 148
48) *Comm.* Matt. 25:31, III, 175
49) *Comm.* Heb. 12:27, p. 337 f.
50) *Comm.* John 12:31, II, 369. See also III, xxv, 11. n. 25.
51) *Comm.* Isa. 65:17, IV, 398 f.

of the deliverance and subjection of Christ's kingdom and Christ himself to God (the Father). For, as soon as the restoration is complete, the role of Calvin's Chalcedonian Mediator is at an end: *telos* becomes *finis*, perfection and completion become termination and even, in a sense, cessation. This entire conception depends on Calvin's exegesis of I Cor. 15:24-28. Paul teaches, first, that Christ shall deliver the kingdom to the Father, "When he shall have abolished all rule" (v. 24). Calvin takes this to mean not simply that the enemies of God shall be destroyed, but also that every form of distinction and rank which is connected with this present order shall be set aside [52]. Still more decisive is Calvin's inference from "(Christ) must reign *until* he has put all his enemies under his feet", (v. 27) that Christ will not reign thereafter. He can indeed speak of the eternal kingdom of Christ, but by this he means insofar as Christ is *God* the Son, one with the Father to whom he transfers the kingship. The next step, then, is Paul's statement: "the Son himself will also be subject to the Father" (v. 28). Calvin asserts in systematic commentary: "Let us wait patiently until Christ shall vanquish all his enemies, and shall bring us, along with himself, under the dominion of God, that the kingdom of God may be in every respect accomplished in us" [53]. Further, in one of his sermons, Calvin announces that when he is called viceroy of God (*lieutenant de Dieu,* the same term Calvin applies to earthly magistrates), Christ is the one (but merely the) means (*moyen*) through which God himself reigns [54]. Finally, Calvin's conclusion rests on the phrase, "that God may be all in all" (v. 28).

What Calvin means when he says that God shall be *all in all* is that we shall behold him and be united with him immediately (unmediatedly). Always before and elsewhere Calvin emphasizes the necessity of Christ coming and assuming our humanity and exercizing the office of Mediator between God and man, *on account of the enemies and the enmity between us and him*. Now that the enemies and the enmity are destroyed, however, Calvin sees the mediatorship of Christ and in a certain sense (or measure, or way, *quodammodo*) *Christ's humanity standing in the way* of this immediate relation between God and man. "Then the *velum* (the veil of Christ's flesh) will fall and we shall behold the glory of God who

---

52) *Comm.* I Cor. 15:24, II, 27.
53) *Comm.* I Cor. 15:27, II, 31.
54) *Sermon* on Eph. 1:19—23, CR LXXIX, 339.

rules his own kingdom; Christ's humanity which *hinders the perfect view of God* will no longer stand in the middle" [55]. This demonstrates that our parable of the humanity of Christ as a suit of armor worn by the Son of God comes uncomfortably close to correctly representing the last stage of that *Heilsgeschichte* which is Calvin's Christology. What remains if the Christian, whose blessing and very survival have otherwise depended on union with Christ, can no longer depend on his union with the exalted God-*man*? Calvin seems to think of a *spiritual* contemplation of God, but the foundation which otherwise anchors his "spiritualizing tendency" to the Gospel is shaken when he says of the Holy Spirit, the earnest ("guarantee" or "first installment" would be more modern translations of *aparchē*) of our inheritance of eternal life: "So long as we are in this world, our warfare is sustained by hope, and therefore this earnest is necessary; but when the possession itself shall have been obtained, the necessity and use of the earnest will then cease" [56]. When the single word *quodammodo* is the only explicit reservation which allows us to conjecture that the humanity of Christ, through which alone we are united with God, does not — according to Calvin — simply evaporate or dissolve into Christ's divinity [57], and when "the necessity and use of" Christ's Spirit "will cease", we have few weapons with which to defend Calvin's eschatology in this area. Our only consolation is our agreement with Quistorp that we are not to carry these more or less isolated ideas *ad absurdam* and that Calvin himself did not draw the implicit consequences of the end of Christ's humanity for humanity as such, and for the effective result of God's total *Heilsgeschichte*.

Finally, Calvin brings us briefly to consider the eternal blessedness and damnation of God's creatures following the Last Judgment and the transfer of Christ's kingdom to the Father. Since Calvin rejects purgatory as unbiblical [58], a great gulf is fixed between the two groups of people, as is clearly symbolized in the metaphorical bosom of Abraham [59]. In describing this blessedness, Calvin again

---

55) *Comm.* I Cor. 15:27, II, 32 f. (author's transl.).

56) *Comm.* Eph. 1:14, p. 209.

57) This again is an idea *expressed* by Servetus and rejected by Calvin, who also sees (IV, xvii, 29) that it is implied by Lutheran ubiquity. In describing the end of the *Heilsgeschichte,* however, Calvin allows his own mind to drift in this direction.

58) III, xxv, 5.

59) *Comm.* Gen. 49:19, II, 465.

strongly emphasizes the metaphor of spiritual warfare: just as the soldier's material rewards can only come after the victory of his cause, so the rewards of spiritual warfare are bestowed in the blessedness of God's eternal kingdom. The believers then participate in the final victory and triumph of Christ over his enemies and theirs [60]. "Then Paul will enjoy the triumph of the many victories that he had obtained under Christ's auspices, and will lead forth in splendor all the nations that have, by means of his ministry, been brought under Christ's glorious yoke"; then we shall see the crowning of faithful warriors with the crown of life, which is the highest honor and joy of the *miles Christi;* and even see the entrance of the resurrected bodies, "which God trains under the banner of the cross, and honors with the glory of victory" [61]. Individual Christians are also like pilgrims who, after finishing their course, "return to Christ" [62]. All of this seems to lend support to the oft-repeated charge that Calvin's eschatology is individualistic. Yet actually the individual members of Christ's one body are rewarded, the individual units and men of one vast victorious army are being decorated. Calvin generally makes implicit and often explicit reference to the church as a whole: "... this prophecy may be applied to the whole church, which is assailed not for one day only, but is perpetually crushed by fresh attacks, until at length God shall exalt it to honor" [63].

Considering Calvin's sense of rigid justice and logical balance in all areas, we cannot expect him to leave the reprobate undamned. To be sure, all men deserve damnation, and every rebel who is not selected to be saved from it falls beneath the eternal curse, the wicked men to go join the devil and his angels in eternal fire and everlasting destruction [64]. Finally, it may be of interest to note that for Calvin — the so-called spiritualizer who sought a less inhumane *means* of execution for Servetus — the eternal torture of the damned is essentially spiritual, the Biblical pictures being purely figurative (this, of course, is commensurate with his view of Christ's descent into hell).

---

60) See Quistorp, *op. cit.,* p. 153.

61) *Comm.* II Cor. 1:14, II, 130; III, xxv, 8 (Allen).

62) *Comm.* II Cor. 5:9, II, 225.

63) *Comm.* Gen. 49:19, II, 465. Quistorp also ultimately recognizes this, *op. cit.,* p. 186.

64) *Comm.* Matt. 25:43, III, 182 f.

Just as the relation of Calvin's eschatology to his theology as a whole is that of the capital stone which completes the building, final victory and the triumphant state is the final Act without which the drama of spiritual warfare would remain agonizingly incomplete, leaving us in the confusion Camus called Sisyphus labor: unending and therefore fruitless struggle. Eschatology may not be the driving force of Calvin's theology, but it is the necessary conclusion. This solid achievement is forced upon Calvin as part of the *Heilsgeschichte* which marks him, in the judgment of Wilhelm Pauck, ultimately not as a theologian of the sovereignty of God, or of predestination or providence, or of justification by faith, but as a profoundly Biblical theologian [65]. On the one hand, it is solely because of this "Biblicism" or "Biblical realism" that Quistorp can speak of Calvin as the Reformation's leader in bringing eschatology again to its rightful place of honor in the heart of the evangelical faith. On the other hand, when Calvin measures the consequences of his basic theological decisions against Biblical eschatology, he reveals some of the most important limitations and weaknesses of his thought. The church today urgently needs Biblical scholars who, like Calvin, are not afraid to formulate a Christian theology, and theologians who, like Calvin, are bold enough to measure their work by the most exacting of all standards — the written form of the Word of God.

---

65) W. Pauck, "Calvin's Institutes of the Christian Religion", *Church History* XV (1946), pp. 17—27.

EPILOGUE: MODERN WARFARE WITH THE SPIRIT'S SWORD

In our Preface to Calvin's drama we said that we were not going to climb mountains (proceed historically), we were going to investigate a house (proceed systematically). Now that we have reached the Epilogue to Calvin's drama we realize that we have explored Calvin's house, the theatre in which he lived and worked. And though we have visited it "dressed" in the scenery and costumes of one particular drama we have come to know it all quite intimately. Or perhaps we are so much at home in Calvin's "house" precisely because we have experienced always only the same play. As we have seen how the whole house "works" together, however, we have discovered that all along we have been mountain-climbing, too, after all. The actors and the spectators we have met — Martin Bucer, Hapsburg Holy Roman Emperor Charles V, Copernicus, Elizabeth I of England, Erasmus of Rotterdam and Basel, Francis I of France, Galileo, Henry VIII, Ignatius of Loyola, Martin Luther, Nicholai Machiavelli, the Marys — Bloody and Scot, Melanchthon, Michelangelo, Servetus, Zwingli, to name a few in simple alphabetical order — have taken us out of Calvin's theatre onto the streets and highways of the sixteenth century. Outside, in "real" life, we discover that the drama inside Calvin's house, the *warfare with the Spirit's sword* which answers the petition "deliver us from Evil", describes man living in that wild mountain pass of history as tellingly as Ephesians 6 describes man in the similar world of the first century of our era. Then, when we reverse our vantage we discover that the Epilogue to Calvin's drama cannot be a mere summary of spiritual warfare in the sixteenth century; it must be Prologue to that of our own time, challenging us to *modern warfare with the Spirit's sword.*

This fact is transparent because the good fight against Evil is as unmistakably imperative today as in any crucial age in history. Except where man emulates the ostrich, hell bulks ominously beneath the thin skin of modern reality. This may appear odd in the impersonal technological age unless we take seriously Robert Ardrey's contention (in *African Genesis*) that *homo faber*, "man the toolmaker", has always been the euphemism for man the forger of weapons; or unless we remember that technology has always — at least until now — been developed (first) for the sake of destructive war: civil, mechanical, and electrical engineering — bridges and roads, machines, power, communications (military intelligence); the chemistry of molecules — conventional explosives; nuclear physics — uranium, hydrogen, cobalt bombs. The unrelenting imminence of a war of destruction drives us to consider *the war of reconciliation,* the good fight with the Spirit's sword. It is this which justifies, indeed demands of theology, a thorough study of a soldier-dramatist of the *militia Christi.* No more appropriate subject could be found than this Founding Father of modern Anglo-Saxon culture who lived, created, fought in such a mountain pass of history as the sixteenth century. From Calvin we have to learn that warfare is still necessary, and that precisely in our materialistic century it has to be spiritual, i. e. defined by use of the Spirit's healing sword and not fought with Evil's destructive weapons or for evil ends.

Thus, our Epilogue retains the terminoloy "with the Spirit's sword" because the intellectual problems of man's spiritual struggle remain the same as formulated in the first century (especially by Paul), and in the sixteenth century by Calvin and Loyola. Walter Stuermann, mathematician and Calvin scholar, has taken the first steps toward a twentieth century formulaion of evil as a theological problem in *Logic and Faith,* his contribution to the Westminster communication series. Evil becomes a problem when it enters the field of force defined by the tension between God's goodness and his power, which Stuermann symbolizes as g and p (which we shall capitalize here). Since the problem thus created is logically insoluble, theology has toyed with the concepts of limited goodness (which Stuermann calls G') and limited power (P'). Mathematically, these four variables offer us four possible combinations with which to meet the dilemma of evil. Stuermann describes them as GP, G'P, GP' and G'P'. (We have dealt with this formulation as a paradigmatic *formal* problem for the logic of theology in *The Common Quest,* Chapter III, "Theology as a Science". Its primary *material* use, however, is at the base of spiritual warfare.)

GP′ (unlimited goodness, but limited power) is a proposed so-lution to the problem of evil, tempting not only to simple purists willing to sacrifice the scope and intensity of God's sovereignty to preserve his goodness, but to all the virile souls tempted by Gnostic and Manichean dualism, from Marcion and the young Augustine through Luther and his northernmost disciples. If God be he who *reveals* himself as unsullied goodness in Jesus, the reality of evil demands that there must also be some other God, a demi-urge, a *deus absconditus,* or else a Satanic counterpoise. Such a view at best, however, condemns "the kingdom of the world" to existence out-side redemptive reach and theological ethics are ultimately so irrelevant that some *Unmensch,* some inhuman Hitler, can leap into the power void.

Stuermann himself has the courage of Calvin's conviction and opts for the exploration of G′P (limited goodness but unlimited power). What is gained is scope, the vast interstellar spaces and forces of the cosmos known to modern science and expressed in Calvin's panergistic omni-potent God. But the God who operates in *all* is responsible for all, including the destructive works of Evil. Though Calvin sees this danger and shrinks back from saying G′P, he never really escapes Castellio's charge that "Calvin's God is worse that the devil".

G′P′ (which leaves God limited in both dimensions) is as modern as the relativist ethic, and just as ethically impotent and unsatis-fying. It is the Pelagian pluralism which levels God to man and makes both appealingly indecisive and forgivable. It is oriented to-ward an impartial fairness and exhaustive completeness which is neither Biblical (in the theological co-ordinate) nor realistic (in the pragmatic one).

This survey throws us back on the logically impossible classic assertion GP: God is both perfectly good and all-powerful, even in the presence of Evil — that sum of forces which destroy men and relationships — which is operative in human history. "P" emphasizes the forces which *bear* upon man and "G" asserts ulti-mate faith in man's destiny — beyond his Fall into sin and death. Only this "insoluble" formulation of the problem does justice to the ethical tensions within which man exists. Only the tension be-tween G and P is compatible with the Christological paradox of the *unio personalis* of the Mediator who reconciles in his person and work infinite and finite, powerful and impotent, offended Creator and offending creature. *That God took upon himself in Christ all the evils which oppress man, within and without, is the only Christian answer to the problem of evil.* And every age of theology must learn *how* to express this answer correctly, relevantly, and beautifully for the men and women of its own time.

This brings us to the dissonance sounded in the symbolism of the title for our Epilogue: *Modern* warfare with the Spirit's *sword.* The sword is simply not an effective modern weapon. This makes *Calvin's* "theology of spiritual warfare" (and Paul's for that matter) now charmingly obsolete. It must be replaced by one which *meets* the *terms* of modernity. We cannot meet the terms of modernity by such a simple substitution as that in the linguistic equation: we must now fight the good fight with the Spirit's ICBM. The unavoidable question, What does "modern" mean for theology in this case? is not answered, because "ICBM" is not yet a rich enough symbol, for all its mighty and modern sound. To be sure, "modern" means "technological", but even "technological" goes beyond machines to the men and nations who not only shape them but are in turn shaped by them. Thus, the technological wars of the twentieth century, both brush-fire police-action and cosmic conflagration, cry out for a total peace offensive by all of man's political institutions against the enemies of the race which erupt from deep within him. The same *demonic forces* alternatively *take the shape* of race riots and poverty riots around the world, challenging the social structures and economic channels designed to harness and bridle all energies. Finally, the towering, teeming concrete canyons of Manhattan symbolize the forces which threaten to crush the human psyche. These pressures compel us to cry: Has a human species yet been evolved which is sufficiently flexible, tough, and resourceful to endure the presence of the technological monster vulnerable man has made?

Whence shall come the power and the tools to deal with these demons? In "Theology as a Craft of Conduct" (Chapter IV of *The Common Quest*) we have· attempted to explore the avenues of dialogue along which theology and the "social" or "behavioral" sciences may attack such problems. In this dialogue, they provide techniques of analysis and evaluation for the description and prediction of "social processes". Theology contributes through the essential task of prescription it is enabled to undertake by virtue of its more conscious attention to the ultimate good, and to the related proximate goods for man which underlie *all* meaningful efforts of political science, economics, sociology, and psychology. This last-named discipline and the very description of its problems with the mechanistic-yet-self-transcending psyche reminds us that ethics cannot live by science and its logic alone: Calvin is right in using art — above all dramatic and narrative — to express in the *metaphor* of spiritual warfare his answer to the almost overwhelming existential ethical problems engendered by Evil. All the weapons of natural science and of the related crafts of human conduct are not enough; the tools of art, too, must be flung into the fray.

When we turn to the modern arts with this in mind they shout at us that they have been at this task long before us who are scientists of society and of theology. For the last fifty years many artists have spent their major creative energies describing and attempting to deal with Evil, with the demonic, with chaos, the irrational, the grotesque, the non-representable, the dissonant, the painful, the absurd. And theology, from its side, has limped with snail-like pace toward its encounter with the modernity mirrored by art. Calvin's mind had the clarity and power to rediscover and retain something close to the heart of the Bible's Gospel *and* to express it in the lingua franca of the Renaissance which defined his modernity. Jonathan Edwards began with Calvin's Bible — as the Reformers had with Augustine's — which he translated into the exciting new language of Newton's physics and Locke's psychology. And we, "theologians of modernity . . ."?

It is a problem of symbols, of communication; yet it is not as though we merely needed to agree on an International Morse Code we all understood anyway. Rather, our problem of communication demands that we understand how symbols work: *what* they are trying to get at: *how* they convey this to the symbolizer; *how* he translates them into other symbols which he thinks may communicate them to "less symbolic" men; and then *how* he transmits them into the ether which separates him from the neighbor he has been told to love.

Theology always begins and begins again with the Bible, but only a museum-piece theology can afford to end there. When Albert Camus says to one of his characters in *The Fall,* "You know the Bible; you interest me", he does not mean that the problem of communication is solved thereby, but that the problems and the proposed solutions may now begin to operate on us and on each other. "You know the Bible" and thus you are heir to an inexhaustible treasury of symbols and presumably, therefore, you are at least aware that symbolization is a problem. We have been using the Bible's *personalized* symbolism for Evil: Satan, Lucifer, Diabolos, Sin, Death, Flesh, Law, and Calvin has encouraged us to do so — as though they somehow "spoke" to modern man and had not received the death-blow in the eighteenth century. We are eternally in the debt of the Enlightenment which banished forever the superstitious shapes which pointlessly plagued ancient and medieval man. We must not leap back over that firebreak created by the burning glass of Enlightenment's Reason. It is no good to react against it as does Romanticism by apotheosizing the Irrational, whether like the nineteenth century French novelists catalogued in the Carmelites' *Satan* or like Paul Tillich who — after all due regard is paid to his daring symbolic experiments — ultimately depends on the assumption that the mystic ontology (he might prefer neontology) of Jakob Böhme and the German Idealists really speaks to our "modernity". "Satan" and the Spirit's "Excalibar" are still there but, like Arthur Adamov who cannot find a word for what people used to call God, we no longer know their *proper* names.

At the beginning of modern theology — stands Karl Barth. At first, he symbolized Evil or Darkness as Culture and Culture-theology in that pioneering period, 1919—33. Then in the presence of the demonic state (Tillich had earlier developed the concept of the self-absolutizing "demonic" from philosophical roots) Barth discovered [1] that the angelic-demonic forces known to Biblical apocalypticism — especially Daniel, Paul, Mark 13 and Matthean parallels, and Revelation — symbolize variant forms of the state. His unique discovery, however, was that because of the decisive Christ-event even the demonic state is already now objectively under the lordship of Christ. The systematic contemplation of creation required by writing his *Dogmatics* led him to a higher level of symbolism than the history of Christian thought has usually provided. Therefore he carried on his discussion of Evil (*das Nichtige,* the Negational) with Martin Heidegger and Jean-Paul Sartre in *Church Dogmatics* III, 3 because "that is where the demons reside, nowadays". (It may well be that theology's dialogue with modernity about evil *must* begin in Marburg, 1924—28, in the matrix of theo-

---

1) With the help of Günther Dehn's article on the "powers" of Rom. 13:1 ff., and possibly Martin Dibelius, *Die Geisterwelt im Glauben des Paulus.*

logical existentialism where Being and Time, myth and history, and creative existence-unto-death met — but that is another book. This is where Rudolf Bultmann began, but his preoccupation with the *Weltbild* (cosmographic) *problem* leads him to the conclusion that in the New Testament the demonic powers "really express only a specific understanding of existence". Thus, for example, he seems slightly miffed that the author of Eph. 2:1-3 contaminates his discussion of trespasses, sins, passions, and desires with talk about the prince of the power of the air.) Barth leaves us with a feeling that the true church today lives again in a pre-Constantinian era powerless in the power politics of this world and therefore radically free for its own life and theology. Theoretically, Barth's theology is free to forge new weapons with modern terminological tools — always provided that dogmatics proves them on the testing range of the Biblical witness. In practice, Barth tends to limit his service to renovating proven weapons, to rethinking classic Christian dogma, theology's indispensably primary task — if indeed there are others. Reinhold Niebuhr has embodied the conviction that there is another task, that the true test of theology is its relevance to man's needs for love and justice. His encounter with social and political life drove him beyond the Pelagian pretense to the realization that evil is greater than the sum of man's wickedness, and that the Biblical Satan like Tillich's "demonic" is a symbol for that reality.

These all are tantalizing suggestions, fragments of solutions to the predicament expressed by the facts that *spiritual warfare* must be fought in the *modern* world, but that we do not know precisely what weapons the Spirit provides in an era when swords and shields and breastplates are ludicrous in comparison with sophisticated rocketry, electronics and nuclear power. Since, as Calvin reminds us, the warfare corresponds to the weapons, our ignorance of the weapons means that we do not yet really understand the modern warfare against evil, either. What symbols, what logical techniques, what language shall we borrow to express GP and the meaning of the reconciliation (in the Mediator) of man estranged from God and from himself? Art, science and even philosophy offer tantalizing fragments crying for a synthesis. Since Hebrew, Greek and Latin are classic raw materials for the theologian and modern man has a new math, the tempter tempts us to the premature formulation of an ethical tour de force, to be unwitting false prophets, to think we have solved war and plumbed the secret depths of social, racial and personal explosives with *agapē* plus *eros* plus *charitas* equals *zedek* plus *mishpat* plus *dikaiōsunē* equals *shalom* plus *eirēnē* plus *pax* equals peace, peace, peace — where there is none to be found. To do this would be to write off the Evil which frustrates ethics, and by self-deception to serve the strategy of the enemy. We must be content to work and wait until we understand better how to express and implement the spiritual warfare in which half-knowing we win some skirmishes today. Here, we must be content with what Calvin has taught us about his time, and about the nature of Christian truth, and about ourselves.

The good fight he has fought against evil with the Spirit's sword, his life's blood spent in struggle to the death, has brought us hard won truths: that God is great and good and purposeful; that man is good and weak, too weak for Evil which is active and powerful; that therefore for man *vivere militare est,* man is inevitably engaged in the fight of his life; that we are given the strength and morale to wage this *spiritual* warfare by the victory of the Mediator which has decided its ultimate outcome in our favor. There are few truths modern man more needs to learn. Few men have contributed so much as John Calvin to our instruction.

FOOTNOTES

Key to Abbreviations
(For full titles see the Bibliography)

CR — Volume in the Corpus Reformatorum (NOT CO, volume of the *Calvini opera,* which begins with vol. XXIX of the CR).

OS — *Johannis Calvin Opera Selecta,* ed. P. Barth and W. Niesel.

CL — Correspondence in Latin within the CR.

CF — Correspondence in French (Herminjard).

CE — Calvin Translation Society selection from the correspondence.

CG — German translation of selection from the correspondence (Schwarz).

EA — Erlangen Ausgabe of Luther's Works.

WA — Weimar Ausgabe of Luther's Works.

Comm — Calvin's Biblical Commentaries *ad loc.*

e. a. — Emphasis added by present author.

I, i, 1 — Book, chapter, section of LCC edition of the 1959 Institutes.

BIBLIOGRAPHY

Allers, Rudolf, ed., *Anselm von Canterbury, Leben, Lehre, Werke,* Vienna: Thomas-Verlag Jakob Hegner, 1936.

Anselm of Canterbury, *Cur Deus Homo?,* (Migne, J.-P., *Patrologia latina,* Vols. CLVIII—CLIX), Paris, 1844—64.

— *De Casu Diaboli,* (Migne, J.-P., *Patrologia latina,* CLVIII—CLIX), Paris, 1844—64.

Aulén, Gustav, *Christus Victor,* tr. by A. C. Hebert, The Macmillan Co., 1931.

Bainton, Roland H., *Here I Stand: A Life of Martin Luther,* Abingdon Press, 1950.

— *Hunted Heretic,* The Beacon Press, 1953.

— "The Left Wing of the Reformation", *The Journal of Religion* XXI (1941), 2, pp. 124—34.

Barth, Karl, *Kirchliche Dogmatik,* Zollikon-Zürich: Evangelischer Verlag, 1955 ff.; Engl. tr.: *Church Dogmatics,* tr. by G. T. Thomson, G. W. Bromiley, T. F. Torrance et al, Charles Scribner's Sons, 1955 ff.

— *Rechtfertigung und Recht* (Theologische Studien, No. 1), Zollikon-Zürich: Evangelischer Verlag, 1938: Engl. tr.: *Church and State,* tr. by G. Ronald Howe, London: Student Christian Movement Press, 1939 (also in *Community, State and Church,* Anchor Books, 1960).

Barth, Peter, *Das Problem der natürlichen Theologie bei Calvin* (Theologische Existenz Heute, No. 18), Munich: Chr. Kaiser Verlag, 1935.

Battenhouse, Roy W., "The Doctrine of Man in Calvin and in Renaissance Platonism", *Journal of the History of Ideas* IX (1948), pp. 469 f.

Berger, Heinrich, *Calvins Geschichtsauffassung,* Zürich: Zwingli-Verlag, 1955

Blume, F., *Die evangelische Kirchenmusik,* Potsdam: Athenaion, 1931.

Boehmer, Heinrich, *Der junge Luther,* Gotha: Flamberg, 1925 (3rd edn., Heinrich Bornkamm, ed., 1939); Engl. tr. (from the 2nd edn. of 1929): *Road to Reformation: Martin Luther to the Year 1521,* tr. by John W. Doberstein and Theodore G. Tappert, Muhlenberg Press, 1946.

Bohatec, J., *Budé und Calvin: Studien zur Gedankenwelt des französischen Frühhumanismus,* Graz: Böhlau, 1950.

— *Calvins Lehre von Staat und Kirche,* Breslau: Marcus, 1937.

— *Calvin und das Recht,* Feudingen: Buchdruck und Verlags-Anstalt, 1934.

Boisset, Jean, *Sagesse et sainteté dans la pensée de Jean Calvin,* Paris: Presses Universitaires de France, 1959.

Borgeaud, Charles, *Histoire de l'Université de Genève, L'académie de Calvin 1559—1798,* 4 vols., Geneva: Georg, 1900—1934.

Breen, Quirinus, "John Calvin and the Rhetorical Tradition", *Church History* XXVI (1957), pp. 3—21.

— *John Calvin: A Study in French Humanism,* Wm. B. Eerdmans Publishing Co., 1931.

Brennan, R. E., *Thomistic Psychology,* The Macmillan Company, 1941.

Père Bruno de Jesus-Marie, O. C. D., ed., *Satan,* 1951. (Based on a volume of the series Collection de Psychologie Religeuse: Etudes Carmelitaines.)

Brunner, H. Emil, *The Christian Doctrine of Creation and Redemption (Dogmatics,* Vol. II), tr. by Olive Wyon, The Westminster Press, 1952.

— *Man in Revolt,* tr. by Olive Wyon, Charles Scribner's Sons, 1939.

Brunner, Peter, *Vom Glauben bei Calvin,* Tübingen: J. C. B. Mohr, 1925.

Buesser, Fritz, *Calvins Urteil über sich selbst,* Zürich: Zwingli-Verlag, 1950.

Cadier, Jean, *Calvin — L'homme que Dieu a dompté,* Geneva: Labor et Fides, 1958; Engl. tr.: *Calvin, the Man God Mastered,* tr. by O. R. Johnston, London: Intervarsity Fellowship Press, 1960.

Calvin, John, *The Commentaries of John Calvin,* various translators, 46 vols., Edinburgh: Calvin Translation Society, 1843—1855 (reprinted by Wm. B. Eerdmans Publ. Co., 1948—50).

— *Calvin's Commentaries,* ed. by David W. Torrance and Thomas F. Torrance, Edinburgh: Oliver and Boyd and Wm. B. Eerdmans Publ. Co., 1959 ff.

— *Institutes of the Christian Religion,* tr. by John Allen, 7th edn. revised, 2 vols., The Westminster Press, 1936.

— *Institutes of the Christian Religion,* ed. by John T. McNeill, tr. by F. L. Battles (The Library of Christian Classics, Vols. XX—XXI), The Westminster Press, 1960.

— *The Letters of John Calvin,* ed. by Jules Bonnet, tr. by Bonnet, Constable and Gilchrist, 4 vols. (Calvin Translation Society 1855—7), Presbyterian Board of Publication, 1858.

— *Joannis Calvini opera quae supersunt omnia,* ed by G. Baum, E. Cunnitz, E. Reuss, 59 vols. (*Corpus Reformatorum,* vols. XXIX sqq.), Brunswick, 1863—1900.

— *Tracts and Treatises on the Reformation of the Church,* tr. by Henry Beveridge, 3 vols., Edinburgh: Calvin Translation Society, 1844 (reprinted with notes and introduction by Thomas F. Torrance, Wm. B. Eerdmans Publ. Co., 1958).

Cantimori, Delio, *Eretici italiani del Cinquecento,* Florence, 1939; German tr. by Werner Kaegi, *Italienische Haeretiker der Spätrenaissance,* Basel: Benno Schwabe & Co., 1949.

Choisey, E., "Calvin et la science", *Recueil de la Faculté de Théologie Protestante,* University of Geneva, 1931.

Church, F. C., *The Italian Reformers 1534—64,* Columbia University Press, 1932.

Cullmann, Oscar, *Die ersten christlichen Glaubensbekenntnisse* (Theologische Studien, No. 15), Zollikon-Zürich: Evangelischer Verlag, 1943; Engl. tr. *The Earliest Christian Confessions,* tr. by J. K. S. Reid, London: Lutterworth Press, 1949.

Dee, Simon Pieter, *Het Geloofsbegrip van Calvijn,* Kampen: J. A. Kok, 1918.

Denifle, F., Heinrich, S., and Weiss, A. M., *Luther und Luthertum in der ersten Entwicklung,* 3 vols., Mainz: F. Kircheim, 1904—9; Engl. **tr.** (from 2nd revised edn.); *Luther and Lutherdom from Original Sources,* Somerset, O.: Torch Press, 1917.

De Quervain, Alfred, *Calvin, sein Lehren und Kämpfen,* Berlin: Furche Verlag, 1926.

Dibelius, Martin, *Die Geisterwelt im Glauben des Paulus,* Göttingen: Vandenhoeck, 1909.

Doumergue, Emile, *Jean Calvin, les hommes et les choses de son temps,* 7 vols., Lausanne: G. Bridel, 1899—1917; Neuilly (Seine): La Cause, 1926—7.

Dowey, Edward A., Jr., *The Knowledge of God in Calvin's Theology,* Columbia University Press, 1952.

Ebstein, Wilhelm, *Dr. Martin Luthers Krankheiten und deren Einfluss auf seinen körperlichen und geistigen Zustand,* Stuttgart: Enke, 1908.

Emmen, Egbert, *De christologie van Calvijn,* Amsterdam: H. J. Paris, 1935.

Erichson, D. Alf., *Bibliographia Calviniana, Catalogus Chronologicus Operum Calvini,* Nieuwkoop: B. de Graaf, 1960 (unchanged reprint of Berlin edn. of 1900).

Erikson, Erik H., *Young Man Luther: A Study in Psychoanalysis and History* (Austen Riggs Monograph No. 4), Norton, 1958.

Favre-Dorsaz, André, *Calvin et Loyola, Deux Réformes* (Bibliotheque Historique), Paris and Bruxelles: Editions Universitaires, 1951.

Fife, Robert H., *The Revolt of Martin Luther,* Columbia University Press, 1957.

Forstman, H. Jackson, *World and Spirit: Calvin's Doctrine of Biblical Authority,* Stanford University Press, 1962.

Foster, H. D., "Calvin's Programme for a Puritan State in Geneva 1536—41", *Harvard Theological Review,* Vol. 1 No. 4 (Oct. 1908).

Froehlich, Karlfried, *Die Reichgottesidee Calvin,* Munich: Chr. Kaiser Verlag, 1922.

— *Gottesreich, Welt und Kirche bei Calvin,* Munich, E. Reinhardt, 1930.

Fuhrmann, Paul T., *Instruction in Faith (1537), by John Calvin,* tr. with a historical forward and explanatory notes, The Westminster Press, 1949.

Goedke, K., *Grundriss zur Geschichte der deutschen Dichtung,* 2 vols., Hannover and Dresden: L. Ehlermann, 1859 ff.

Gilson, Etienne, *L'Esprit de la philosophie médiévale,* Paris: Vrin, 1932; Engl. tr.: *The Spirit of Medieval Philosophy,* tr. by A. H. C. Downes, Charles Scribner's Sons, 1936.

Goumaz, Louis, "Calvinisme et Liberté", *Les Cahiers de "Foi et Vérité",* Geneva, 1951.

Greenlaw, R. W., ed., *Protestantism and Capitalism: The Weber Thesis and its Critics,* D. C. Heath & Co., 1959.

Griffith, C. R., *Principles of Systematic Psychology,* University of Illinois Press, 1943.

Grisar, Hartmann, *Luther,* 2nd edn., 3 vols., Freiburg im Breisgau: Herdersche Verlagshandlung, 1911; Engl. tr. F. M. Lamond, ed. by Luigi Cappodelta, 6 vols., London: Kegan Paul, Trench, Truebner & Co., 1913—7.

— *Martin Luthers Leben und sein Werk,* Freiburg i. Br., 1927; Engl. tr.: *Martin Luther, His Life and Work,* tr. by Frank J. Eble, ed. by Arthur Preuss, Newman Press, 1950.

Harnack, Adolf, *Militia Christi, Die christliche Religion und der Soldatenstand in den ersten drei Jahrhunderten,* Tübingen, J. C. B. Mohr, 1905.

Hasse, F. R., *Anselm von Canterbury,* Leipzig: W. Englemann, 1852.

Hausrath, Adolf, *Luthers Leben,* 2 vols., Berlin: G. Grote, 1905 (new edn. by H. von Schubert, 1914).

Herminjard, Aimé Louise, *Correspondance des Réformateurs dans les pays de langue française . . .,* 9 vols., Geneva: H. Georg, 1866—97 (reprinted Nieuwkoop: B. de Graaf, 1965 ff.).

Heussi, Karl, *Kompendium der Kirchengeschichte,* 10th edn., Tübingen: J. C. B. Mohr, 1949.

Holl, Karl, "Johannes Calvin", *Gesammelte Aufsätze zur Kirchengeschichte,* III, pp. 254—284, Tübingen: J. C. B. Mohr, 1932.

Hunter, A. M., *The Teaching of Calvin, a Modern Interpretation,* 2nd edn., Glasgow: J. Clarke, 1950.

Imbart de la Tour, Pierre, *Les origines de la Réforme, IV: Calvin et l'Institution chrétiene,* Paris, 1935; Germ. edn.: *Calvin. Der Mensch — die Kirche — die Zeit,* Munich: Georg D. W. Callwey, 1936.

Jacobs, Paul, *Prädestination und Verantwortlichkeit bei Calvin* (Beiträge zur Geschichte und Lehre der Reformierten Kirche, No. 1), Neukirchen, Kreis Moers: Buchhandlung des Erziehungsvereins, 1937.

Jansen, J. F., *Calvin's Doctrine of the Work of Christ,* London: James Clarke & Co. Ltd., 1956.

Kingdon, R. M., *Geneva and the Coming of the Wars of Religion in France, 1555—63* (Travaux d'humanisme et Renaissance, xxii), Geneva: Librarie E. Drog, 1956.

Klingner, Erich, *Luther und der deutsche Volksaberglaube* (Palaestra, LVI), Berlin: Mayer & Mueller, 1912.

Koestlin, Julius, *Martin Luther, sein Leben und seine Schriften,* 5th edn. (ed. by Gustav Kawerau), 2 vols., Berlin: A. Duncker, 1903; Engl. trans.: *The Life of Luther,* Charles Scribner's Sons, 1911.

Kolfhaus, Wilhelm, *Vom christlichen Leben nach Johannes Calvin* (Beiträge zur Geschichte und Lehre der Reformierten Kirche, No. 7), Neukirchen, Kreis Moers: Buchhandlung des Erziehungsverein, 1949.

Küchenmeister, G., Friedrich, H., *Dr. Martin Luthers Krankheitsgeschichte,* Leipzig, 1881.

Lang, A., "Calvin Schizoid?" *Reformierte Kirchenzeitung* 81 (1931).

Lewis, C. S., *The Screwtape Letters,* The Macmillan Company, 1943.

Lindsay, Thomas M., *A History of the Reformation* (International Theological Library), 2 vols., Charles Scribner's Sons, 1916.

Littel, Franklin, "The Anabaptists and Christian Tradition", *The Journal of Religious Thought* IV (1947), 2, pp. 168—171.

Loyola, Ignatius of, *The Spiritual Exercises of St. Ignatius,* tr. by L. J. Puhl, The Newman Press, 1951.

Luther, Martin, *Dr. Martin Luthers sämtliche Werke,* 1st edn., 65 vols., Erlangen, 1826 ff.

— *D. Martin Luthers Werke, kritische Gesammtausgabe,* eds. J. K. T. Knaake et al, 57 vols., Weimar, 1883 ff.

Macchioro, Vittorio, *Martin Luther, ein Held des Glaubens,* Gotha, 1929.

Mackinnon, James, *Calvin and the Reformation,* London: Longmans, Green & Co.

Mattiessen, Emil, *Der jenseitige Mensch: Eine Einführung in die Metapsychologie der mystischen Erfahrung,* Berlin and Leipzig: W. de Gruyter & Co., 1925.

McNeill, J. T., "The Democratic Element in Calvin's Thought", *Church History* XVII (1949), pp. 153—171.

— *The History and Character of Calvinism,* Oxford University Press, 1954.

— ed., *John Calvin on God and Political Duty,* 2nd edn., Library of Liberal Arts, 1956.

Mercier, Charles, "L'esprit de Calvin et la démocratie", *Revue d'histoire ecclésiastique* XXX (1934).

Moltmann, Jürgen, ed., *Calvin-Studien, 1959,* Neukirchen, Kreis Moers: Buchhandlung des Erziehungsverein, 1960.

Mone, F., *Schauspiele des Mittelalters,* 2 vols., Karlsruhe: C. Macklot, 1846.

Muehlhaupt, Erwin, *Die Predigt Calvins, ihre Geschichte, ihre Form und ihre Grundgedanken* (Arbeiten zur Kirchengeschichte, No. 18), Berlin: De Gruyter, 1931.

Neuenhaus, Johannes, "Calvin als Humanist", *Calvinstudien,* publ. by the Reformierte Gemeinde Elberfeld, Leipzig: R. Haupt, 1909. (Also in *Reformierte Kirchenzeitung* 32 (1909), pp. 2—5; 9—12.)

Niesel, Wilhelm, *Calvin Bibliographie, 1901—1959,* Munich: Chr. Kaiser Verlag, 1961.

— "Calvin und die Libertiner", *Zeitschrift für Kirchengeschichte,* XLVIII (1929).

— *Die Theologie Calvins,* 2nd edn., Munich, Chr. Kaiser Verlag, 1957; Engl. tr.: *The Theology of Calvin,* tr. by H. Knight, The Westminster Press, 1956.

Northcott, Cecil, *John Calvin* (Brief Biographies, No. 3), London: Lutterworth Press, 1946.

Obendiek, Harmannus, *Der alt böse Feind, das biblisch-reformatorische Zeugnis von der Macht Satans,* Neukirchen bei Moers: Erziehungsverein, 1930.

— *Der Teufel bei Martin Luther* (Furche-Studien, No. 4), Berlin: Furche-Verlag, 1931.

— *Satanismus und Dämonie in Geschichte und Gegenwart,* Berlin: Furche-Verlag, 1928.

Osborn, Max, "Die Teufelliteratur des XVI. Jahrhunderts", *Acta Germanica* III, 3 (1893).

Otten, Heinz, *Calvins theologische Anschauung von der Prädestination,* Munich: Chr. Kaiser Verlag, 1938.

Palm, F. C., *Calvinism and the Religious Wars,* Henry Holt and Co., 1932.

Parker, T. H. L., *The Doctrine of the Knowledge of God: A Study in Calvin's Theology,* Wm. B. Eerdman's Publishing Co., 1959.

— *The Oracles of God,* London: Lutterworth Press, 1947.

— *Portrait of Calvin,* London: Student Christian Movement Press, 1954.

Pauck, Wilhelm, "Historiography of the German Reformation during the past twenty Years", *Church History* IX (1940), pp. 305—40.

— "Calvin's Institutes of the Christian Religion", *Church History* XV (1946), pp. 12—27.

Pfister, Oskar, *Calvins Eingreifen in die Hexer- und Hexenprozesse von Peney*

1545 nach seiner Bedeutung für Geschichte und Gegenwart, Zürich, Artemis, 1947.

Quistorp, Heinrich, *Die letzten Dinge im Zeugnis Calvins: Calvins Eschatologie,* Gütersloh: C. Bertelsmann Verlag, 1941; Engl. tr.: *Calvin's Doctrine of the Last Things,* tr. by H. Knight, John Knox Press, 1955.

Rade, Martin, *Zum Teufelsglauben Luthers* (Marburger theologische Studien, Heft 2: Rudolf-Otto-Festgruss), Gotha: Leopold Klotz Verlag, 1931.

Ritschl, Otto, *Die reformierte Theologie des 16. und 17. Jahrhunderts in ihrer Entstehung und Entwicklung (Dogmengeschichte des Protestantismus,* Vol. III), Göttingen, 1926.

Roskoff, Gustav, *Geschichte des Teufels,* 2 vols., Leipzig: F. A. Brockhaus, 1869.

Rouse, Ruth and Neill, Stephan C., eds., *A History of the Ecumenical Movement, 1517—1948,* The Westminster Press, 1954.

Scheel, Otto, *Martin Luther, vom Katholizismus zur Reformation,* Tübingen: J. C. B. Mohr, 1916.

Schmidt, Albert-Marie, *John Calvin and the Calvinistic Tradition* (Men of Wisdom), tr. by Ronald Wallace, Harper and Brothers, 1960.

Schroten, Hendrik, *Christus, de Middelaar bij Calvijn,* Utrecht: P. den Boer, 1948.

Schulze, Martin, *Calvins Jenseitschristentum in seinem Verhältnis zu den religiösen Schriften des Erasmus,* Görlitz: Rudolf Dülfer, 1902.

Schwarz, R., *Johannes Calvins Lebenswerk in seinen Briefen,* Tübingen: J. C. B. Mohr, 1909.

Seeberg, Reinhold, *History of Doctrines,* tr. by C. E. Hay, Baker Book House, 1956.

Servetus, Michael, *The Two Treatises of Servetus on the Trinity,* tr. by E. M. Wilbur (Harvard Theological Studies, No. 16), Harvard University Press, 1932.

Smith, Preserved, *The Age of the Reformation,* Henry Holt and Co., 1920.

— "Luther's Early Development in the Light of Psychoanalysis", *American Journal of Psychology* XXIV (1913).

Stuermann, Walter E., *Calvin's Concept of Faith,* University of Tulsa Press, 1952.

— *Logic and Faith: A Study of the Relations between Science and Religion* (Westminster Studies in Christian Coummunication), The Westminster Press, 1962.

Thomas Aquinas, *Basic Writings of St. Thomas Aquinas,* ed. by A. C. Pegis, 2 vols., Random House Inc., 1945.

Thurneysen, Eduard, *Die Lehre von der Seelsorge,* Zollikon-Zürich: Evangelischer Verlag, 1946.

Tillich, Paul, *The Interpretation of History,* tr. by N. A. Rosetski and Elsa L. Talmay, Charles Scribner's Sons, 1936.

Torrance, T. F., *Calvin's Doctrine of Man,* London: Lutterworth Press, 1949.

Trinkhaus, Charles, "Renaissance Problems in Calvin's Theology", *Studies in the Renaissance* III, ed. by W. Peery, University of Texas Press, 1954.

Van Buren, Paul, *God in our Place, the Substitutionary Character of Calvin's Doctrine of Reconciliation,* Edinburgh: Oliver and Boyd, 1957.

Warfield, B. B., *Calvin and Calvinism,* ed. by E. D. Warfield, et al, Oxford University Press, 1931.